EQUALITY BEFORE THE LAW

This book presents a defence of the value of equality within law which is neither purely formal nor an entirely speculative theory of justice. It does this by combining a theoretical with a doctrinal project.

At the theoretical level, it argues that there is a distinct and meaningful conception of equality before the law which can be separated from concerns of distributive justice. It therefore rejects the claim that legal equality is merely formal. Rather, it is grounded in the equal moral status of all legal subjects. The demand that individuals be treated in accordance with the principle of equality before the law, then, requires that they not be treated in ways that would deny their equal moral standing. This principle of moral equality is the fundamental normative basis of the rule of law.

This general claim is applied, in the second half of the book, to anti-discrimination law. It is argued here that the wrong of wrongful discrimination consists in implicit or explicit denial of the equal moral status of legal subjects. This is also a core wrong that the common law seeks to remedy via judicial review and is thus intimately tied to legality itself.

In the final chapter, these two strands are brought together to defend the idea that law is a public asset which must be directed towards advancing the best interests of those it governs. This kind of equality principle, one which sets the outermost limits of the use of public power, must look beyond individual rights claims. It manifests a fundamental commitment to substantive equality – understood as collective flourishing – without tying it to group-based distributive concerns which arise from distinct social and historical contexts and require the exercise of political authority to choose among a range of plausible options for their resolution.

Hart Studies in Constitutional Theory: Volume 6

Hart Studies in Constitutional Theory

Series Editors

The *Hart Studies in Constitutional Theory* series publishes thought-provoking works of scholarship addressing diverse aspects of constitutional theory in a concise and crystalline manner. Authors writing for this series cover a wide range of perspectives, methods, and regions, to enhance our understanding of constitutions as central institutions of modern public life. Taken together, the books in this series aim to challenge established wisdom and advance original ideas.

This series is a natural home for books interrogating the concepts and structures of constitutions on the national, the supranational and the international level. Its guiding philosophy is that the task of constitutional theory is not only to delineate the basic structures of government and to protect human rights, but also more broadly to offer methods for grappling with the social, political, and economic problems societies face today.

The series is open to theoretical, normative, analytical, empirical and comparative approaches, stemming from legal studies as well as from political philosophy and political science. In its ambition to become a global forum for debate about constitutional theory, the series editors welcome submissions for monographs as well as edited volumes from all parts of the world.

Recent titles in this series:

Proportionality and Facts in Constitutional Adjudication
Anne Carter

The Methodology of Constitutional Theory
edited by Dimitrios Kyritsis and Stuart Lakin

A Constitutionalist Approach to the European Convention on Human Rights: The Legitimacy of Evolutive and Static Interpretation
Lisa Sonnleitner

Judicial Avoidance: Balancing Competences in Constitutional Adjudication
Carolina Alves das Chagas

Constitutionally Conforming Interpretation – Comparative Perspectives: Volume 1: National Reports
Edited by Matthias Klatt

Equality Before the Law: Equal Dignity, Wrongful Discrimination, and the Rule of Law
Michael P Foran

Equality Before the Law

Equal Dignity, Wrongful Discrimination, and the Rule of Law

Michael P Foran

•HART•
OXFORD • LONDON • NEW YORK • NEW DELHI • SYDNEY

HART PUBLISHING

Bloomsbury Publishing Plc

Kemp House, Chawley Park, Cumnor Hill, Oxford, OX2 9PH, UK

1385 Broadway, New York, NY 10018, USA

29 Earlsfort Terrace, Dublin 2, Ireland

First published in Great Britain 2023

A catalogue record for this book is available from the British Library.

A catalogue record for this book is available from the Library of Congress.

Library of Congress Control Number: 2023942366

ISBN: HB: 978-1-50996-494-9
ePDF: 978-1-50996-496-3
ePub: 978-1-50996-495-6

Typeset by Compuscript Ltd, Shannon

Series Editors' Foreword

EQUALITY IS A core moral value and a fundamental commitment that is found in constitutions around the globe. As Sandra Fredman has convincingly pointed out, equality is key to such vital questions as addressing stigma, stereotyping and prejudice; redressing disadvantage; enhancing voice and participation; accommodating difference; and achieving structural change.

These challenges are particularly acute in our times. Climate change triggers concerns about transgenerational equality. Other crises, such as pandemics, wars, including those of the economic kind, and democratic regression, all give rise to 'exponential' inequalities. The legal status and social condition of all kinds of minorities depend on our understanding of equality rights. That is true when it comes to issues like gender diversity; questions of distributive justice in sector-specific areas like education, where overrepresentation calls for desegregation measures; equal opportunities for political representation (such as the right to vote or quotas for the composition of parliaments); or decent socio-economic and health protections. In all these areas, the success or failure of the initiatives undertaken depends on our capacity to spell out equality's role and meaning regarding the exercise of public power.

As pressing and complex as all these problems are, we risk losing sight of the overall coherence of the constitutional system if we get bogged down in the particular complexities they each contain. Worse, equality is prone to becoming a vehicle for controversial political agendas inspired more by political activism than analytical rigour. Achieving holistic and coherent approaches to the design, justification and operation of equality as a constitutional principle requires, first and foremost, sound theory.

As such, and unimpressed by the temptations of 'scholactivism', Michael Foran provides a lucid and coherent defence of equality within the law, combining theoretical and doctrinal considerations. We thus welcome this new addition to our series to deepen our theoretical understanding of equality. The reader will find a thorough and convincing account of why and how the respect for the equal moral standing of all legal subjects is no less than the normative fundament of the rule of law.

Maartje de Visser
Charles Barzun
Matthias Klatt
Singapore/Charlottesville/Graz, September 2023

Acknowledgements

THIS BOOK WOULD not have been possible without the support and guidance from those around me, to only some of whom is it possible to give particular recognition here.

My deep gratitude goes first to Professor Trevor Allan, who has expertly guided me through the doctorate that became the foundation of this book. His unwavering support was matched only by his insightful and rigorous criticism. He is an intellectual hero of mine and it has been an honour to have had the opportunity to work with and learn from him.

I owe a great debt to many others. My thanks to Matthew Kramer, Ryan Meade, Colm O'Cinneide, Adam Tomkins, Adrian Vermeule and Lars Vinx for their kind and generous support both intellectually and professionally; to Shona Wilson-Stark for her council and her unwavering optimism and humour. Particular thanks must be given to Alison Young who has been an inspiration and a role model to me and to Chris McCorkindale who has been a better mentor and friend than I deserve.

I would not have come to the end of this process with my sanity intact without the support of the great friends that I have made along the way. My undying love and gratitude to Alex Allan, Stephen Bogle, Jonathan Brown, Giordana Campagna, Conor Casey, Emma Curren, Jinal Dadiya, Angela Daly, Rebecca Freund, Jelena Gilgorijevic, Pablo Grez, María Ithurria, Nick Kilford, Agnes Lindberg, Khomotso Moshikaro, Sinead O'Brien, Matt Psycharis, Aime Rankin, John Ritzema, Alex Schwartz, Rajiv Shah, So Yeon Kim, Yuan Yi Zhu and Tony Zhou. I owe a deep debt to Sean Fleming for his advice, empathy, and support during this entire process.

Special thanks must be given to those who were instrumental in my journey to begin this project. Niamh Connolly has been a mentor to me from the moment that I first stepped into her office eight years ago. Without her support and encouragement, I would not have even considered academia as a viable option for me. Before that, however, there was Ryan McCarthy. Words cannot express what I owe to this man, nor the ways in which he surpassed what could ever be expected of an educator. He gave me so much more than guidance or encouragement: he made me believe in myself and in the capacity of a kid from Tallaght to reach heights others believed to be shut off to students like me with backgrounds like mine.

Finally, I would like to thank Verity Stuart and Kate Whetter at Hart Publishing for their encouragement and hard work throughout this process. I am indebted to Maria Skrzypiec for her excellent copyediting support.

Above all else, I am grateful to my parents, who have sacrificed more than anyone could ask for to see me pursue my education. Their love and support have meant the world to me and can never be repaid.

Go raibh míle maith agaibh go léir

Contents

Introduction: Constitutional Value and Constitutional Theory

At the most foundational level, the term 'constitution' connotes the body of legal rules and principles which establish and maintain the relationship between ruler and ruled within a sovereign state.[1] But what is the precise nature of this relationship? Do constitutional principles such as the rule of law place limits on its scope or character? If so, do these limitations tell us anything about how we relate to one another in the eyes of the law? Some have argued that constitutional governance, appropriately respectful of the rule of law, manifests a particular kind of relationship between legal officials and legal subjects: one of reciprocity and respect.[2] It is not possible to assess the merits of these kinds of claims without first settling contentious methodological issues relating to constitutional scholarship.

On one view, the British constitution is best conceived as a coherent body of fundamental principles derived from the rule of law, the separation of powers, and the sovereignty of Parliament.[3] These principles form an overarching unity of legality, legitimacy, and fundamental value, grounded within the particular institutional history of the common law. This theory – common law constitutionalism – places constitutional law within this framework of fundamental principles, their meaning expounded and developed by the common law courts. Statute, on this view, plays a supplementary role, adding to and helping to shape and define the constitutional order. However, it is ultimately legal principle which operates as the lens through which statutory meaning is gleaned. As Laws puts it, 'An Act of Parliament is words on a page. Only the common law gives it life'.[4]

This approach presents a very particular account of constitutional theory, one which is compatible with a particular account of the proper place of value

[1] See J Laws, *The Common Law Constitution* (Cambridge University Press, 2014) 4.

[2] See L Fuller, *The Morality of Law*, rvsd edn (Yale University Press, 1969); TRS Allan, *The Sovereignty of Law: Freedom, Constitution, and Common Law* (Oxford University Press, 2013); J Raz, 'The Law's Own Virtue' (2019) 39 *Oxford Journal of Legal Studies* 1.

[3] Allan, *The Sovereignty of Law* (n 2); TRS Allan, *Law, Liberty, and Justice: The Legal Foundations of British Constitutionalism* (Clarendon Press, 1993); TRS Allan, *Constitutional Justice: A Liberal Theory of the Rule of Law* (Oxford University Press, 2001); *cf* T Poole, 'Dogmatic Liberalism? T.R.S. Allan and the Common Law Constitution' (2002) 65 *Modern Law Review* 463.

[4] Laws (n 1) 6; *cf* J Goldsworthy, 'The Myth of the Common Law Constitution' in *Parliamentary Sovereignty* (Cambridge University Press, 2010); T Poole, 'Back to the Future? Unearthing the Theory of Common Law Constitutionalism' (2003) 23 *Oxford Journal of Legal Studies* 435.

within legal interpretation.[5] Under the theory of common law constitutionalism, fundamental common law values such as equality and fairness become operative in the correct interpretation of both statute and precedent. On this view, correct answers to constitutional questions cannot be provided by recourse to detached empirical observation. The centrality of legal principle, normatively engaged and constantly evolving, ensures that judges do not merely apply legal rules which are in no way shaped or informed by interpretative adjudicative reasoning. Rather, they become custodians of constitutional value, responsible for applying a body of law which they protect and sustain with integrity and appropriate respect for fundamental rights and the public good.[6] To answer questions of constitutional theory and law, as they arise within the common law, is to offer justifications for existing or proposed practice, justifications which cannot be neatly separated from deeper commitments to constitutional values.

In contrast, academic scholarship typically attempts to present the law 'as it is', focusing on judicial practice and thereby committing to the idea that the British constitution can be fully accounted for, if this is possible at all, only by reference to empirical fact, abstracted from interpretation.[7] The inevitable result is that theoretical and doctrinal disagreement is sidelined, confined to the realm of contested or uncertain law which must be addressed by the higher courts before it can be resolved. On this account, the law is conceived as an archipelago – 'an array of discrete islands, posited by authoritative legal institutions, surrounded by an empty sea, where lawyer or judge must supplement the law by a form of quasi-legislation'.[8] Unless and until a higher court has made an authoritative statement as to whether, for example, public authorities act lawfully when they dismiss employees because they are homosexual, there is no law on this matter.[9] There is only external academic speculation. Should the court decide that certain public authorities can lawfully dismiss employees on the basis of their sexuality, then that is the law and speculation must cease, to be replaced by evaluation. The Supreme Court, on this view, becomes incapable of making legal mistakes except insofar as the Court itself later declares a mistake to have been made. This approach is neatly summarised by Robert H Jackson's famous observation, speaking on behalf of the US Supreme

[5] See D Oliver, *Common Values and the Public-Private Divide* (Butterworths, 1999).

[6] This is the principal theme of Allan's early work in constitutional theory; Allan, *Law, Liberty, and Justice: The Legal Foundations of British Constitutionalism* (n 3); Allan, *Constitutional Justice: A Liberal Theory of the Rule of Law* (n 3); TRS Allan, 'Dworkin and Dicey: The Rule of Law as Integrity' (1988) 8 *Oxford Journal of Legal Studies* 266. On legal officials as custodians, see Raz (n 2).

[7] See eg JAG Griffith, 'The Political Constitution' (1979) 42 *Modern Law Review* 1; HLA Hart, 'Positivism and the Separation of Law and Morality' (1958) 71 *Harvard Law Review* 593; M Kramer, *In Defence of Legal Positivism: Law without Trimmings* (Oxford University Press, 1999).

[8] Allan, *The Sovereignty of Law* (n 2) 334.

[9] *R v Ministry of Defence, ex p Smith* [1996] QB 517.

Court, that 'we are not final because we are infallible, but we are infallible only because we are final'.[10]

Yet, lawyers often disagree with the Court. Our scholarship is replete with academic analysis explaining why superior courts have got it wrong. How do we make sense of this? Are scholars who disagree with particular judgments simply explaining why they would have *preferred* an alternative outcome? Are they merely bringing their own private values and politics to bear in an external evaluation? We can, of course, point to examples of scholars doing exactly this. However, there is a vast literature which explicitly argues that, in given cases, the court has erred in its *legal* analysis. Must this scholarship be described as nothing more than work in detached speculation or evaluation? There is another method of engaging with legal practice that rejects, at least implicitly, an account of law as determined only by reference to authoritative pronouncements from recognised sources such as the Supreme Court. Lawyers who disagree with the court on a matter of law need not do so externally, only evaluating legal decisions by reference to detached moral or political considerations. It is possible to offer an alternative *interpretation* of the law, one which focuses on how a particular decision has failed to account for or appropriately weigh important legal principles.[11]

The common law must be construed as a body of legal principles and not collapsed into the judgments and rules which derive from these principles. However, once this is accepted, a question arises as to how these principles relate to and inform judicial practice. If the law is a collection of principles and not simply the pronouncements of an authorised source, it becomes possible that superior courts may be mistaken as to the correct answer to a particular legal question. Principles, unlike rules, are not all-or-nothing standards. They have weight and must be appropriately balanced against one another. The correct balance, leading to the correct statement of law, will necessarily require a morally engaged interpretation that brings the interpreter's opinion to bear on the pertinent legal materials. The law on any issue is never the incontrovertible product of authoritative decree; it is always an informed assessment of how best to balance competing legal principles. Legal interpretation, of statute or case law, is a normatively engaged practice which demands a degree of moral or political judgement; it is not merely a work in linguistics or an empirical search for objective legislative intention.[12] A lawyer may, of course, offer a prediction as to how the court will decide a 'hard' case which raises a contested or previously unaddressed legal issue. However, they may also reasonably add that, in their

[10] *Brown v Allen*, 344 US 443 (1953).

[11] See R Dworkin, *A Matter of Principle* (Clarendon Press, 1986); R Dworkin, *Law's Empire* (Harvard University Press, 1986).

[12] Allan, *The Sovereignty of Law* (n 2) 4–6. See also *Anisminic Ltd v Foreign Compensation Commission* [1969] 2 AC 147; TRS Allan, 'Law, Democracy, and Constitutionalism: Reflections on Evans v Attorney General' (2016) 75 *Cambridge Law Journal* 38.

informed and considered opinion, the court would be making a legal error if it decides one way rather than another. This is not to say that they are necessarily bringing external values and politics to bear in their evaluation of a given decision. Rather, the dissenting lawyer or judge is offering a rival interpretation of the relevant legal considerations. Among these considerations are legal and constitutional values.

Legal interpretation raises important questions concerning the proper relationship between legal practice and political or moral theory, particularly in public law where values such as liberty and equality are necessarily engaged. How then are we to conceptualise this relationship? Peter Cane argues that academic debate in this area has 'diverted attention away from legal values and on to styles of legal and theoretical scholarship'.[13] The result of this focus on political theory, according to Cane, is a shift towards external values that contribute little to public law because of their abstract nature and the presence of intractable disagreement concerning their practical implications for given cases. A more valuable approach is to focus on the values internal to the law itself and, in particular, the common law: 'judge-made law provides a framework of values into which legislation is introduced and within which the forward-looking outcome-oriented values of legislation have to be accommodated'.[14]

We can thus distinguish between two kinds of value in this context: the private, external values which lawyers and others may draw upon to evaluate the law, and those values internal to law, derived from but also informative of the common law. On Cane's view, this distinction is represented as one between background and foreground values. Background values, found in the interaction between legislative and judicial functions, include accountability, representation and judicial deference. Foreground values are provided by existing political theories such as liberalism or republicanism; they are external to and provide a basis for criticising the law. However, while Cane's account captures an important distinction between internal and external perspectives which helps to explain the difference between interpretation and evaluation, there remain important connections between immanent and critical values.

Any neat distinction between internal and external value must be challenged if it denies the capacity for moral value to guide one's understanding of legal practice.[15] While public law enjoys a degree of autonomy from abstract

[13] P Cane, 'Theory and Values in Public Law' in P Craig and R Rawlings (eds), *Law and Administration in Europe: Essays in Honour of Carol Harlow* (Oxford University Press, 2003) 14.

[14] ibid 6. This distinction between legal value and outcome-oriented value is addressed in detail in Ch 2 below. Note, however, that it is quite contestable whether the common law should be described as judge-'made' law. An alternative and much older view is that judges act as interpreters for a body of law which transcends their individual decisions. See G Postema, *Bentham and the Common Law Tradition* (Oxford University Press, 1986) Ch 1.

[15] See P Craig, 'Theory and Values in Public Law: A Response' in P Craig and R Rawlings (eds), *Law and Administration in Europe: Essays in Honour of Carol Harlow* (Oxford University Press, 2003); Allan, *The Sovereignty of Law* (n 2) 334–40.

political theory, it nevertheless maintains a deep and enduring connection to a normatively engaged interpretive enterprise; one which depends on but does not collapse into 'pure' moral reasoning. While a judge or lawyer cannot abandon the practice that they seek to interpret and determine legal issues only by reference to political or moral values, this does not mean that such values cannot become internal legal values, should the practice embrace, for example, democratic governance. Once parliamentary sovereignty is understood to refer to a democratically elected Parliament in a system of universal suffrage, democracy (and its associated commitment to moral equality) becomes an internal value, one which can guide adjudication and interpretation.[16] However, once this is done and the practice is interpreted in light of these internal values, one cannot then ignore the practice in determining precisely what a given value requires in this context. On this understanding, the common law is not just a collection of principles, but also a collection of hundreds of years of precedents wherein these principles are tested, refined, and, if necessary, abandoned. Abstract political or moral value is forged through the fires of legal practice to become a unified web of legal principle, appropriately attuned to institutional history and the lessons learned from confronting hard cases which challenge existing understanding.[17]

While there may be some values which seem not to be contingent upon development of practice in this manner, they will often entail additional value commitments once properly understood. Take, for example, the notion of analogical reasoning, essential for common law adjudication and the rule of law. From this we can derive a commitment to coherence and consistency such that legal principle preserves the integrity of the legal order. But we can also derive a commitment to legal equality which explains why coherence and consistency matter in the first place. Without a commitment to some notion of equality, much of our practice becomes unintelligible. Why does legality demand general rules rather than the particularised commands of an authority? Why must judges situate their decisions within a body of rules and principles? Why not just decide each case as it comes, with no reference to general rule or institutional history? The answer cannot be provided without recourse to values which themselves underpin a commitment to coherence and consistency.[18] However, this does not mean that legal analysis collapses into abstract comparison of political value. The rule of law operates as mediator between political theory and legal practice, manifesting in a body of principles which are grounded in the nature and structure of law itself. This inevitably has an impact upon the content of law and the kinds of ends that can legitimately be pursued within a legal system,

[16] See for example the judgment of Lady Hale in *A v Secretary of State for the Home Dept* [2004] UKHL 56, [237]–[238].

[17] See TRS Allan, 'The Moral Unity of Public Law' (2017) 67 *University of Toronto Law Journal* 1.

[18] For consistency itself is only contingently and instrumentally valuable. See Ch 2 below.

further collapsing any neat distinction between an external and fully internal account of legal value.[19]

Nevertheless, the mere fact that a value is recognised as being contained within the common law is not enough to ensure the protection of concrete rights or the enforcement of specific duties which might derive from it. Such protection necessarily depends upon interpretive judicial practice, informed by robust conceptual understanding. As Elliott notes, '[w]hether – and, if so, to what extent – *values* acknowledged at common law can be regarded as *rights* properly so-called turns upon the rigour with which courts are able to protect them and the resulting degree of constitutional resilience that they exhibit in the face of legislative or administrative infraction'.[20]

In addition, *which* rights and duties derive from particular constitutional values is also a matter of interpretation, appropriately attuned to the history and practice of the common law. Values can serve as the normative foundation for particular rights, explaining why they must be granted protection. However, this does not mean that anything that can be traced back to a recognised value has constitutional status. The value of liberty grounds many common law rights and duties, including the right to a fair trial, *habeas corpus*, and many more. But this does not mean that any proposed right which is informed by a commitment to liberty can be or is recognised by and enforceable under the common law. Values necessarily exhibit a degree of indeterminacy; they cannot be invoked free from the interpretive enterprise and must always be brought into conversation with legal practice and theory if they are to have any real purchase.

I. EQUALITY AS A FUNDAMENTAL VALUE

The focus of this book is on one particular constitutional value, vital to the legitimacy of any legal order: equality. Constitutional governance under the rule of law rests on a fundamental commitment to the moral equality of persons. Despite the many differences that exist between us, one thing we share, according to this commitment, is an equality of worth or status.[21] No one is or should be treated as an inferior to others by any public authority claiming to be legitimate. To respect moral equality, the state cannot play favourites: it cannot single out some individuals or groups as morally superior to others. This connection between legitimacy and appropriate respect for moral equality, embodied in the

[19] See M Foran, 'The Rule of Good Law: Form, Substance and Fundamental Rights' (2019) 78 *Cambridge Law Journal* 570; J Gardner, 'The Supposed Formality of the Rule of Law' in *Law as a Leap of Faith: Essays on Law in General* (Oxford University Press, 2012); *cf* P Craig, 'Formal and Substantive Conceptions of the Rule of Law' [1997] *Public Law* 467.

[20] M Elliott, 'Beyond the European Convention: Human Rights and the Common Law' (2015) 68 *Current Legal Problems* 85, 96.

[21] The connection between equal worth and equal status will be explored in Ch 3 below.

ideal of impartiality, has been remarkably underexplored within constitutional scholarship in the United Kingdom,[22] although there has been some work in legal and political philosophy more generally.[23]

In 1994, Jeffrey Jowell published a paper arguing that equality was a fundamental constitutional principle.[24] He quite rightly noted that the value of equality has been neglected as a topic of study within British public law, especially when compared to its place within scholarship pertaining to other constitutional regimes. The result is that the fundamental connection between equality and legitimacy within the common law has been obscured. To Jowell, it is a 'fundamental precept', 'constitutive of democracy' that people should be regarded as having equal moral worth, free from unjustified discrimination.[25] In the years since its publication, the judiciary have, at times, been explicit in their support of 'the equality principle' and have recognised its fundamental constitutional importance.[26]

However, as we will see throughout this book, the concept of equality can be interpreted to mean and require a great variety of things, being embraced by practically all modern political and moral philosophies.[27] There is, nevertheless, a core unifying commitment to appropriately respecting the equal moral status of persons. While different theories offer alternative methods of showing this respect, what unifies them as equality theories is this fundamental belief in the equal worth and dignity of persons. The question that we are left with, then, is whether this commitment to respecting equal moral worth or status is, properly understood, a foundational legal principle within the common law constitution.

Given the methodological constraints of an interpretive approach to constitutional law, it is important to make sense of the practice and institutional history that we are attempting to analyse. This raises difficulties, given the particular history of the United Kingdom, much of which is premised upon inequalities not just in distribution of resources but of precisely the kinds of status or worth claims mentioned above. A legally enshrined aristocracy,

[22] Allan is a notable exception: Allan, *The Sovereignty of Law* (n 2); TRS Allan, 'Questions of Legality and Legitimacy: Form and Substance in British Constitutionalism' (2011) 9 *International Journal of Constitutional Law* 155; Allan, *Constitutional Justice: A Liberal Theory of the Rule of Law* (n 3) chs 5, 8; Allan, *Law, Liberty, and Justice: The Legal Foundations of British Constitutionalism* (n 3) Ch 7.

[23] See R Dworkin, *Sovereign Virtue: The Theory and Practice of Equality* (Harvard University Press, 2000); R Dworkin, *Is Democracy Possible Here?* (Princeton University Press, 2006); W Sadurski, *Equality and Legitimacy* (Oxford University Press, 2008).

[24] J Jowell, 'Is Equality a Constitutional Principle?' (1994) 7 *Current Legal Problems* 1.

[25] ibid 7.

[26] See in particular *Matadeen v Pointu* [1999] 1 AC 98, and the comments of Lady Hale in *A v Secretary of State for the Home Dept* [2004] UKHL 56, [237]–[238]. See also Lord Woolf et al, *De Smith's Judicial Review*, 8th edn (Sweet & Maxwell, 2018) paras 11.061–11.068; N Bamforth, 'Conceptions of Anti-Discrimination Law' (2004) 24 *Oxford Journal of Legal Studies* 693.

[27] See in particular Ch 2.

operative within a monarchical state, which is structured, even in its modern manifestation, around a division between commoner and Lord, is difficult to reconcile with a deep commitment to moral equality. This is particularly true given a number of structural elements within the British constitutional order. The aristocracy might not have the power that it once had within the United Kingdom, but it is still legally enshrined to such a degree that legislation must pass through a second chamber of unelected elites and be approved, even if only formally, by an unelected, hereditary monarch before it can have the force of law. The sovereignty of Parliament, under the British system, is the sovereignty of the *King in* Parliament.

Nevertheless, one cannot ignore the monumental shifts that have occurred within British public law since the early modern period. There have been profound changes to the structure and normative foundations of the British constitution, moving the monarchy and the lords from the centre to the periphery, reflecting a fundamental shift of legal and political power away from the aristocracy and onto the commons. The expansion of the franchise provided a new democratic basis for the legal constraints on the arbitrary exercise of state power and shifted the foundations of legitimacy away from Hobbesian notions of absolute sovereignty towards the values and precepts of democratic constitutionalism. The result has been the gradual removal of real monarchical power and a fundamental change in the legal conceptualisation of the relationship between legal official and legal subject.

Equality has come to form a core aspect of the British constitutional order, ensuring that governance functions in a manner which is compatible with the equal dignity of persons and the associated legal and moral obligations which derive from that commitment. Equality before the law or legal equality is central to both representative democracy and the rule of law, each in turn forming the bedrock of the modern notion of political equality – the formal equality of status of persons within the electoral and law-making process. Political equality now underpins the foundations of UK public law, including legislative supremacy, the primacy of the Commons, and the accountability of government to Parliament.[28]

Having said all of this, it would be wrong to assume that it is only in modern times that equality has been recognised as a constitutive element of our law. The common law has deep roots. It is born from an ancient, if fragmented, tradition which views law as a public asset – a common good – which must be directed towards advancing the best interests of all the governed.[29] Aristotle, Aquinas,

[28] See M Gordon, *Parliamentary Sovereignty in the UK Constitution: Process, Politics, and Democracy* (Hart Publishing, 2015) 34. See also Allan, *Constitutional Justice: A Liberal Theory of the Rule of Law* (n 3) 243–81.

[29] See A Vermeule, *Common Good Constitutionalism* (Polity Press, 2022); RH Helmholz, *Natural Law in Court: A History of Legal Theory in Practice* (Harvard University Press, 2015); R Heinrich, *The Natural Law* (Liberty Fund, 2012).

and Coke were all operating within very different constitutional orders. Yet, they shared something in their understanding of the relationship between posited law and background, unwritten, principles of morality and justice. To modern positivism, law is very little more than the product of sovereign will, at most embracing non-legal social rules of recognition or change.[30] While there are many differences in how law was conceived pre-positivism, one thing which remains constant is the refusal to equate law – even posited law – with the mere will of those with political authority.

Conceived as such, law cannot remain neutral on the good life. It must be justified as a plausible attempt at the common good, intended to improve the lives of its subjects by facilitating their flourishing among a community of moral equals. On this view, the common law is 'a local variant' of the classical Roman and European tradition, the *ius commune*.[31] Common law shares 'the classical legal cosmology in which civil positive law gives specification to, and is interpreted in light of, general background principles of natural law and the law of nations, understood as enduring commitments of the legal order'.[32] One such principle is equality before the law and this fundamental commitment to natural justice has remained a core part of legal reasoning, lasting in one form or another from the ancient Roman world up to our modern common law principles of administrative justice.

In addition to common law principle, equality has worked its way into British public law in two other important respects. First, the United Kingdom has ratified both regional and international equality and human rights treaties including UN and Council of Europe treaties guaranteeing the right to non-discrimination. The incorporation of Article 14 of the European Convention on Human Rights (ECHR) into domestic law via the Human Rights Act 1998 further solidifies anti-discrimination rights, notwithstanding the fact that it only applies to discrimination in the enjoyment of ECHR rights. Second, this is echoed in the introduction of domestic legislation through the Equality Act 2010 where expanded protection is offered in employment and other private contexts, but only on the basis of protected characteristics. Importantly, while Article 14 offers protection on the basis of an open-ended ground of 'personal status', the Equality Act only covers wrongful discrimination on the basis of a finite list of enumerated grounds. It is to the common law constitution that we must turn if we are to provide an account of wrongful discrimination which is unmoored from these constraints.

[30] See HLA Hart, *The Concept of Law*, 2nd edn (Oxford University Press, 1994); Hart (n 7).

[31] Vermeule (n 29) 5. Indeed, the very name 'common law' derives from the *ius commune*: F Pollock and F Maitland, *The History of English Law before the Time of Edward I*, 2nd edn (Liberty Fund, 2010) 176. See also TJ McSweeney, *Priests of the Law: Roman Law and the Making of the Common Law's First Professionals* (Oxford University Press, 2019).

[32] Vermeule (n 29) 55.

Scholarship and judicial analysis rarely place equality in so prominent a position when describing the core pillars of British constitutional law. This is a constitution in constant but gradual evolution. This book seeks to problematise this marginalisation of legal equality by exploring the ways in which contemporary understandings of key constitutional principles such as the sovereignty of parliament and the rule of law presuppose the moral equality of persons. In particular, it will be shown that the rule of law can only be fully understood when one accounts for the central role that equal dignity plays in our conception of legality. The connection between moral equality and legality is ancient, embraced by classical natural lawyers such as the Stoics and the early Sophists as well as the later Roman jurists who were emphatic that by natural law, all men are equal.[33] Posited law during this time, by permitting slavery and other forms of unjust discrimination, manifestly failed to respect this truth, however. Similarly, the historical approach of the common law to the value of equality or the principle of non-discrimination is often said to be lacklustre at best, displaying what McColgan describes as a 'marked lack of concern'.[34] While the common law has seemingly failed to properly articulate a coherent conception of legal equality, it would be wrong to presume that this represents a failure in the *capacity* of the common law to provide such a conception, given the deep connection between common law and natural law.[35] Indeed, if one is appropriately attuned to constitutional principle and value, in addition to the rules which derive from the adjudicative process, it becomes increasingly difficult to deny the central role that equality plays as a value which underpins the common law constitution.[36]

This book seeks to provide a conceptual framework through which to view the different ways that the value of equality manifests within British public law. It will begin by defending equality as a constitutional value itself. The principle of equality before the law is often characterised as procedural or formal in nature and consequently of minimal value. Recent scholarship has offered a more nuanced representation of this critique, maintaining that the principle is procedural in nature but emphasising its instrumental importance. The first chapter challenges that characterisation, arguing that equality before the law is best interpreted as a foundational constitutional principle which entails substantive commitment to the content of legal principle. Equality before the law, as an independent constitutional principle, should not be confused with the broader value of equality, nor with the rule of law: it incorporates aspects of both, mandating that legal subjects, including legal officials, be treated as

[33] *Dig* 50.17.32. On the ancient Greek natural law embracing of moral equality, see M Foran, 'Equal Dignity and the Common Good' (forthcoming) *Harvard Journal of Law and Public Policy*.

[34] A McColgan, *Discrimination, Equality and the Law* (Hart Publishing, 2014) 11.

[35] See Helmholz (n 29).

[36] M Foran, 'The Cornerstone of Our Law: Equality, Consistency, and Judicial Review' (2022) 81 *Cambridge Law Journal* 249.

prima facie equals in the creation, interpretation, and application of the law. It is not simply a requirement to apply the law to appropriate cases regardless of its content: as a foundational constitutional principle, informed by constitutional value, it cannot be described as morally inert.[37]

Constitutional provision for equality before the law should be interpreted as informed by a commitment to treating legal subjects as moral equals whose dignity must be respected. Any analysis of the common law constitution must adequately account for and give proper recognition to this fundamental constitutional principle. But this interpretation raises some important challenges. The idea of treatment as equals commits us to the position that legal subjects have equal moral status, but how we respect that equality does not manifest itself as a matter of logic. Chapter 2 addresses the fact that multiple ways of treating individuals as equals exist. At a very basic level there can be deontic, rights-based equality principles and utilitarian equality principles, or other broadly teleological, goal-orientated equality principles. It is a matter of value which conception is chosen. Notwithstanding this, it seems that general principles of the common law constitution and, in particular, the rule of law, might lend guidance in our determination of which values best underpin the concept of legal equality. There appears to be a distinctly legal account of equality that has a general affinity with deontology and right-based accounts of morality, one which does not collapse equality into other values such as liberty or autonomy, but which also can be distinguished from the demands of distributive justice, traditionally understood to fall within the constitutional purview of the legislature and executive.

It is thus vital to have a sufficiently nuanced account of the rule of law and its connection to both human dignity and human equality. That is the task of Chapter 3, where it will be argued that legal equality represents the coming together of two important moral concepts which, when analysed in isolation from each other, are vulnerable to powerful critiques. Respect for both dignity *and* equality is central to the foundations of our constitutional order and vital for a coherent understanding of the rule of law which affords appropriate weight to the values which underpin the common law itself. Ultimately, the demand that individuals be treated in accordance with the principle of equality before the law requires that subjects of the law not be treated in ways that would amount to a denial of their equal moral standing but also that they be treated in accordance with the standards of the rule of law: equality before the law entails the appropriate protection of law, of which respect for equal dignity is an integral part.

From here, the book turns to address the prime way that equal dignity might be violated: wrongful discrimination. Chapter 4 offers a conceptual framework for identifying what discrimination is as an action, as well as instances where

[37] On the moral and political salience of constitutional principle and value, see J Laws, 'Law and Democracy' [1995] *Public Law* 72.

it will be wrongful and unjustified. At its core, discrimination is a relational concept: to discriminate, A must treat B less favourably than A does or would treat C on the basis of some property, P. As such, unjustified forms of discrimination amount to comparative wrongs. A key argument in this chapter is that there is a particular kind of wrongful discrimination, what Deborah Hellman calls demeaning discrimination, that directly affronts the moral equality of persons.[38] My account draws upon Hellman's understanding of discrimination as being wrongful in an expressive sense, and combines it with the deontic account of wrongful discrimination offered by Benjamin Eidelson.[39] The result is an account of discrimination that is sufficiently attuned to the importance of expressive wrongdoing, while remaining grounded within a respect-based account of wrongful discrimination.

There may be times when discrimination is unjustified purely by virtue of the harmful consequences that it produces. However, constitutional principle demands some form of deontic wrongdoing before it can justify judicial interference with executive action. To that end, Chapter 5 sets out a defence of the current approach to judicial review for wrongful discrimination, which conceives of it as an instance of unreasonable conduct. The principle of non-discrimination, when understood to be an aspect of rationality review, has been criticised for deficiencies in both coherence and consistency.[40] However, it will be shown that, once we place reasonableness review within its appropriate context, where the rule of law is contrasted with unreasonableness, it becomes clear that unjustified, wrongful discrimination between persons or groups is and has long been prohibited as unlawful misuse of public power – even if what constitutes 'wrongful' in this context has been subject to change through time. We can determine whether a form of discrimination is wrongful only by reference to legal principle and the existing grounds for review provide ample resources to do so.

Nevertheless, there remains a concern that the existing principles of judicial review are not sufficiently attuned to the distributive demands of equality. In particular, a specific conception of substantive equality is invoked to explain the inadequacy of our current constitutional order. Chapter 6 draws on many of the previous chapters to address the distinction between acts of wrongful discrimination and failures to achieve diversity-based distribution goals which violate precepts of distributive justice and what has been termed substantive equality. It is often argued that anti-discrimination rights are ultimately concerned with redressing group-based disadvantage and furthering these telic equality or distributive goals.[41] This chapter challenges that assumption, arguing that

[38] D Hellman, *When Is Discrimination Wrong?* (Harvard University Press, 2011).

[39] B Eidelson, *Discrimination and Disrespect* (Oxford University Press, 2015).

[40] See A Lester and G Bindman, *Race and Law* (Penguin, 1972); B Hepple, *Race, Jobs and the Law in Britain* (Penguin, 1970); McColgan (n 34).

[41] T Khaitan, *A Theory of Discrimination Law* (Oxford University Press, 2015).

anti-discrimination rights are best conceived as examples of formal equality by virtue of their focus on deontic wrongdoing. In contrast, the various principles of substantive equality are unified by reference to a telic or goal-oriented approach to equality which focuses on bringing about the transformation of social and legal structures to better advance diversity, representation and distributive justice. It is here that the public sector equality duty contained within the Equality Act 2010 becomes salient, by requiring public authorities to pay sufficient attention to the importance of advancing these distributive goals.

While specific lists of protected characteristics or specific policies to advance the relative position of distinct groups within society often form part of equality law in our contemporary context, that is primarily the result of a tailoring of more general equality commitments to the specific context and policy goals of contemporary nation states. But it is wrong to presume that the only way that equality manifests as a constitutional principle is either as deontic principles of right action, best determined and enforced by courts, or group oriented distributive policies, best determined by legislatures and administered by executives. A commitment to the moral equality of persons also manifests within constitutional principle as a commitment to the common good: to the idea that law is a public good, to be directed towards public ends, and cannot be privatised for the pursuit of the private ends of rulers. Once this is accepted, we are then faced with the possibility that there may be a role for legal officials, including judges, to determine what constitutes plausible conceptions of the public good and to develop mechanisms for addressing circumstances where administrative action is not in pursuit of any plausible conception of the public good. That is the subject of the final chapter. It will be argued that the rule of law is committed to the idea that law must be directed towards public ends and that this manifests a commitment to equality. Properly understood, public ends are those which are directed towards the benefit of all, affording appropriate respect for the moral equality of persons while seeking to facilitate the flourishing of each and every member of the community.

Drawing all of this together, we can conclude that the value of equality has a vital role to play in any legal order. It provides a normative underpinning for the public nature of law; it grounds the legal concept of non-discrimination and assists in our understanding of why wrongful discrimination is wrongful, as well as our comprehension of the more politically orientated distribution goals associated with substantive equality. It also allows us to distinguish between those goals which are inherent within the rule of law and those which constitute a legitimate policy choice from within a range of reasonable options. Only the former is within the inherent jurisdiction of a court of law tasked with determining the lawfulness of administrative action.

Without a coherent understanding of legal equality, any theory of the constitution is incomplete. The central role that equality plays in constitutional interpretation is buttressed by the important connection between equality and legitimacy. Nevertheless, this legitimacy runs both ways: the demands of equality before the law must be respectful of the separation of powers and the appropriate limits on the role of the judge within a constitutional order which leaves certain decisions to other constitutional actors. Full respect for the equal dignity of persons very likely demands some degree of distributive justice and certainly requires those with legal authority to actively pursue the collective flourishing of the polity. Under our constitutional settlement, however, that demand must be met through the legislative and executive processes. Judicially enforceable common law equality rights within public law must attach to a breach of constitutional principle and the rule of law, focused on an instance of administrative wrongdoing which falls outside a range of plausible conceptions of the common good.

A theory of the constitution must account for the normativity of constitutional law: for the reasons why we as legal subjects are under a duty to obey the law and why legal officials must respect the distinctive moral status of the legal subject. A principle of moral equality, understood to demand that legal subjects be treated with equal dignity and not wrongfully discriminated against, is the fundamental normative basis of the common law constitution, one without which a constitutional order could not be said to be legitimate or to deserve the obedience of legal subjects. It is essential in this regard to provide a detailed analysis of legal equality, both conceptually and morally. For too long has equality been sidelined within common law constitutional theory. What follows is not an attempt to provide an exhaustive analysis of this value. It is nevertheless a step in the right direction.

1

Legal Equality: Form and Substance

MANY CONSTITUTIONAL FRAMEWORKS contain some provision for the principle of equality before the law.[1] Usually these provisions are associated with the protection of both procedural and substantive rights that legal subjects have as against the misuse of governmental power. In particular, there is a strong connection between modern provisions for legal equality and the protection of anti-discrimination rights. In contrast, philosophical analysis of the principle of equality before the law has generally resulted in the conclusion that the concept is empty, circular, or merely procedural. As a result, many scholars have concluded that equality before the law is of minimal value.[2] This chapter challenges those accounts and argues that modern constitutional frameworks are not mistaken to draw a connection between legal equality and fundamental constitutional law. Equality before the law is best conceived as a substantive constitutional principle which informs the content of fundamental legal principles and rules. It should not be confused with the abstract value of equality, nor with requirements that laws be sufficiently general or that there be congruence between laws as enacted and as applied.[3] Equality before the law incorporates aspects of both the rule of law and the more abstract value of equality, mandating that legal subjects, including legal officials, be treated as moral equals in the creation, interpretation, and application of the law. Equality before the law is the grounding moral principle of the common law constitution, without which a constitutional order cannot be said to be legitimate, nor could fidelity to law be achieved.

The orthodox position operates within a theoretical framework which is premised on the claim that the principle of equality before the law is synonymous with and exhausted by the maxim that 'likes should be treated alike'.[4]

[1] See eg Canadian Charter for Rights and Freedoms, s 15(1); Constitution of South Africa, s 9(1); Constitution of India, Art 14; Constitution of Ireland, Art 40; Constitution of the United States of America, Amend 14.

[2] See P Westen, 'The Empty Idea of Equality' (1982) 95 *Harvard Law Review* 537; C Peters, 'Foolish Consistency: On Equality, Integrity, and Justice in Stare Decisis' (1996) 105 *Yale Law Journal* 2031; C Peters, 'Equality Revisited' (1997) 110 *Harvard Law Review* 1210; H Frankfurt, 'Equality and Respect' in *Necessity, Violation and Love* (Cambridge University Press, 1994).

[3] On congruence, see L Fuller, *The Morality of Law*, rvsd edn (Yale University Press, 1969) Ch 2.

[4] See Aristotle, 'Nicomachean Ethics' in J Barnes (ed), *The Complete Works of Aristotle* (Princeton University Press, 1984) V.3. 1131a10-b15; Aristotle, 'Politics' in Barnes (ibid) III.9.1280a-15, III. 12.

When viewed through this lens, the principle becomes vulnerable to a powerful critique of emptiness and circularity.[5] However, recent scholarship has argued that the principle of equality before the law exerts pressure on adjudicators to act in accordance with their previous decisions should there be multiple permissible options available to them.[6] This approach continues to maintain that equality before the law requires nothing more than that like cases be treated alike, but argues that such a principle may not be completely empty or circular. It has also led to calls for consistency to be classed as an independent ground of judicial review.[7]

It is a mistake to construe the principle of equality before the law as wholly contained within the maxim that like cases should be treated alike. This is but one requirement among many. Equality before the law can reasonably be associated with a number of distinct principles, varying from the requirement of congruence between laws as enacted and applied to the prohibition of wrongful discrimination on the part of legislators, judges, or other legal officials or even to a fully fleshed-out theory of distributive justice. This chapter, in its examination of these requirements, will suggest that equality before the law, as a foundational constitutional principle, manifests both procedural and substantive requirements which are all informed by a commitment to treating legal subjects as moral equals. Consequently, there is no meaningful distinction between equality *before* the law and equality *in* the law, or even the equal *protection* of the law. These are all different labels which can be attached to the same fundamental constitutional commitment. What will be required to adequately meet this requirement will be the subject of the rest of this book.

1282b19-23; Westen (n 2) 539–540; K Simons, 'The Logic of Egalitarian Norms' (2000) 80 *Boston University Law Review* 693, 698, 727–728; J Rawls, *A Theory of Justice*, rvsd edn (Harvard University Press, 1971) 50–51.

[5] Westen (n 2). Westen's original article prompted a number of critical responses. See S Burton, 'Comment on "Empty Ideas"; Logical Positivist Analyses of Equality and Rules' (1982) 91 *Yale Law Journal* 1136; E Chemerinsky, 'In Defence of Equality: A Reply to Professor Westen' (1983) 81 *Michigan Law Review* 575; K Greenawalt, 'How Empty Is the Idea of Equality?' (1983) 83 *Columbia Law Review* 1167; K Karst, 'Why Equality Matters' (1983) 17 *Georgia Law Review* 245. These critiques resulted in greater reflection from Westen and culminated in the publication of his 1990 book (P Westen, *Speaking of Equality: An Analysis of the Rhetorical Force of 'Equality' in Moral and Legal Discourse* (Princeton University Press, 1990). This book marked a substantial departure from the arguments made in his 1982 article, moving from a claim that equality is completely empty towards an argument which puts greater stress on the nuances of egalitarian norms. The extent of this departure is seen starkly when one notes that his original article is not cited in the 1990 book and that he explicitly disavows its title in the preface to the book (ibid xix–xx).

[6] F Thomsen, 'Concept, Principle, and Norm – Equality Before the Law Reconsidered' [2018] *Legal Theory* 1.

[7] See M Elliott, 'Consistency as a Free-Standing Principle of Administrative Law?' (*Public Law for Everyone*, June 2018) www.publiclawforeveryone.com/2018/06/15/the-supreme-courts-judgment-in-gallaher-consistency-as-a-free-standing-principle-of-administrative-law/; A Schymyck, 'Vulnerable Detainees in Prison Illustrate the Need for Consistency as a Ground of Review' (*UKCLA Blog*, February 2020) www.ukconstitutionallaw.org/2020/02/24/alex-schymyck-vulnerable-detainees-in-prison-illustrate-the-need-for-consistency-as-a-ground-of-review/; *cf* M Foran, 'The Cornerstone of Our Law: Equality, Consistency, and Judicial Review' (2022) 81 *Cambridge Law Journal* 249.

The proceeding analysis focuses primarily on jurisprudential arguments relating to legal equality as a philosophical concept. Nevertheless, it should be stressed that correctly understanding the nature of this principle is a necessary precondition for its legal enforcement. Operating broadly within an interpretivist framework, some of the arguments advanced below will draw on both theory and doctrine to present this principle in its best light.[8] As such, the claim here is that one can best account for the divergent requirements of this principle by reference to a general obligation to treat legal subjects as moral equals. Many of the themes and concepts discussed below will be dealt with in greater detail in subsequent chapters. For now, the goal is to defend the claim that legal equality should be interpreted substantively such that it is concerned with ensuring appropriate respect for moral equality, rather than simply formal requirements of consistency.

I. TREATING LIKE CASES ALIKE

In the 1980s and 1990s, theoretical debates concerning the nature of equality centred around the argument posed by Peter Westen that it was an empty concept.[9] This critique was extremely influential and was arguably the catalyst for a shift within anti-discrimination scholarship away from equality-based accounts towards liberty-based accounts.[10] Such a reconceptualisation has the potential to significantly undermine the place of anti-discrimination rights within a principle of legal equality. Additionally, the mantle of Westen's original critique was taken up by others in the late 1990s, who argued that equality is a self-contradictory and absurd norm.[11] This critique is highly relevant for public

[8] See TRS Allan, *The Sovereignty of Law: Freedom, Constitution, and Common Law* (Oxford University Press, 2013) 333–49; J Laws, *The Common Law Constitution* (Cambridge University Press, 2014); R Dworkin, *Taking Rights Seriously* (Harvard University Press, 1977) 227–228; Simons (n 4) 720–21; TRS Allan, *Law, Liberty, and Justice: The Legal Foundations of British Constitutionalism* (Clarendon Press, 1993) 140; J Waldron, *One Another's Equals: The Basis of Human Equality* (The Belknap Press of Harvard University Press, 2017).

[9] Another notable strand of this critique has been proposed by Joseph Raz. See; J Raz, *The Morality of Freedom* (Clarendon Press, 1988) Ch 9.

[10] See E Holmes, 'Anti-Discrimination Rights without Equality' (2005) 68 *Modern Law Review* 175; T Khaitan, *A Theory of Discrimination Law* (Oxford University Press, 2015) 113–15, 130–34; S Moreau, 'In Defense of a Liberty-Based Account of Discrimination' in D Hellman and S Moreau (eds), *Philosophical Foundations of Discrimination Law* (Oxford University Press, 2013); S Moreau, 'What Is Discrimination?' (2010) 38 *Philosophy & Public Affairs* 143; S Moreau, 'Discrimination as Negligence' (2010) 40 *Canadian Journal of Philosophy* 123; *cf* D Hellman, 'Equality and Unconstitutional Discrimination' in Hellman and Moreau (ibid); D Hellman, 'Two Concepts of Discrimination' (2016) 102 *Virginia Law Review* 895; D Hellman, *When Is Discrimination Wrong?* (Harvard University Press, 2011); S Fredman, *Discrimination Law*, 2nd edn (Oxford University Press, 2011) Ch 1. There has, however, been a gradual revival of equality-based discrimination theory. See eg S Moreau, *Faces of Inequality: A Theory of Wrongful Discrimination* (Oxford University Press, 2020); B Eidelson, *Discrimination and Disrespect* (Oxford University Press, 2015).

[11] Peters, 'Equality Revisited' (n 2). This article also prompted a number of replies. See K Greenawalt, '"Prescriptive Equality": Two Steps Forward' (1997) 110 *Harvard Law Review* 1265;

lawyers interested in the principle of equality before the law as it rests upon the association of equality with the maxim of natural justice that like cases should be treated alike.[12]

According to Westen, the determination of like cases, for the purposes of legal equality, is dependent upon the applicability of pertinent legal rules. He argues that 'likes should be treated alike' means that people for whom a certain treatment is prescribed by a standard should all be given the treatment prescribed by the standard'.[13] This is also the approach taken by legal theorist HLA Hart in his discussion of justice in the administration of law where he notes that 'this meaning connotes the principle of treating like cases alike, though the criteria of when cases are alike will be, so far, only the general elements specified in the rules'.[14] Thus, on this conception, the principle of equality before the law (when understood to require only that like cases be treated alike) means that legal rules should be applied to those that they purport to apply to. This being the case, proponents of this view argue that talk of equality adds nothing to this analysis; the only thing that equality provides in this context is the consistent application of legal rules, or, more precisely, the application of legal rules: if a rule is not being applied consistently it is not being applied. Similarly, Joseph Raz argues that 'all principles can be regarded as principles of equality in virtue of their generality' but that this kind of equality is quite trivial.[15] Absent from this analysis is any account of *why* generality in principle is desirable in the first place. More precisely, to collapse concerns over the arbitrary or capricious exercise of power into mere triviality is to fail to take seriously the values of generality and non-arbitrariness as important, constitutive elements of the rule of law.

This understanding of equality as generality maps quite closely onto many of the aspects of Lon Fuller's requirement of congruence between official action and declared rule contained within the rule of law.[16] To Fuller, a lack of congruence

J Sarnoff, 'Equality as Uncertainty' (1999) 84 *Iowa Law Review* 377; C Peters, 'Slouching Towards Equality' (1999) 84 *Iowa Law Review* 801; J Sarnoff, 'I Come to Praise Morality, Not To Bury It' (1999) 84 *Iowa Law Review* 819.

[12] Westen himself defined equality as 'the position in law and morals that "people who are alike should be treated alike", and its correlative, that "people who are unalike should be treated unalike"': Westen (n 2) 539–40. His focus on the relevant likeness being between 'people' differed slightly from other scholars, who considered the principle of equality before the law to be concerned with like 'cases' being treated alike. This, however, did not change the core of Westen's argument as his definition of likeness eschewed any analysis that might hinge upon a focus on persons over cases. This is because, for Westen, determinations of likeness were premised on the applicability of some moral or legal rule to both parties. As such, persons were only alike under law where the legal cases that pertained to them were sufficiently alike. The importance of this conclusion will be elucidated further below.

[13] ibid 547.

[14] HLA Hart, 'Positivism and the Separation of Law and Morality' (1958) 71 *Harvard Law Review* 593, 623–24.

[15] Raz, *The Morality of Freedom* (n 9) 218.

[16] Fuller (n 3) 81–91. However, it is not exhaustive of his principle of congruence. Fuller argued that congruence also required what we might call 'procedural due process' including the right to representation by counsel, to cross-examination, and to appeal: ibid 81.

between judicial action and statutory law threatens to undermine the entirety of the legal order through the consequent breach of a number of other aspects of the rule of law, resulting in 'a failure to articulate reasonably clear general rules and an inconstancy in decision manifesting itself in contradictory rulings, frequent changes in direction, and retrospective changes in law'.[17] Thus, equality before the law, on this account, ensures that we are subject to the same body of laws, but that is itself an empty statement with respect to equality. If laws are being applied to those they should be applied to, then, while we are 'equally' subject to the same laws, fidelity to the rule of law is really guiding this principle. Equality appears to be adding nothing. If this were all that legal equality required, absent an underlying normative rationale, then Peters would be right when he concludes that we could remove the term 'equal' from the Equal Protection Clause of the US Constitution without changing the meaning of the clause.[18]

However, Frej Klem Thomsen has recently argued that it would be wrong to conclude from this that equality before the law is an empty principle. He argues that the principle that like cases should be treated alike does indeed have something to say independently from the demand for rule application in circumstances where a court has a number of permissible options in its adjudication of a case. In such cases, Thomsen argues that the principle of equality before the law exerts pressure on judges to treat like cases according to the same (non-discriminatory) permissible action that has most frequently occurred in previous cases. The force of this principle is directly proportional to the proportion of previous cases that have been decided in that manner.[19]

This argument rescues the principle of equality before the law from the charge of emptiness levied by Westen and ties it to the doctrine of precedent. Thomsen's principle of equal treatment, what he refers to as 'procedural legal egalitarianism', is now a viable candidate for one of the requirements of equality before the law because, on this interpretation, it is grounded within an equality framework which is independent from simple rule application, unmoored from an underlying moral rationale. Equal treatment in this sense is not inherently valuable. Nevertheless, the principle that like cases should be treated alike can instead be seen as instrumentally valuable such that a high degree of adherence to it would be necessary for maintaining a state of internal coherency and integrity within a legal system.[20] As such, it is an important aspect of the rule of law,

[17] Fuller (n 3) 82.

[18] Peters, 'Equality Revisited' (n 2) 1258.

[19] Thomsen (n 6) 13, 19. The requirement of non-discrimination contained within this principle will be explored in greater detail below. For now it is sufficient to note that Thomsen does not consider this requirement of non-discrimination to manifest anything in the way of a substantive principle of equality before the law. To him, this principle is completely procedural.

[20] See R Dworkin, *Law's Empire* (Harvard University Press, 1986); TRS Allan, 'Dworkin and Dicey: The Rule of Law as Integrity' (1988) 8 *Oxford Journal of Legal Studies* 266; Fuller (n 3) 81; TRS Allan, 'Principle, Practice, and Precedent: Vindicating Justice, According to Law' (2018) 77 *Cambridge Law Journal* 269.

even if it may be departed from in circumstances where it would require the duplication of wrongful treatment. Thus, he argues that the principle that like cases should be treated alike is not inherently morally desirable and should not be followed in circumstances where it would require that a person 'be treated *wrongly* simply because another, identically situated person has been treated wrongly'.[21]

This conception of legal equality views it as synonymous with and exhausted by a commitment to treating like cases alike where like cases are determined by reference to legal rules as opposed to moral principles. The result is the almost complete subsumption of equality before the law into the doctrine of precedent. It is not entirely clear if this principle even belongs under the umbrella of equality before the law, strictly speaking. It seems to have its home more within the ambit of the rule of law than equality before the law, if we are drawing sharp distinctions between these two constitutional principles. Put another way, it would be unclear on this reading what work the value of equality would be doing beyond grounding the procedural demand for consistency in treatment. Even here, it would not provide anything to determine *when* departure from consistent treatment is permissible, beyond a generic claim that it would be justified if consistent treatment would be wrongful. How wrongfulness is to be assessed in this context seemingly has nothing to do with the value of equality.

The argument advanced by Westen and Thomsen is committed to the view that equality principles presuppose the existence of other prescriptive rules which do the real normative work, thus rendering restatement of those rules superfluous. It does not account for how equality could form the basis of independent moral principles that may in some cases inform the substance of legal rules. This alternative approach represents a uniquely legal conception of equality, fundamentally tied to principles of good governance in the best interests of the governed.[22] Legal equality may not guarantee substantive justice, but it places substantive restrictions on the character of juridical relations operative within a legal system, and manifests within law a commitment to respecting the dignity and moral equality of legal subjects. What follows is an examination of some of the other principles which, when properly understood, are associated with equality before the law. These principles move beyond the procedural requirements mentioned above and manifest substantive restrictions on the content of legal rules.[23]

[21] Peters, 'Equality Revisited' (n 2) 1212. Peters argues that this wrong can take the form of undeserved positive treatment as well as undeserved negative treatment.

[22] See J Raz, 'The Law's Own Virtue' (2019) 39 *Oxford Journal of Legal Studies* 1.

[23] It should be stressed, however, that this kind of constitutional substantiveness is distinct from that which typically corresponds with the term 'substantive equality'. Here, substantive defines principles which affect the content of law and not those which pursue transformative social goals. See Ch 6 below.

II. EQUAL SUBJECTION TO LAW

AV Dicey, in *An Introduction to the Study of the Law of the Constitution*, defined the rule of law as 'the absolute supremacy or predominance of regular law as opposed to the influence of arbitrary power, and excludes the existence of arbitrariness, of prerogative, or even of wide discretionary authority on the part of the government'.[24] As such, he stressed that 'Englishmen are ruled by the law, and by the law alone'.[25] To elaborate upon this, he posited three meanings of the rule of law.[26] He expressed one of these meanings as guaranteeing 'not only that no man is above the law, but (which is a different thing) that here, every man, whatever be his rank or condition, is subject to the ordinary laws of the realm and amenable to the jurisdiction of the ordinary tribunals'.[27] Dicey referred to this as the 'idea of legal equality' and argued that it had been pushed to its utmost limit within England.[28] Core to this understanding of equality before the law is the notion of equal subjection of all to governance by law. It may be the case that certain classes of persons (for example, soldiers) are subject to legal duties that ordinary citizens are not and, as such, may be said to be subject to different laws. However, Dicey quite rightly stressed that this is not inconsistent with the principle of equal subjection to law so long as those persons, or any other legal officials, are not *exempted* from the application of ordinary law or the legal duties which are entailed by it.[29]

Consider the case of *M v Home Office* to elucidate this point.[30] M was a citizen of Zaire who came to the United Kingdom seeking asylum. His applications were rejected, as were his requests for judicial review of those decisions. However, while his latest application for judicial review was pending, he was deported. Upon learning of this deportation, the court ordered his return. The Secretary of State refused to comply, convinced that the application for asylum had been correctly rejected and that the deportation was lawful. The High Court proceeded to hold him in contempt of court for failing to obey a judicial order. This case illustrates a number of key aspects of the principle of equal subjection to law and the connection between that principle and the separation of powers. Of central concern was the ability of government to place itself above the law or, more precisely, to usurp the judicial function and decide for itself the applicability of a given legal rule to its present circumstances. The court held that, even if the Crown itself was immune from the judicial process, the government, and by extension its ministers and departments, were not. Lord Templeman stressed

[24] AV Dicey, *An Introduction to the Study of the Law of the Constitution* (JWF Allison ed, Oxford University Press, 2013) 119.
[25] ibid.
[26] ibid 183–206.
[27] ibid 193.
[28] ibid.
[29] ibid 194.
[30] *M v Home Office* [1994] 1 AC 377.

that 'the proposition that the executive obey the law as a matter of grace and not as a matter of necessity is a proposition which would reverse the result of the Civil War'.[31] In so holding, the court reiterated a long-standing commitment of the common law to the principle of equal subjection to law. While one could interpret the judgment in this case by reference to the rule of law alone, such a reading would fail to account for a key normative underpinning that equal subjection to law provides. In this case, a breach of the rule of law amounted to one organ of state attempting to place itself beyond the reach of law, undermining equal subjection to law.

This being said, Dicey's conception, if it is interpreted as a purely procedural constraint on government is open to the charge of emptiness expressed above. As Marshall stresses, 'the prescription of equality in law, as in morals, seems sometimes to fall away into an empty formality'.[32] Again, the issue here is not that there is no value in ensuring that law applies to those that it purports to apply to. No, the problem is that such an understanding could be explained by reference to consistency without any recourse to an underlying commitment to equality.[33] Such an interpretation would seem to collapse his second requirement of legal equality into the first. No man may be above the law in the sense that all must follow it. However, Dicey seems to have envisaged an additional requirement, one which prevented the existence of legally enshrined exemptions to law for legal or political rulers.

Marshall argues that Dicey's conception of legal equality, leaving aside his rejection of overly-broad discretionary powers, is purely procedural.[34] The two procedural constraints that he identifies from Dicey are: (1) that everyone is to be (equally) subject to general laws rather than individualised commands or mob rule; and (2) that everyone is to be (equally) covered by a body of law that is 'impartially applied without fear, favour, or anything similar, by an independent judiciary'.[35] Aspects of these constrains are certainly procedural. But these procedural constraints simply require that legal enactments are properly applied to those that they are supposed to apply to. It is the equivalent of demanding that one enforces the rules and not break them. References to equality here are superfluous except as a basic requirement of consistency and the doctrine of precedent mentioned above. That being said, other aspects of these principles are evidently more substantive. They clearly manifest more than the requirement of congruence between judicial action and legislative pronouncement; equal

[31] ibid 395.

[32] G Marshall, *Constitutional Theory* (Clarendon Press, 1971) 137.

[33] Leaving aside the argument that the rule of law is itself committed to fundamental moral equality; Allan, *Law, Liberty, and Justice: The Legal Foundations of British Constitutionalism* (n 8) 22, 163–83.

[34] Marshall (n 32) 137–38. It should be noted that the rejection of discretionary powers is clearly an example of the principle of equality before the law amounting to substantive restrictions on legal enactments.

[35] ibid 138.

subjection to law limits the potential scope of legal enactments by requiring that those enactments be general in nature, thus excluding particularised punishment of named individuals, for example. In addition, the idea that law be impartially applied without fear or favour by an independent judiciary clearly presupposes a minimum degree of independence and impartiality within the law such that it be conceived primarily as a public asset and not the emanations of the private whims of rulers.

In this sense, the principle of equal subjection to law is closely related to requirements of generality associated with the rule of law. Law must be expressed in the form of general rules and not determined solely on the basis of ad hoc adjudicative decisions.[36] Following Dicey, the rule of law may also require generality in aim: that laws be impersonal, applied only to general classes, and contain no proper names, to be contrasted with blatant arbitrariness or caprice.[37] Thus, it is not open to lawmakers to enact a bill of attainder. This would manifestly breach the principle of equality before the law.[38] Crucially, it would be the content of the law that was at issue, not the procedure by which it came to be.[39] As such, the principle of equality before the law, if it includes requirements of equal subjection to law and generality in aim, must consequently limit the content of legal rules such that particularised laws or enactments which attempted to grant unjustified immunities would be pre-emptively precluded from the class of legitimate legal aims. What is more, full conformity with the second aspect of Dicey's conception of legal equality would require adherence to some principle of the independence of the judiciary.[40] Any legislation attempting to abolish the judicial branch or to radically curtail the judicial role, properly understood, would be in violation of the rule of law and the principle of legal equality, both of which are tied to this ideal of impartiality and the classical natural law maxim of *nemo judex in causa sua*.[41]

Another aspect of the principle of equal subjection to law is the requirement that all legal subjects be full legal persons under the law, entitled to hold the same rights and be bound by the same duties as others. In concrete terms,

[36] Fuller (n 3) 46–47.

[37] See Marshall (n 32) 136–37; TRS Allan, *Constitutional Justice: A Liberal Theory of the Rule of Law* (Oxford University Press, 2001) 122–23. Note, however, that Fuller would not consider these requirements to be contained within his generality desideratum; to him, these belonged within the realm of external morality and the doctrine of fairness, not the more foundational requirement that there be a system of general rules.

[38] Allan, *The Sovereignty of Law* (n 8) 93–94, 140–41.

[39] See J Gardner, 'The Supposed Formality of the Rule of Law' in *Law as a Leap of Faith: Essays on Law in General* (Oxford University Press, 2012) 198–201. Here the common assumption that requirements of generality amount to formal or procedural restraints on law is challenged and rebutted. See also M Foran, 'The Rule of Good Law: Form, Substance and Fundamental Rights' (2019) 78 *Cambridge Law Journal* 570.

[40] See also J Raz, 'The Rule of Law and Its Virtue' in *The Authority of Law: Essays on Law and Morality*, 2nd edn (Oxford University Press, 2009) 216–17.

[41] *cf* A Vermeule, 'Contra Nemo Iudex in Sua Causa: The Limits of Impartiality' (2012) 122 *Yale Law Journal* 384.

this manifests as a complete rejection of legally enshrined slavery. A slave is not a legal subject: he is denied the protection of law and the capacity to bear legal rights. To be a slave is to be cast out from the system of juridical relationships; to be a mere object of proprietary claims.[42] No legal system claiming to uphold a principle of legal equality could countenance an institution of slavery, where persons entitled to the protection of law are instead subject only to the whims of another. In this sense, we can see starkly the distinction between subjection to law and subjection to the arbitrary will of a master, one which echoes Dicey's distinction between the rule of law and arbitrary power. When abstracted to the perspective of the legal system as a whole, the position of the slave mirrors the position of those denied the protection of the rule of law. Nigel Simmonds makes this point when he argues that 'to be governed by law is to enjoy a degree of independence from the will of others'.[43] This is to be contrasted with an interpretation of liberty which views it as pertaining to the range of choices of which one can avail oneself. It is possible for a slave to have a greater range of options open to them than a free man. Indeed, this was particularly the case in ancient Rome where some slaves had access to vast amounts wealth and social privilege relative to many free persons.[44] Nevertheless, Simmonds is right to stress that this does not make the slave free. Clearly freedom entails more than simply a wide range of possibilities open to an individual; it must at a minimum include some degree of independence from the arbitrary interference of others.[45] It is only through subjection to law that this independence can be secured. As Simmonds notes:

> [w]hen a citizen lives under the rule of law, it is conceivable that the duties imposed upon him or her will be very extensive and onerous, and the interstices between these duties might leave very few options available. Yet, if the rule of law is a reality, the duties will have limits and the limits will not be dependent upon the will of any other person.[46]

Thus, equal subjection to law, necessarily entailing subjection to the rule of law and not man, emphatically rejects any system of slavery. To be subjected to law is to be protected by the rule of law and the principles of legality which recognise the dignity and autonomy of the legal subject as a locus of juridical

[42] NE Simmonds, *Law as a Moral Idea* (Oxford University Press, 2008) 101; NE Simmonds, 'Rights at the Cutting Edge' in M Kramer et al, *A Debate Over Rights* (Clarendon Press, 1998) 113, 165–67. Note that there may be times when a slave enjoys some legal protections, for example against excessive violence from his master. Those protections are dependent upon law and, to that extent, a slave may have legal rights. However, this is a narrowly defined exception to the nature of slavery as a denial of subjection to law and might be better seen as analogous to the protections offered to animals within contemporary legal systems.

[43] Simmonds, *Law as a Moral Idea* (n 42) 101.

[44] R Gamauf, 'Slaves Doing Business: The Role of Roman Law in the Economy of a Roman Household' (2009) 16 *European Review of History* 331.

[45] Simmonds, *Law as a Moral Idea* (n 42) 101, 141–42, 156.

[46] ibid 101.

relationship; a rights and duty bearer.[47] Equal subjugation to law, like the requirement that like cases be treated alike, is derived from and obtains meaning and coherence as a result of this more foundational commitment to a moral vision of equality.

There is strong evidence to suggest that this interpretation of legal equality has been accepted by the British courts, notwithstanding an historical deference to the capacity of Parliament to disregard fundamental constitutional principles. This can be seen quite clearly in the case of *Somerset v Stewart*, a landmark decision of the Kings Bench in 1772, which held that the common law was incapable of supporting chattel slavery.[48] The decision of the court, given by Lord Mansfield held that '[t]he state of slavery is of such a nature that it is incapable of being introduced on any reasons, moral or political, but only by positive law'. Reaffirming that it was not simply the case that slavery had not been authorised by statute, Lord Mansfield noted that '[i]t is so odious, that nothing can be suffered to support is, but positive law'. As such, the common law was incapable of supporting slavery. What is it about slavery that makes it so odious that the common law cannot support it? Of course, there are basic moral commitments that explain the odiousness of slavery. But it seems that there is a distinctly legal, constitutional reason for objecting to slavery: to countenance slavery is to deny the equal subjection and protection of law to all and consequently to run afoul of constitutional commitments to the rule of law and legal equality.[49]

In the context of historical common law reasoning, these commitment were derived from the natural law tradition which has consistently set itself against slavery. Thus, the early Sophists drew upon idea of natural law to ground a commitment to the unity of all men, whether Greek or barbarian, as belonging to the same race and possessive of the same fundamental essence.[50] From here, Alkidamas advances the core insight that 'nature made no one a slave' which was eventually taken up by Roman imperial jurists, such as Florentinus and Ulpian, preserved in Justinian's *Corpus iuris civillis*. Florentinus stressed that slavery is 'against nature',[51] and Ulpian similarly argues that under the law of nature, there are no slaves because 'all human beings are equal'.[52] Where slavery exists, it is by virtue of the positive law and in direct contrast with the natural law. In this, Ulpian identified the ground for the natural law rejection of slavery: that all

[47] See J Waldron, 'How Law Protects Dignity' (2012) 71 *Cambridge Law Journal* 200; Allan, *The Sovereignty of Law* (n 8) 96; Foran (n 39).

[48] *Somerset v Stewart* [1772] 98 ER 499 (KB), [1772] 20 St Tr 1. See also F Shyllon, *Black Slaves in Britain* (Oxford University Press, 1974); E Fiddes, 'Lord Mansfield and the Sommersett Case' (1934) 50 *LQR* 499.

[49] See Allan, *Law, Liberty, and Justice: The Legal Foundations of British Constitutionalism* (n 8) Ch 7.

[50] See H Rommen, *The Natural Law: A Study in Legal and Social History and Philosophy* (T Hanley tr, Liberty Fund, 1998) Ch 1.

[51] *CIC Dig* 1.5.4 preface.

[52] *CIC Dig* 50.17.32.

humans possess the same fundamental value by virtue of the kind of being they are: persons. There are many reasons why slavery is morally reprehensible, but one which has been recognised since the time of Rome is that slavery fundamentally disrespects the moral equality of persons.

Natural law principles helped to inform common law doctrine and could be invoked in hard cases to help further or correct the common law.[53] When Lord Mansfield held that the common law 'works itself pure by rules drawn from the fountain of justice',[54] he meant the laws of nature.[55] As such, natural law could be relied upon as a source of common law where no positive law could be found. In holding that slavery was so odious that it was presumptively unlawful, Lord Mansfield relied heavily upon the natural law because by its dictates, discovered through reason, all men were free. It could only be introduced via the positive law or the *ius gentium*. Because England had no such law, Somerset could not lawfully be treated as a slave within its jurisdiction. In fact, for all its fame, *Somerset* did not establish much in the way of new precedent. Previous case law had accepted that it was 'against the law of nature for one man to be a slave to another' and so 'if the plaintiff had any right to the servitude of this negro, that right is now divested by his coming into England' because 'by Magna Charta, and the laws of England, no man can have such a property over another'.[56] In this sense, natural law maxims relating to the moral equality of persons were sources of common law; they could be drawn upon to answer more concrete questions.[57]

Thus we can see that the principle of equality before the law did not simply manifest in a procedural requirement or in the idea that differentiation in treatment should be justified. It also provided substantive principles to inform precisely what would count as an unjustified distinction between persons. As we explore these more substantive restrictions on legal content it is worth stressing that, notwithstanding the substantive nature of the principle of equality before the law, the ability of Parliament to ignore those requirements is an entirely separate issue. While there is clearly support for equal subjection to law expressed in a refutation of the capacity of the common law to sanction an institution of slavery, the judgment in this case did not amount to a ringing endorsement of the capacity of the common law to actually overturn or limit posited laws which

[53] See DJ Ibbetson, 'Natural Law and Common Law' (2001) 5 *Edinburgh Law Review* 4; JCH Wu, 'The Natural Law and Our Common Law' (1954) 23 *Fordham Law Review* 13; *cf* TJ McSweeney, *Priests of the Law: Roman Law and the Making of the Common Law's First Professionals* (Oxford University Press, 2019).

[54] *Omychund v Barker* (1744) 1 Atk 22, 33; 26 ER 15, 23. See also *James v Price* (1773) Lofft 219, 220; 98 ER 619, 621; *Jones v Randall* (1774) 1 Cowp 37; 98 ER 954, 955.

[55] See N Poser, *Lord Mansfield: Justice in the Age of Reason* (McGill-Queen's University Press, 2013) 214–16.

[56] *Chamberline v Harvey* (1696) 5 Mod 182, 190, 87 ER 596, 600.

[57] See eg *Manby v Scot* (1661–62) 1 Keb 69, 363; 83 ER 826, 996: 'There being no presidents we must resort to the law of Nature.'

would introduce slavery into England. Lord Mansfield's decision is premised on the fact that no such enactments existed. It is likely that, had they been in force at the time of this decision, the court would not have ordered Somerset to be discharged.

The concept of odious law is quite important here and would have been familiar to anyone knowledgeable of the continental jurists at this time.[58] Odious law referred to posited law which was incompatible with natural law principles. A statute authorising slavery is an obvious example. Continental jurists would treat such posited law in a very similar manner to how the Human Rights Act 1998 demands UK judges treat domestic legislation which is incompatible with the European Convention on Human Rights (ECHR): by interpreting it, as far as possible, to be compatible with natural law principles of justice and, where they could not, confining its application as much as possible. Statutes which were in harmony with the natural law were given an expansive interpretation, whereas odious law was not.

This is so, even though an odious statute may not necessarily have been struck down or voided. Under some institutional arrangements, they may be. But this is a peripheral issue.[59] It is true that many back of the napkin summaries of the natural law tradition begin and end with the maxim *lex inusta non est lex*, crudely and incompletely translated as the idea that an unjust law is no law. But this is incomplete even taken in abstraction from the rest of the natural law tradition. Lex is posited law, understood to be a good faith attempt to more concretely determine the requirements of the natural law – *ius*. It is not generally taken to be something which exists in abstraction from this connection to justice. *Lex* is an interpretation of *ius*, as applied to specific contexts. Thus, as early as the Institutes of Gaius, it was understood that 'considerations of civil law can destroy civil but not natural rights'.[60] But this was first and foremost a maxim about the interpretation of law, not the capacity of judges to strike down statute. Where the option existed to interpret positive law compatibly with natural law, it was taken over an odious interpretation. This is exactly what happened in *Somerset*. Positive law which permitted slavery did exist, but it was foreign to England. When faced with an interpretation of common law that would be as odious as slavery, the common law courts favoured an interpretation which was compatible with natural law requirements of justice.

Slavery, the institution which most fundamentally undermines the principle of equal subjection to law, is incompatible with the common law. A decision to breach or set aside that principle in favour of enforcing an Act of Parliament is one which brings the ostensible conflict between the rule of law and parliamentary

[58] See RH Helmholz, *Natural Law in Court: A History of Legal Theory in Practice* (Harvard University Press, 2015) 108–109.

[59] ibid 69–75.

[60] *G Inst* 1.158 (F de Zulueta trans, 1946).

sovereignty into sharp focus, but that is a separate issue.[61] For now, it suffices to note that Somerset's case signifies a deeper understanding of what 'equal' means when we speak of equality before the law, one which establishes some level of basic equality in status as between individuals within the state, as opposed to simply requiring that governmental officials obey the law, whatever its content may be.[62] The common law may be informed by a concept of equality before the law that could never support the establishment of slavery, even if it may yield to the principle of parliamentary sovereignty. Even here, however, it is important to stress that legislation is interpreted by reference to these background common law principles and so it is not quite so clear as to say that legislation permitting slavery might still be given legal effect. True, it might. But it would also be given as limited an effect as plausibly defensible, precisely because of the common law presumption in favour of equality before the law.

III. NON-DISCRIMINATION

Principles of non-discrimination seem to be obviously and intrinsically linked to the concept of equality before the law. Indeed, when one ponders what equality before the law might require within a contemporary constitutional system, often non-discrimination is the first thing that comes to mind. Other aspects of the principle, such as adherence to the doctrine of precedent and a commitment to equal subjection of law are rarely seen as prime or emblematic instantiations. Nevertheless, while principles of non-discrimination are regularly associated with equality before the law, they are often seen as contained within the other requirements set out above. For example, Thomsen considers non-discrimination to be a necessary element of the principle that like cases should be treated alike.[63] Recall, however, that Thomsen considers determinations of likeness to arise non-comparatively, by reference to specific legal rules as opposed to determinations that individuals are moral or legal equals. He argues that two cases are alike 'in the sense required for equality before the law *iff* they share the set of permissible actions, that is, if the court ought non-comparatively to treat them the same'.[64] Thomsen's commitment to the belief that determinations of likeness must be made non-comparatively results in him facing conclusions which he finds intuitively unsatisfying.[65] Not wishing to conclude that treating like cases alike could

[61] See Allan, *The Sovereignty of Law* (n 8) 133–68; Allan, 'Principle, Practice, and Precedent: Vindicating Justice, According to Law' (n 20); TRS Allan, 'Questions of Legality and Legitimacy: Form and Substance in British Constitutionalism' (2011) 9 *International Journal of Constitutional Law* 155.

[62] On equality and status, see J Waldron, *Dignity, Rank, and Rights* (Oxford University Press, 2012); Waldron, *One Another's Equals: The Basis of Human Equality* (n 8).

[63] Thomsen (n 6) 9–11.

[64] ibid 8.

[65] ibid 10–11.

be compatible with blatantly wrongful discrimination, whilst holding steadfast to the claim that determinations of likeness must be done by reference only to existing rules rather than moral principles, he must then locate a requirement of non-discriminatory treatment within the concept of like *treatment*. A principle that likes should be treated alike contains: (i) a determination of likeness; and (ii) a commitment to treat those like cases alike – like treatment.[66] He argues, in addition to this, that:

> A court treats two cases alike *iff* 1) the court φ's in case A and φ's in case B, and 2) φ'ing does not requires [*sic*] the court to distinguish on the basis of a property that case A and case B do not share.[67]

This additional requirement of non-discrimination or non-arbitrariness as a component of like *treatment* (and in no way related to determinations of like cases or like persons) appears from nowhere. It is not grounded in or informed by any explicit theoretical foundation; it exists entirely to prevent equality before the law from being compatible with wrongful discrimination on the part of adjudicative bodies such as courts without having to concede that likeness may be determined by reference to moral truth. Thomsen and I are in agreement that non-discrimination is an aspect of equality before the law. However, his explanation for why this is the case is unsatisfactory. He simply asserts that a principle of equality before the law which fails to prohibit wrongfully discriminatory application of law would be intuitively unpalatable.

A principle of non-discrimination arises because we consider individuals who differ with regard to a particular characteristic to nevertheless be sufficiently alike (in spite of that difference) by virtue of their *moral* equality. It is not something that is inherent within the concept of like treatment; it originates from a determination of likeness which is comparative in terms of moral worth. Where there is overlap between equal treatment and non-discriminatory treatment, it occurs at the point of determining likeness. It is only when the moral equality of two individuals is recognised – when we see them as alike despite some other difference – that we can conclude that treating them differently would amount to a moral or legal wrong in a given context. To that end, there is nothing special about the requirement of like treatment; the important moral work is done entirely by determinations of likeness. Once we have done that, a requirement of equal treatment demands only that treatment accorded to one is consistent with the treatment accorded to the other. Of course, it is no surprise

[66] It should be noted that Thomsen's description of this requirement as one of non-discrimination might also be described as a requirement of non-arbitrariness, as a common interpretation of discrimination would require that decisions be made on the basis of very particularised grounds such as race or sex but not necessarily parentage. See Khaitan (n 10) Ch 2; T Khaitan and S Steel, 'Wrongs, Group Disadvantage and the Legitimacy of Indirect Discrimination Law' in H Collins and T Khaitan (eds), *Foundations of Indirect Discrimination Law* (Hart Publishing, 2018).

[67] Thomsen (n 6) 10.

that this has led many to conclude that equal treatment may not be desirable in circumstances where it requires the duplication of wrongful treatment.[68]

In contrast, a principle of non-discrimination focuses only on the prohibition of certain kinds of wrongful treatment. It does not mandate uniformity in treatment. This is of vital importance. Too often it is assumed that equal treatment *means* non-discriminatory treatment. Rather, equal treatment demands far more than the prohibition of unjustifiable less favourable treatment. It requires that likes are afforded the same treatment regardless of what that treatment is. Non-discrimination, as it manifests within law, is instead focused on prohibiting particular forms of unjust or wrongful treatment.[69] One principle *mandates* consistency in action, the other *prohibits* certain actions. The equal treatment principles which we have in mind for our purposes then are exactly those that Thomsen identifies: the equal treatment of like cases in accordance with the doctrine of precedent. He is wrong to think that this is all that equality before the law requires, but it may be all that it requires in the way of equal treatment. Thomsen is entirely correct to conclude that this principle may yield in circumstances where the duplication of wrongful treatment is threatened. Non-discriminatory treatment, however, is a free-standing principle which may be more central to the common law constitutional order due to its intrinsic value and its connection to the concept of non-arbitrariness.[70]

Modern constitutional frameworks are therefore not wrong to draw a connection between legal equality and non-discrimination.[71] For example, in 1954, the US Supreme Court had, in a landmark case, declared that state laws establishing segregated schools for Black and white pupils were in breach of the Fourteenth Amendment to the Constitution, which holds that no state shall 'deny to any person within its jurisdiction the equal protection of the laws'.[72] The case, *Brown v Board of Education*,[73] overturned the decision of *Plessy v Ferguson*,[74] which had promoted a doctrine of 'separate but equal' that was based on the notion that 'equality of treatment is accorded when the races are provided substantially equal facilities, even though these facilities be separate'.[75] In *Brown*, the court concluded that '[s]eparate educational facilities are

[68] ibid 23–25; Peters, 'Foolish Consistency' (n 2); M Kramer, *In Defence of Legal Positivism: Law without Trimmings* (Oxford University Press, 1999) Ch 2.

[69] Even indirect discrimination is concerned with decisions that are *discriminatory* in effect not simply unequal in effect. See Holmes (n 10).

[70] Indeed, the classic example of complete arbitrariness is treatment which discriminates on the basis of hair colour: *Associated Provincial Picture Houses Ltd. v Wednesbury Corpn* [1948] 1 KB 223, 229.

[71] See eg Canadian Charter for Rights and Freedoms, s 15(1); Constitution of South Africa, s 9(1); Constitution of India, Art 14; Constitution of Ireland, Art 40.

[72] Constitution of the United States of America, Am 14, s 1.

[73] *Brown v Board of Education*, 347 US 483 (1954) (SC).

[74] *Plessy v Ferguson*, 163 US 537 (1896) (SC).

[75] *Brown v Board of Education of Topeka* (n 73) 489.

inherently unequal', and that, as such, those who are subject to segregation have been denied equal protection of the laws guaranteed by the Fourteenth Amendment.[76]

It should be noted, however, that often judicial decisions concerning the precise nature of the principle of equality before the law leave much to be desired. The *Brown* decision is a prime example. The court made little effort to substantiate any connection between the Fourteenth Amendment and principles of non-discrimination save a bare assertion that segregated educational systems are inherently unequal. Nevertheless, it is possible for an informed reader to present a more charitable interpretation of the Fourteenth Amendment and the cases which flow from it.

While *Brown* operates within a constitutional framework that is quite distinct from the British common law system, I suggest that the court nevertheless relied on a similar interpretation of equality before the law that I wish to advance: namely, that this is a substantive principle which affects legal content and entails respect for the equal moral status of legal subjects. Only this could explain how the equal protection of law might require the state to act in a non-discriminatory manner. Nothing within a formal or procedural interpretation can explain why faithfully and consistently applied, but wrongfully discriminatory, laws violate legal equality.

Another example of equality before the law entailing principles of non-discrimination, this time in the UK context, is the Belmarsh case.[77] This case concerned the indefinite detention without trial of foreign suspected terrorists under anti-terrorism law.[78] UK law prevented British nationals from being detained indefinitely without trial. However, non-nationals seemingly did not have that protection. The House of Lords held that such discrimination against non-nationals was not compatible with the ECHR and issued a declaration to that effect. For our purposes, attention should be drawn to the judgments of Lord Hoffmann and Baroness Hale. Lord Hoffmann dissented from the majority, agreeing that the appeal should be allowed but grounding this decision in a denial that there was a public emergency of the kind needed to justify detention. However, he also indicated strong disagreement with the majority focus on the ECHR, instead wishing to emphasise an incompatibility between the Constitution and any law that attempted to imprison an individual indefinitely without trial.[79] As such, this case may have been decided by reference to UK constitutional law independently of the ECHR. With that in mind, the following extract from the judgment of Baroness Hale may be hinting towards the principle of equality before the law that is of interest to us:

[76] ibid 496.
[77] *A v Secretary of State for the Home Dept* [2004] UKHL 56.
[78] Anti-Terrorism, Crime and Security Act 2001, s 23.
[79] *A v Secretary of State for the Home Dept* (n 77) [97].

> Democracy values each person equally. In most respects, this means that the will of the majority must prevail. But valuing each person equally also means that the will of the majority cannot prevail if it is inconsistent with the equal rights of minorities. … No one has the right to be an international terrorist. But substitute 'black', 'disabled', 'female', 'gay', or any other similar adjective for 'foreign' before 'suspected international terrorist' and ask whether it would be justifiable to take power to lock up that group but not the 'white', 'able- bodied', 'male' or 'straight' suspected international terrorists. The answer is clear.[80]

This aspect of her judgment is grounded in fundamental principles of legal equality. The decision of the court in *Brown* and the implications of Baroness Hale's judgment in the Belmarsh case evidently rejected an understanding of legal equality as simply the application of laws to those the laws purport to apply to, regardless of their content. As this chapter has argued, that understanding represents only one aspect of the principle of equality before the law. At its core, equality before the law demands that individuals be treated as legal and moral equals. Such treatment seems now to necessitate non-discrimination in the creation, interpretation, and application of law. As Allan stresses:

> [i]t is not sufficient for laws or government policies to be accurately applied to particular persons, in accordance with their true meaning or proper interpretation; the associated distinctions made between persons, or groups of persons, must also be capable of justification.[81]

IV. EQUALS BEFORE THE LAW

The principle of legal equality is informed by a conception of the rule of law which limits the ability of legal officials to exempt themselves from their own laws and enact non-general laws such as bills of attainder. However, as has been argued above, equality before the law, properly understood, also requires limitations to be placed on the way in which the state draws distinctions between persons or groups of persons, requiring non-discrimination in some form or another.

Acceptance of these conclusions would signify a notable shift in our understanding not only of the principle of equality before the law but also of the rule of law itself. Requirements of generality ensure that all are subject to the same laws of justice, preventing lawmakers from enacting legislation which singles out particular individuals or groups for adverse treatment. This guarantees some basic degree of equality as between citizens and lawmakers as well as between individual citizens themselves. Principles of non-discrimination build upon and

[80] ibid [237]–[238]. See also *Ghaidan v Godin-Mendoza* [2004] UKHL 30, [132]: 'Democracy is founded on the principle that each individual has equal value.'

[81] Allan, *Constitutional Justice: A Liberal Theory of the Rule of Law* (n 37) 2.

deepen this notion of equal citizenship. Legal decisions pertaining to the proper exercise of constituted authority must be informed by a conception of likeness that provides guidance as to the correct understanding of equality before the law; one which allows a court to place substantive limitations on the content of specific laws in accordance not only with the principle of equality but also with the rule of law, of which legal equlity is a foundational tenet.[82] This conception is premised on an understanding of equality before the law as guaranteeing 'the protection of *equal laws*, not merely the equal application of the laws'.[83] It is thus essential for courts to have due regard to this principle when interpreting statute and common law alike.

Even the doctrine of precedent, informed by the principle that like cases should be treated alike, while not necessarily informed by a conception of equal citizenship in its determination of like cases, is premised upon a commitment to respecting the equal legal status of legal subjects as all being subject to the same body of laws consistently applied. Similarly, the principle of equal subjection to law establishes and vindicates the principle that both ruler and ruled are sufficiently alike that requiring one set of laws for one and another for the other would amount to an infringement of basic justice.

This conception of likeness has clearly changed over time, as social attitudes have changed to more accurately reflect the demands of moral equality. We need only cast our gaze back one hundred years to encounter a much more restricted understanding of who counts as a moral equal. Constitutional and common law jurisprudence has all too often been used to deny the equal moral status of persons. Examples abound, but two will suffice to establish the point. First, the historic exclusion of women and certain classes of men from many of the aspects of full citizenship throughout the common law world.[84] Second, the legal status of non-whites, particularly Blacks, in the United States and elsewhere. The case of *Dred Scott v Sandford* represents one of the most stringent denials of moral equality one can imagine: the complete denial of equal legal status to an ethnic group.[85] The Court ruled that Blacks:

> are not included, and were not intended to be included, under the word 'citizens' in the Constitution, and can therefore claim none of the rights and privileges which that instrument provides for and secures to citizens of the United States. On the contrary, they were at the time considered as a subordinate and inferior class of beings ...[86]

Contemporary judicial analysis of the principle of equality before the law is wise to reject such reasoning. Nevertheless, as we have seen above, it would be

[82] See generally Allan, *Law, Liberty, and Justice: The Legal Foundations of British Constitutionalism* (n 8); Allan, *Constitutional Justice: A Liberal Theory of the Rule of Law* (n 37); Allan, *The Sovereignty of Law* (n 8).

[83] Allan, *Law, Liberty, and Justice: The Legal Foundations of British Constitutionalism* (n 8) 163.

[84] See S Fredman, *Women and Law* (Oxford University Press, 1997) Ch 2.

[85] *Dred Scott v Sandford*, 60 US 393 (1857).

[86] ibid 404–405.

unwise to presume that these blatant errors mean that equality has only recently been recognised as an important legal value. While *Dred Scott* represents one of the worst of these failures, *Somerset* represents a great success, drawing far more directly upon the classical common law and natural law traditions than the odious decisions which reject moral equality altogether.

Legal equality means very little if it does not entail a commitment to viewing persons as *equals* before the law. This recognition that past mistakes are mistakes is essential to the integrity of the common law constitution, even if it is not, by virtue of its mistakenness, determinative of legal principle.[87] Correct understandings of this principle deepen and extend our conception of likeness, forcing us to cast our gaze into the social domain and explore how the state distinguishes between persons or groups of persons. Ronald Dworkin provides us with a clear exemplification of this conception of equal moral status when he insists that government must show equal concern and respect for all legal subjects.[88] This conception has clearly informed the judgment of Baroness Hale in the Belmarsh case and is the normative core which grounds the principle of equality before the law. There will inevitably be times when legal officials fail to live up to this ideal, just as there will always be failures to properly respect the separation of powers or the right to access to courts. But this should not be reason to abandon our commitment to the moral equality of persons, just as instances of injustice should not be reason to stop striving for justice.

The notion of equal concern and respect is seen as embodying a 'deeper conception of equality than the superficial conception of equalising material benefits or burdens'.[89] Here Dworkin draws a distinction between what has been described as superficial 'equal treatment' and deeper 'equal concern' or 'treatment as an equal'. Using the example of a father with two children, one of whom is dying from a disease that is only making the other uncomfortable, he argues that one does not show equal concern for both children if they flip a coin to decide which child shall receive the remaining dose of medicine.[90] To Dworkin, this shows that 'the right to treatment as an equal is fundamental, and the right to equal treatment, derivative'.[91] On this reading, the principle of equality before the law requires the state to recognise and respect the fact that all citizens are *equals* before the law, not simply that they should be *treated* equally before the law.[92]

[87] See G Postema, 'Integrity: Justice in Workclothes' (1997) 82 *Iowa Law Review* 821, 828–31.

[88] Dworkin (n 8) 227–28. See also Simons (n 4) 720–21; Allan, *Law, Liberty, and Justice: The Legal Foundations of British Constitutionalism* (n 8) 140; Waldron (n 8).

[89] Simons (n 4) 721.

[90] Dworkin (n 8) 227.

[91] ibid.

[92] See also Waldron's analysis of the importance of moral equality for modern political and legal theory: Waldron, *One Another's Equals: The Basis of Human Equality* (n 8); *cf* R Dahl, *On Political Equality* (Yale University Press, 2006); N Smith, *Basic Equality and Discrimination: Reconciling Theory and Law* (Ashgate, 2011).

This analysis is illuminating; however, it also presents us with a new problem, namely, how one is to determine what 'treatment as an equal' requires. Considerable confusion and uncertainty abounds within this area of law as a result of a failure to adequately answer that question. If two or more things share equal moral status, certain actions may be required to adequately respect that fact, and certain actions may be prohibited. The idea of treatment as equals commits us to the position that legal subjects have equal moral status, but how we respect that equality does not manifest itself as a matter of logic.[93] Multiple ways of treating individuals as equals exist. It is a matter of value which conception is chosen. This means that equality is not empty, but, just like notions of justice or legality, it is considerably more complex than scholars sympathetic to the Westen critique presume. This being said, it is not necessarily open to us to interpret this principle in whatever way we wish. As an interpretative concept operating within a legal system, conceptions of equality before the law must adequately fit with the jurisdictional context within which they operate and maintain a degree of internal coherency such that requirements are non-contradictory. The values which are to be incorporated to substantiate the meaning of this principle must arise from or at least not contradict those which have been elucidated through the jurisdictional history of a given legal system.

The correct interpretation of the principle of equality before the law is so often confused and unclear precisely because there is no single principle of equality. Rather, there are multiple principles of equality which are themselves informed by divergent political ideologies and conceptions of justice.[94] Following from this, we can conclude that the concept of equality in the abstract, and the principle of equality before the law specifically rest on 'multiple normative foundations'.[95] Thus, while Fredman recognises that '[t]he choice between different conceptions of equality is not one of logic but of values or policy',[96] this still leaves us with the difficult task of presenting a coherent theory given that the law is routinely informed by a number of contradictory conceptions of equality.

This being said, the principle of equality before the law should not be confused with the broader concept or value of equality. The scope of this principle concerns the constitutional relationship between the state and its legal subjects. As such, equality before the law has little to say about interactions between private individuals. Such concerns must be dealt with through other

[93] S Fredman, *Discrimination Law*, 2nd edn (Oxford University Press, 2011) 2.

[94] See P Shin, 'Is There a Unitary Concept of Discrimination?' in D Hellman and S Moreau (eds), *Philosophical Foundations of Discrimination Law* (Oxford University Press, 2013); C O'Cinneide, 'The Uncertain Foundations of Contemporary Anti-Discrimination Law' (2011) 11 *International Journal of Discrimination and the Law* 7.

[95] Khaitan (n 10) 8. Indeed, many scholars working within discrimination law theory reject any connection between non-discrimination and equality, preferring a liberty-based account. See Holmes (n 10); Moreau, 'In Defense of a Liberty-Based Account of Discrimination' (n 10); Khaitan (n 10) 130–34.

[96] Fredman, *Discrimination Law* (n 93) 2.

areas of the common law and the ordinary legislative process.[97] Nevertheless, as this chapter has shown, the principle of equality before the law has quite a lot to say about the products of the legislative process and manifests both procedural and substantive restrictions on law. This is in direct contrast with the approach taken by Thomsen and other scholars sympathetic to the Westen critique. Thomsen explicitly draws a distinction between what he refers to as equality *in* the law and equality *before* the law. Equality *in* the law is described as entailing rights and duties contained within positive law 'i.e. the *content* of the law, and mandates something like the absence of certain distinctions in the distribution of these'.[98] In contrast, equality *before* the law is seen as pertaining to the practices of legal officials, what he describes as 'the *process* of the law, and mandates something like the absence of certain distinctions in its application'.[99]

To Thomsen, a violation of equality *in* the law occurs when a state enshrines racial distinctions in law and a violation of equality *before* the law occurs when a judge 'wittingly or unwittingly' allows racial prejudice to cloud her judgement in the application of racially neutral law. This distinction is ultimately untenable. These are not two neatly separable and alternative conceptions; they are two requirements of the same principle, each unintelligible without the other. The prohibition of racial prejudice in the administration and application of law is evidently informed by a principle of non-discrimination and non-arbitrariness. However, once we accept that equality before the law entails respect for such a principle, it would be completely arbitrary to not also prohibit discriminatory or arbitrary legal content. Why should equality before the law prohibit *unconscious* racial discrimination if it does not prohibit *deliberate* racial discrimination? Equally, is there not an internal contradiction in a principle which prohibits discrimination in the content of law, but which does not also prohibit discriminatory application of facially neutral law? If we are to agree with Thomsen's dichotomy, we are faced with the task of explaining why equality before the law mandates non-arbitrariness or non-discrimination in the application of law but not in the creation of law, as if the problem with discriminatory application had nothing to do with the discriminatory nature of the treatment and everything to do with a lack of congruence between law as enacted and as applied. If part of the problem (from the perspective of legal equality) is indeed the discriminatory nature of the treatment, then this must surely view discriminatory legal content as also a threat to equality before the law.

In his description of the principle of equal treatment, Thomsen relies on an example of a court sentencing individuals disparately by virtue of their parentage.[100] It is clear that the issue which arises here is not with the fact that legal rules are

[97] See Equality Act 2010; B Hepple, *Equality: The Legal Framework*, 2nd edn (Hart Publishing, 2014).

[98] Thomsen (n 6) 3.

[99] ibid.

[100] ibid 5–6.

not being applied; in this example, sentencing decisions are left to the discretion of the judge. No, the problem with treating individuals differently on the basis of parentage arises because a distinction is being drawn on the basis of a normatively irrelevant characteristic such that the decision is unreasonable and unjustified. It is clear that the point of contention here is the distinction itself, not the lack of congruence between legislative pronouncement and official action. If this reading is correct and Thomsen's requirement of non-discrimination within the definition of equal treatment excludes specific kinds of distinctions that may be drawn by legal officials, it seems completely arbitrary to conclude that a breach of the principle of equality before the law occurs when a *court* draws such distinctions (Thomsen's equality before the law) but not when a *legislature* does (his equality in the law). It simply cannot be the case that the principle of equality before the law prohibits the drawing of arbitrary or discriminatory distinctions by a court but has nothing to say about those exact same distinctions being drawn by a legislature or an administrative body. Ultimately, if the principle of equality before the law is entirely procedural and pertains only to principles of rule application then it cannot entail a requirement of non-arbitrariness or non-discrimination. If it does entail such a requirement, that requirement must apply to all organs of state, including the legislature.

From the perspective of the legal subject, it makes little difference if discrimination comes in the form of a faithfully applied discriminatory statute or the arbitrary (mis)use of official discretion. It is almost senseless to have a right not to be racially discriminated overtly but no right to have legal rules applied without racial bias or vice versa. Equality before the law, properly understood, cannot entail one of these requirements without also entailing the other. Once we see these principles as derivative of this broader principle of equal citizenship, it becomes easier to interpret Thomsen's analysis in its proper context. His mistake lies in the location of the requirement of non-discrimination: it does not arise by virtue of a requirement of equal treatment; it is grounded in a commitment to treating legal subjects as legal and moral equals, as all viable equality principles are.

The best way to account for the divergent requirements that have come to be associated with equality before the law is to recognise that this constitutional principle is informed by conceptions of likeness that relate to the moral status of individuals or groups within the legal sphere. The principle of equality before the law must be informed by this conception of equality which ensures that all are *equals* before the law not simply that they be treated equally. This raises a considerable difficulty relating to how one is to respect this equal moral status. While it is clear that determinations as to the best way to 'treat equals as equals' is a matter of values, not logic, it is not immediately clear which values should inform interpretations of the principle of equality before the law nor which conceptions of equality are best for this purpose. What *is* clear is that, whichever conceptions are chosen, they must be harmonious and cannot contradict one another. This does nothing to assist judges in their choice of conception except in the crucial respect that it prevents them from interpreting the principle of equality before the law in a manner which is self-contradictory. Whichever decision is made must be made consistent with what has come before it or must be willing to depart from and abandon those principles.

The fact that much of these requirements can be described by reference to the rule of law as much as to equality before the law indicates that there is a close and intimate connection between the rule of law and the notion of equal citizenship. Equality before the law, when viewed in this manner results in us shifting our focus from determining likeness by reference to existing legal rules towards a conception of likeness which can inform and affect the content of those very rules. At a minimum, equality before the law tempers the doctrine of precedent and the notion that like cases should be treated alike by demanding that conclusions regarding the differential treatment afforded to particular cases be justified. As Allan notes;

> The demand for justice is an appeal to fundamental equality, insisting that the differential treatment of different persons or groups be justified – consistent with the principles that we espouse as the appropriate criteria to determine the legitimate exercise of governmental authority.[101]

Equality before the law, like any constitutional principle, is informed by and intimately connected to other constitutional principles such as the rule of law, and the doctrine of precedent. Nevertheless, it is a free-standing pillar of the British constitutional order, in many ways doing a significant amount of normative work to underpin and inform a number of other constitutional principles. Equality before the law is, at its core, the foundation of equal citizenship; any theory of the common law constitution must adequately account for and give proper recognition to the importance of this fundamental precept.

[101] Allan, 'Principle, Practice, and Precedent: Vindicating Justice, According to Law' (n 20) 271.

2

Legal Equality and Social Policy

IN THE PREVIOUS chapter, we mentioned Ronald Dworkin's appeal to deeper notions of equality which move beyond superficial duties to 'equalise' benefits or burdens towards a more fundamental commitment to respect the moral equality of persons. This chapter explores that commitment in greater detail, arguing that the principle of equality before the law could be plausibly interpreted to require adherence to a number of equality principles, but that it cannot reasonably entail respect for all possible equality principles simultaneously. To most legal theorists, the notion of equal concern and respect has a particular association with the work of Dworkin. While the insights offered by his analysis should not be downplayed, it is important to be aware of the place that moral equality and the concept of equal concern and respect hold within much broader debates in the fields of political philosophy, ethics, and even legal history. Indeed, most modern theories of moral or political obligation rely on the notion of human equality in one way or another. As such, a coherent interpretation of the principle of equality before the law will necessarily have to adopt a consistent ethical stance in relation to these foundational debates. It is one thing to say that equality before the law entails respect for the moral equality of persons; it is another thing entirely to adequately unpack precisely what that may require within a particular social, political, and juridical context.

To that end, this chapter argues that we can meaningfully distinguish between equality principles and equalisation principles (what could be called egalitarian principles). An equality principle, broadly construed, is one which is informed by this commitment to respect moral equality, even if it does not mandate any equalisation. When abstracted from the more foundational commitment to respecting moral equality, equalisation principles of the sort I describe, lose much of their intrinsic appeal. This is not to say that they lose their contingent appeal; we can easily imagine how equalisation of treatment, opportunities, or outcomes might bring about desirable social consequences such that they become prudential means to achieve the common good of all members of a community. However, this alone begins to bring to the fore important distinctions between deontological and consequentialist conceptions of equality.

How then is a judge, charged with interpreting a constitutional principle of equality before the law, supposed to decide between these competing conceptions? This chapter suggests that there is much to be found within the common law tradition which can lend guidance to this deliberation. The rule of law and the conception of man inherent within legality have a general affinity with a particular deontological conception of the moral status of the legal subject. Constitutional equality or legal equality is therefore a particular account of how one is to best respect the equal moral status of legal subjects. There is thus something distinctly 'legal' about legal equality: the affinity between the common law and deontology suggests that legal equality is primarily (although not exclusively) concerned with the principled articulation of the rights and duties which accrue by virtue of the foundational commitment to equal dignity that gives meaning to our constitutional order. This principled approach provides reasoned justification for the common distinction between appeal of executive decision and review for legality. The independence of the judiciary and the rule of law demand that judicial review occur on the basis of constitutional principle and not goal-orientated policy concerns which are properly within the purview of the political branches of state.

This conception of equality before the law is not just compatible with the common law constitution; it is arguably the foundation upon which the pillars of British public law rest; the fountain from which other principles spring. Properly understood, principles of democracy, parliamentary sovereignty, the independence of the judiciary, and the rule of law are all fundamentally committed to a particular conception of the moral equality of legal subjects. However, this does not mean that the British constitutional order has always – or even often – respected moral equality in this manner. The fact that legal equality is foundational does not mean that the state is actually adhering to its obligations to respect moral equality. However, to adhere to those obligations, we must first have a coherent picture of what they are.

Once we accept that legal equality is only derivatively concerned with equalisation and that respect for moral equality is fundamental, it becomes clear that constitutional principles derived from this value are similarly grounded in a concern with moral equality rather than equalisation. It is for this reason, for example, that *stare decisis* is ultimately justified by reference to the demand to justify departures from consistent treatment, rather than anything intrinsically or contingently valuable about consistent treatment itself.[1]

I. EQUAL CONCERN AND RESPECT

Ronald Dworkin argues that a constitutional principle of equality before the law necessitates respect for legal subjects as moral equals.[2] By this he means that individuals have a legal right to *treatment as an equal* rather than simply equal

[1] See M Foran, 'The Cornerstone of Our Law: Equality, Consistency, and Judicial Review' (2022) 81 *Cambridge Law Journal* 249.

[2] R Dworkin, *Taking Rights Seriously* (Harvard University Press, 1977) 226–29.

treatment. We have seen in the previous chapter that this occupies a central role within equal protection jurisprudence for Dworkin. All other equality-based rights must necessarily derive from this fundamental right. In this, Dworkin is entirely correct. However, equal concern and respect could mean a great many things and it is not clear from that commitment alone what a right to be treated as an equal actually requires.

Dworkin suggests that we should acknowledge 'the distinction between equality as a policy and equality as a right'.[3] In so doing he seems to be hinting towards a distinction between telic and deontic conceptions of equal concern and respect, what might be crudely described as the contrast between a commitment to *moral* equality and a commitment to *social* equality.[4] Each of these broad approaches will be addressed in turn. However, it is important to note at the outset that Dworkin is wrong to think that drawing a distinction between equality as a right and equality as a social policy is sufficient to resolve these contentious debates. As will be explained below, an advocate of distributive equality can very easily argue that equality as a social policy, the equal or fair distribution of benefits and burdens is also a fundamental right, compliance with which is necessary to properly respect the equal dignity of persons. There must therefore be some stronger reason for embracing one of these conceptions over the other. I will argue that the common law provides such a reason once its connection to respect-based deontology is properly understood. There is nothing within the common law constitution which prohibits policies of redistribution, be they egalitarian or prioritarian in nature. Indeed, as will be explored in the final chapter, the interpretation of what properly falls within the realm of lawful discretion afforded to administrative decision-makers will likely take these principles as emblematic of the kinds of legitimate principles that a public authority can prudentially choose between.[5] However, to claim that the common law *demands* one form of distribution over another would require a quite radical reinterpretation of legal equality.

It is important at this point to stress that a theory of legal equality is not, nor is it intended to be, a complete theory of social justice akin to the work of Rawls.[6] The task before us is to identify a principle of legal equality that sets the boundaries of legislative or executive action within a constitutional order, appropriately respectful of the rule of law and the independence of the judiciary. To that end, there may be aspects of a complete theory of justice that can only

[3] ibid 226.

[4] See A Sangiovanni, 'On the Relation Between Moral and Distributive Equality' in G Brock (ed), *Cosmopolitanism versus Non-Cosmopolitanism* (Oxford University Press, 2013); C Fourie et al (eds), *Social Equality: On What It Means to Be Equals* (Oxford University Press, 2015).

[5] Here we might take inspiration from the 'green light' approach to administrative law. See C Harlow and R Rawlings, *Law and Administration*, 4th edn (Cambridge University Press, 2022); C Casey, 'An Administrative State for the Common Good' (*Ius & Iustitium*, 28 July 2022) www.iusetiustitium.com/an-administrative-state-for-the-common-good/.

[6] J Rawls, *A Theory of Justice*, rvsd edn (Harvard University Press, 1971).

be brought into law through legislative or executive means, regardless of their substantive merit. A theory of equality before the law must adequately fit the practice as we understand it, including a defensible distribution of legislative, executive and judicial power. The focus of this book is only on legal equality: the *constitutional* requirements derived from the equal moral status of persons. Other moral or political ends, even those essential for a complete theory of social justice, would require executive and legislative action to be achieved. It is then a separate question whether our constitutional division of powers should be departed from to empower the judiciary to enforce its vision of social justice, effectively taking on the role of legislature or executive to do so. Even here, however, foundational legal principles can and do serve to both restrain and empower. The rule of law sets both limits on the exercise of state power and duties upon legal officials to act in the public interest.[7] It may not be appropriate for a court to dictate how to act from within a range of defensible options, but it is an inherent jurisdiction of a common law court to determine the scope of that range, precluding unreasonable ends and facilitating the pursuit of good ones.

II. CONSEQUENTIALIST EQUALITY

Teleology is derived from two Greek words: *telos* meaning end, goal, or purpose; and *logos* meaning reason or explanation. Within the field of normative ethics, teleology focuses on identifying certain goals that should be pursued. It is thus closely related to consequentialism and the belief that the outcomes of one's conduct are the ultimate basis for evaluating the rightness or wrongness of that conduct. To a consequentialist, a morally right action is one which will produce a good consequence. Teleology, as it operates within normative ethics, focuses on identifying goals that must be pursued and measuring the morality of actions by reference to how they facilitate or frustrate the pursuit of those goals It is concerned with the purpose or end of, for example, politics or law as forms of social ordering which have purposes or ends as essential aspects of their nature.

Other forms of consequentialism do not necessarily identify end-goals to be achieved but rather, when assessing the morality of a given action, will look to the consequences that have actually been produced or which are likely to occur and assess them against some moral standard such as a desire to reduce overall harm or suffering. Consequentialist ethical theories have the capacity to justify what some would see as inherently evil or wicked actions by reference to the desirable outcomes which might obtain by virtue of the act. For example, a consequentialist might say that the goal of promoting the safety of the populace

[7] See A Vermeule, *Common Good Constitutionalism* (Polity Press, 2022); C Casey, 'Common-Good Constitutionalism and the New Battle over Constitutional Interpretation in the United States' [2021] *Public Law* 765; M Foran, 'Rights, Common Good, and The Separation of Powers' (2023) 86 *Modern Law Review* 599.

outweighs the badness of torturing suspected terrorists, such that torture is morally permissible in some circumstances.[8] It should come as no surprise, then, to learn that these theories can be summarised by the maxim that 'the ends can justify the means'.

The most well-known family of consequentialist theories is utilitarianism, which promotes actions that maximise happiness and well-being for the majority of the population.[9] Unlike many other forms of consequentialism such as egoism or altruism, utilitarianism demands that interests be considered equally: everybody to count for one, nobody for more than one.[10] This principle of equal consideration of interests grounds utilitarianism within an equality-based framework. Utilitarianism is thus a theory of how best to respect the moral equality of persons; one which focuses on the importance of impartiality.[11] Central to this is a commitment to aggregation, according to which all interests count the same, weighted only for their strength and abstracted from the people who hold them.[12] Thus, a utilitarian account of moral equality employs an aggregative conception of 'concern' and 'respect'. To a utilitarian, treating people with equal concern and respect involves 'taking everyone's welfare into account and balancing some interests against others, if necessary, to produce the outcome that is, on balance, best'.[13] This aggregative approach ensures that a utilitarian account of equality remains 'person-neutral', assigning no moral importance as such to who is benefited or burdened, so long as the collective is better off in the end.[14] Remaining person-neutral, according to the utilitarian, is the only way to treat everyone with equal concern and respect, as is required by their equal moral status.

A common critique of utilitarianism is that this person-neutrality means that it lacks sensitivity to distribution such that, for example, (9, 1) is held to be of equal value to (5, 5).[15] As such, utilitarianism could, in principle, allow for highly

[8] See M Bagaric and J Clarke, *Torture: When the Unthinkable Is Permissible* (State University of New York Press, 2007); *cf* JM Arrigo, 'A Utilitarian Argument against Torture Interrogation of Terrorists' (2004) 10 *Science and Engineering Ethics* 543.

[9] See K de Lazari-Radek and P Singer, *Utilitarianism: A Very Short Introduction* (Oxford University Press, 2017).

[10] JS Mill, 'Utilitarianism' in JM Robson (ed), *The Collected Works of John Stuart Mill, Vol X, Essays on Ethics, Religion and Society* (University of Toronto Press, 1969) 257.

[11] P Singer, *Practical Ethics*, 2nd edn (Cambridge University Press, 1993) 21; R Hare, *Moral Thinking: Its Levels, Method, and Point* (Clarendon Press, 1981); J Harsanyi, 'Morality and the Theory of Rational Behaviour' in A Sen and B Williams (eds), *Utilitarianism and Beyond* (Cambridge University Press, 1982).

[12] N Holtug, 'Theories of Value Aggregation: Utilitarianism, Egalitarianism, Prioritarianism' in I Hirose and J Olson (eds), *The Oxford Handbook of Value Theory* (Oxford University Press, 2015) 268.

[13] D Brink, 'The Separateness of Persons, Distributive Norms, and Moral Theory' in RG Frey and C Morris (eds), *Value, Welfare, and Morality* (Cambridge University Press, 1993) 253.

[14] ibid.

[15] Holtug, 'Theories of Value Aggregation: Utilitarianism, Egalitarianism, Prioritarianism' (n 12) 269.

unequal distributions. It is for this reason that Raz rejects the equality-grounding of utilitarianism:

> Bentham's utilitarianism rests on a universal principle which applies to all moral subjects and prescribes equal respect for them all in the sense of considering each pleasure as intrinsically valuable and each pain as intrinsically bad regardless of whose pleasure or pain they are, and depending only on their intensity and duration. The inegalitarian consequences of this theory are so well known that it has become a paradigm case of a moral outlook denying the intrinsic value of equality.[16]

Is it really so obvious that utilitarianism denies the value of equality? Perhaps, if equality is only concerned with the equalisation of distribution. However, if we distinguish equality principles from egalitarian principles, then the inegalitarian consequences of utilitarianism do not necessarily lead us to conclude that this is a paradigm case of a moral outlook denying the intrinsic value of equality. Rather, we could conclude that utilitarianism, by affording equal respect for all moral subjects, is fundamentally premised upon, and grounded within, a commitment to moral equality, even if the way it prescribes one to act in order to adequately provide that respect produces consequences which Raz disfavours.

The highly unequal distributions which utilitarianism might produce evidently raise moral concerns. There are several reasons why these unequal distributions are undesirable. Within consequentialism, egalitarianism offers one explanation, prioritarianism another.[17] Each will be addressed in turn. These critiques are primarily (although not necessarily) motivated by differing accounts for how to best respect moral equality, just as the commitment which gave rise to them, person-neutrality, is also motivated by this concern. Conflicts between utilitarianism and (most) forms of egalitarianism or prioritarianism address a clash of equality-principles: conflicts over how best to interpret the commitment to equal concern and respect, rather than a clash between equality and some other value such as liberty. One thing that each of these three distributional theories share, however, is the reliance on aggregation and consequentialism. The conflicts at play here concern the best goal that is to be pursued, not whether end-goals might be curtailed by countervailing restrictions on the means which might be used to achieve them.

Egalitarianism is most often associated with the pursuit of an equal distribution of benefits and burdens across a community.[18] As Fleurbaey notes, the minimal egalitarian commitment seems to be that 'unequal distributions have something bad that equal distributions do not have'.[19] This can be so for

[16] J Raz, *The Morality of Freedom* (Clarendon Press, 1988) 222.

[17] *cf* R Dworkin, *Law's Empire* (Harvard University Press, 1986) 288–95.

[18] See for example Raz's account of strict egalitarian principles: Raz (n 16) 217–44. See also Holtug, 'Theories of Value Aggregation: Utilitarianism, Egalitarianism, Prioritarianism' (n 12) 273; E Holmes, 'Anti-Discrimination Rights without Equality' (2005) 68 *Modern Law Review* 175.

[19] M Fleurbaey, 'Equality Versus Priority: How Relevant Is the Distinction?' (2015) 31 *Economics and Philosophy* 203, 205.

instrumental or non-instrumental reasons. A non-instrumental egalitarian values equal distribution for its own sake, holding that 'it is in itself bad if some people are worse off than others'.[20] Temkin similarly argues that 'the core, fundamental tenet of substantive non-instrumental egalitarianism is that it is bad for some to be worse off than others'.[21] In contrast, the instrumental egalitarian views equal distribution as contingently valuable to the extent that it helps to secure other desirable outcomes such as social inclusion, crime reduction, or human flourishing.[22]

Egalitarianism, be it instrumental or non-instrumental, is fundamentally comparative in nature: the moral value of a given benefit or advantage to an individual depends on whether others have the same, greater, or lower distribution in comparison to that person.[23] Thus, a distribution to Anthony is made morally better when we know that Albert has received the same distribution. It is made morally worse when we know that Albert has received either a greater or lesser distribution. Importantly, what is salient here it the state of affairs which obtains, and not the act of distributing itself. When abstracted to a society-wide level, egalitarianism is often framed in relation to the relative situation that exists between different social groups. So, distributional differences between various racial, sexual, or economic groups are assessed as unjust by reference to comparative consequentialist principles such as egalitarianism.

Most egalitarian commitments are unintelligible without a prior acceptance of the fundamental moral equality of persons. This is necessarily the case for non-instrumental egalitarianism. However, instrumental egalitarianism may demand equalisation for reasons which are not directly related to moral equality at all, although, many, if not all, of these reasons indirectly presuppose moral equality. In this sense, some egalitarian principles are not necessarily equality principles in so far as the underlying justification of equalisation arises from concern for crime reduction or other normative commitments and not moral equality. Nevertheless, in practice, it is quite difficult to imagine an egalitarian who is not also supportive of fundamental moral equality. Virtually all politically salient egalitarian principles are equality principles.

There are significant nuances within egalitarian thought that must be left unaddressed in this overview, including what is to be equalised, how inequality is

[20] D Parfit, 'Equality and Priority' (1997) 10 *Ratio* 202, 204; Fleurbaey (n 19) 204.

[21] L Temkin, *Equality or Priority in Health Care Distribution* (Mimeo, Department of Philosophy, Rutgers University, 2000) as cited in Fleurbaey (n 19) 205. See also L Temkin, *Inequality* (Oxford University Press, 1993).

[22] However, Raz has argued that all truly egalitarian principles must be non-instrumentally valuable since equalisation is only morally significant when we are distributing goods or ills rather than something valueless such as grains of sand: Raz (n 16) 235.

[23] Holtug, 'Theories of Value Aggregation: Utilitarianism, Egalitarianism, Prioritarianism' (n 12) 273; D Parfit, 'Equality or Priority' in M Clayton and A Williams (eds), *The Ideal of Equality* (Palgrave Macmillan, 2000); *cf* Temkin (1993) (n 21) 200.

to be measured, and the extent to which concerns for efficiency affect the goal of equalisation.[24] Nevertheless, the core commitment of the egalitarian remains a belief that unequal distributions are in some sense morally worse outcomes than equal ones and that equal distribution is a goal that must be pursued.

Some have argued that any moral or political principle which is informed by fundamental moral equality should be called egalitarian. However, if we adopted this approach, we would have to conclude that Marx, Nozick, Scanlon and Singer (among many others) were all egalitarian thinkers. We *could* do that, of course. However, it seems that such an account would gloss over the very real differences which exist between these theories. Are these theories really best understood as competing egalitarian claims? It is better to distinguish between equality-*based* theories and egalitarian theories, where an egalitarian theory is understood to require some degree of equalisation. Within contemporary scholarship, egalitarianism is often associated with the desire to ensure that each individual is placed in certain economic or social conditions relative to the conditions that others are in.

The prioritarian perspective shares much in common with the egalitarian in that both are concerned with *fair* distributions and both critique utilitarianism for its lack of distribution-sensitivity. However, to the prioritarian, there is nothing of intrinsic value in equalisation. Rather, what matters is that people who are worse off are given priority in determining how best to allocate benefits and burdens: 'Benefiting people matters more the worse off these people are'.[25] What is troubling about utilitarianism, from the perspective of the prioritarian, is therefore not that distribution-insensitivity results in unequal distributions, it is that utilitarianism does not give priority to the worse off. As Holtug notes, 'Where utilitarians believe that the moral value of an increase to an individual depends only on the size of the increase, prioritarians believe that it also depends on how well off the recipient would otherwise be.'[26] As such, from the prioritarian perspective, egalitarianism can be critiqued for valuing equal distribution even in situations where people are left worse-off overall.

The primary distinction between egalitarianism and prioritarianism is thus that the egalitarian is concerned with how one is situated relative to how others are situated and the prioritarian is concerned with how one is situated absolutely. According to the prioritarian, the moral value of a given benefit depends only on the size of the advantage and on how well off one would otherwise be – the position of others is irrelevant.[27] Prioritarianism is therefore not relational or comparative in any meaningful sense. Does this mean that principles

[24] Although see Holtug, 'Theories of Value Aggregation: Utilitarianism, Egalitarianism, Prioritarianism' (n 12) 273–77; R Dworkin, *Sovereign Virtue: The Theory and Practice of Equality* (Harvard University Press, 2000); Rawls (n 6).

[25] Parfit, 'Equality or Priority' (n 23) 366, 369, 372; Fleurbaey (n 19) 205.

[26] Holtug, 'Theories of Value Aggregation: Utilitarianism, Egalitarianism, Prioritarianism' (n 12) 277.

[27] ibid.

of prioritarianism are not equality principles? It could. Given that some forms of egalitarianism can reasonably be construed as informed by non-equality-based values, it is entirely possible that prioritarianism could also be informed by concern for liberty or human flourishing and not necessarily moral equality.[28] It is for this reason that some accounts of discrimination law are grounded in the liberty-based commitment to reducing or eliminating advantage gaps between various social groups.[29]

It is important to distinguish what we do from why we do it. Egalitarian and prioritarian principles are distinguishable by reference to what they demand be done, not necessarily by the reasons offered to justify such actions. As such, it is entirely possible that principles of just distribution, be they egalitarian or prioritarian in nature, are fundamentally grounded in non-equality-based values such as liberty, or in prudential concerns relating to the reduction of crime or the promotion of social cohesion.[30] This is not to say that respect for moral equality cannot require commitment to some distributional scheme. Rather, the point is that it does not necessarily do so. Nor does commitment to a distributional scheme necessarily entail a commitment to the value of equality, although it often does. Nevertheless, one could be an egalitarian or a prioritarian and have no particular commitment to the moral equality of persons. Thus, these distributional principles can be said to be only contingently equality-based principles.

III. DEONTIC EQUALITY

We have seen that a basic form of utilitarianism can be critiqued from a consequentialist or teleological perspective due to its potential to produce certain undesirable distributions or for its hindrance of or failure to achieve a stated distributional end. However, there is another family of ethical commitments which have conflicted with the utilitarian project: deontology. This species of normative ethics, derived from the Greek *deon* – meaning obligation or duty – argues that the morality of an action should be determined by reference to whether the action is *itself* right or wrong, according to a set of ethical rules. Deontology is thus often described as obligation-, duty-, or rule-based ethics and is therefore committed to the importance of action over consequences. Deontic moral duties thus specify what one is permitted, forbidden, or required to do without consideration of consequences, except in so far as consequences form a part of the act itself. For example, killing is an act which results in death.

[28] See N Holtug, *Persons, Interests, and Justice* (Oxford University Press, 2010) 204.

[29] T Khaitan, *A Theory of Discrimination Law* (Oxford University Press, 2015); T Khaitan and S Steel, 'Wrongs, Group Disadvantage and the Legitimacy of Indirect Discrimination Law' in H Collins and T Khaitan (eds), *Foundations of Indirect Discrimination Law* (Hart Publishing, 2018).

[30] Raz (n 16) 233–34.

This is not to say that consequences are irrelevant for the deontologist, however. It merely means that the determination of whether an action is wrongful will often be done with regard to the action itself and that, when a deontic duty comes into conflict with pertinent consequentialist concerns, the duty wins out. Where there is no applicable deontic duty, there is no reason why a committed deontologist would be precluded from assessing the permissibility of an act by reference to consequences. While there may be some instances where concern for outcomes will dictate what is the morally right thing to do, there are other times when an action is intrinsically wrongful, regardless of the consequences. Thus, many deontologists will argue that torture is never morally permissible, even if it might save lives.[31] As Raz notes, 'to reject consequentialism is not to claim that the consequences of an action are not among the reasons for or against its performance'.[32] It means only that some valid reasons for action are not included within the consequences of an act and instead relate to the nature of the action itself.[33] As such, it is not the case that any form of reasoning which takes consequences into account must be classed as consequentialist. What matters is whether consequences are ultimately and always determinative of what one ought to do in a given situation. A deontic moral view is one which recognises the existence of moral duties pertaining to acts in abstraction from consequences, even if consequences may be relevant and, in some instances, central to moral reasoning.

The primary difference between the consequentialist and the deontologist, therefore, is that, for the deontologist, this consideration of consequences must yield to a deontic duty, should the duty be engaged. To the deontologist, it is this set of ethical duties which is ultimately determinative of what one ought to do, even if consequences may be relevant and, in some cases, central to the morality of action. For example, a deontic worldview might say that, in general, one should act to save as many lives as possible but not if doing so requires you to engage in torture. To say that, for example, the common law is a deontic system therefore is not to say that consequences do not and cannot enter judicial analysis. Rather, it is to say that the system operates by reference to certain fundamental principles of right action that cannot be infringed, even if infringement might produce desirable consequences.

An important implication of a duty-based morality is the salience of the moral rights which are often correlatively entailed by these duties.[34] Rights

[31] See B Juratowitch, 'Torture Is Always Wrong' (2008) 22 *Public Affairs Quarterly* 91; J Mayerfield, 'In Defence of the Absolute Prohibition on Torture' (2008) 22 *Public Affairs Quarterly* 109; *cf* S Kershnar, *For Torture: A Rights-Based Defence* (Lexington Books, 2011); J McMahan, 'Torture in Principle and in Practice' (2008) 22 *Public Affairs Quarterly* 111.

[32] Raz (n 16) 268.

[33] See D Parfit, *Reasons and Persons* (Oxford University Press, 1984) 104.

[34] On the correlative entailment of rights and duties, see W Hohfeld, *Fundamental Legal Conceptions* (W Cook ed, Yale University Press, 1919). This is not to say that rights and duties are necessarily and always correlatively entailed: Raz (n 16) 170–71.

are justified claims or entitlements to (or not to) perform certain actions, to (or not to) be in certain states, or that others perform (or refrain from performing) certain actions or be (or not be) in certain states.[35] On one reading, duties ground rights such that they are a source of moral entitlements; but duties may be undirected, constituting obligations that are not owed to identified others. The duty on public authorities to act reasonably is one such example. A key feature of deontological ethics is a commitment to the existence of *absolute* rights and duties: those whose claim can never be outweighed by other moral considerations. This is in contrast to prima facie rights and duties, whose claim can be outweighed in this manner. Deontology thus gives us to the tools to explain why certain acts can never be morally justified. As such, if torture is never morally permissible, on one reading, this is because it violates an absolute right derived from a consistent set of moral rules and principles.

Returning to the critique of utilitarianism, many deontological accounts of treatment as an equal necessitate respect for people as rights-bearing individuals whose interests (and rights) cannot be aggregated over. Moral rights and duties are 'not just ordinary reasons to be aggregated and balanced in the ordinary way'.[36] They have peremptory force. As such, it would not be permissible to justify the infringement of certain rights by reference to the cumulative utility, or happiness, or perhaps even distributional fairness, which might obtain from the infringement. To use a well-known example, suppose Jones has suffered an accident in the transmitter room of a television station during the broadcasting of a World Cup match. He is suffering extremely painful electrical shocks, but his injury will not worsen if he is left to suffer until the match has finished.[37] The question we are faced with is whether we should intervene immediately or wait until the match is over. Crucially, 'Does the right thing to do depend on how many people are watching?.'[38] If all that matters here is overall happiness or suffering, then at a certain point there will be enough people getting pleasure from watching the match that, should we aggregate their happiness, it will outweigh the pain felt by Jones. In that case, an aggregative consequentialist would have to accept that Jones should be left to suffer until the match ended.[39] Non-aggregative moral theories such as deontology offer principled reasons for why the right thing to do in this situation would be to intervene immediately, even if many people will be inconvenienced by doing so.

[35] L Wenar, 'Rights', *The Stanford Encyclopedia of Philosophy* (Fall 2015 edn), E Zalta (ed), https://plato.stanford.edu/archives/fall2015/entries/rights/. Rights may be dynamic in that they can give rise to new duties as a result of changing circumstances. See Raz (n 16) 180–86.

[36] ibid 278.

[37] T Scanlon, *What We Owe to Each Other* (Harvard University Press, 1998) 235.

[38] ibid.

[39] See also Sen's example involving the choice whether or not to prevent one man from being beaten up even though the total amount of pleasure gained by the bashers would outweigh the pain felt by the victim; A Sen, 'Rights and Agency' (1982) 11 *Philosophy & Public Affairs* 3, 8–9.

A deontic conception of equality which grounds particular rights could therefore come into conflict with telic or consequentialist conceptions which focus exclusively on consequences or the aggregation of interests. On these accounts, the only way to respect moral equality is to afford people equal recognition as independent moral agents, whose lives and interests have prima facie equal worth.[40] Utilitarianism and other forms of aggregative consequentialism, such as egalitarianism and prioritarianism can thus be critiqued for failing to afford proper attention to the moral rights of individuals. On this conception, equal concern and respect requires recognition of the rights that arise by virtue of our equal moral status and also of the equal weight those, and other rights, should carry. Equality-based deontic theories share the relational character of egalitarian theories and are thus primarily concerned with how one is treated in comparison to others or how certain actions manifest or express the attitude that someone is an inferior in some way.[41] In contrast with consequentialist equality principles such as non-instrumental egalitarianism, a deontic principle is concerned with the wrongness of an act and the relation that has to the breach of a duty or the violation of a right.

Aggregative consequentialism has the potential to infringe upon the rights of some in order to bring about desirable social outcomes. As such, it is argued that requiring one individual to sacrifice so that another can be benefited 'ignores the distinction between persons. … To sacrifice one individual life for another, or one individual's happiness for another's is very different from sacrificing one gratification for another within a *single* life.'[42] Indeed, failing to respect what has come to be known as 'the separateness of persons' has become central to modern critiques of utilitarianism and aggregative consequentialism.[43]

It is, of course, a truism that different people live different lives. If this critique were simply a metaphysical claim about the separateness of persons, it would be exceptionally uninteresting for political and legal theorists. What is of importance for the viability of the separateness of persons as a foil for aggregative consequentialism is the *normative* separateness of persons. By this I mean the important moral implications which arise from the fact that we are individual moral agents with only our own lives to lead. To use a person as a mere means to an end or a vessel of utility, without recognition and respect for the fact that they have their own interests and rights, is to not take seriously the

[40] See B Eidelson, *Discrimination and Disrespect* (Oxford University Press, 2015) 79; B Eidelson, 'Treating People as Individuals' in D Hellman and S Moreau (eds), *Philosophical Foundations of Indirect Discrimination* (Oxford University Press, 2013).

[41] See for example A Sangiovanni, *Humanity without Dignity: Moral Equality, Respect, and Human Rights* (Harvard University Press, 2017) Ch 2.

[42] T Nagel, *The Possibility of Altruism* (Princeton University Press, 1970) 138.

[43] See ibid 132, 138–42; Rawls (n 6) 23–29, 187–88; R Nozick, *Anarchy, State, and Utopia* (Basic Books, 1974) 31–34; B Williams, 'Persons, Character, and Morality' in *Moral Luck* (Cambridge University Press, 1981) 3.

normative distinction between persons.[44] It is to fail to recognise that 'his is the only life he has'.[45] Peter Vallentyne thus explains the problem as follows:

> [I]ndividuals have certain rights that may not be infringed simply because the consequences are better. Unlike prudential rationality, morality involves many distinct centers of will (choice) or interests, and these cannot simply be lumped together and traded off against each other.
>
> The basic problem with standard versions of core consequentialism is that they fail to recognize adequately the *normative separateness of persons*. Psychologically autonomous beings (as well, perhaps, as other beings with moral standing) are not merely means for the promotion of value. They must be respected and honored, and this means that at least sometimes certain things may not be done to them, even though this promotes value overall. An innocent person may not be killed against her will, for example, in order to make a million happy people significantly happier. This would be sacrificing her for the benefit of others.[46]

A focus on equality from the perspective of deontology shifts attention away from the equalisation of resources or the maximisation of utility, towards the rights and duties which flow from recognition of the equal moral status of persons. However, it is important to be clear that a rights-based focus, although naturally affiliated with a deontic ethical framework, does not preclude teleological or consequentialist grounding. In *Taking Rights Seriously*, Dworkin introduces this distinction between equality as a desirable social policy – a goal to be pursued – and equality as a constitutional right.[47] While this distinction can be usefully engaged to describe the conflict between deontological and consequentialist conceptions of equality, I am not convinced that it independently provides any guidance for interpretation of the principle of equality before the law.

The conflict between deontic accounts of equality and consequentialist accounts of equality is not new.[48] If I, as a legal subject, have a right to be treated with equal concern and respect, why should that necessarily entail a right to *deontic* equal concern and respect and not utilitarian equal concern and respect? Put another way, can we not see the right to equality as entailing a right to equality as a social policy – a right to certain outcomes or distributions? A deontic account does not have exclusive use of rights or duties; rather its value lies in the ability to explain the wrong of an act in the act itself.

Reliance on requirements of equal concern and respect on their own evidently cannot tell us whether a deontic or a telic interpretation should be preferred by

[44] Rawls (n 6) 26–27.

[45] Nozick (n 43) 32–33.

[46] P Vallentyne, 'Against Maximizing Act Consequentialism' in J Dreier (ed), *Contemporary Debates in Moral Theory* (Blackwell, 2006) 29.

[47] Dworkin, *Taking Rights Seriously* (n 2).

[48] See T Nagel, 'Equality' in M Clayton and A Williams (eds), *The Ideal of Equality* (Palgrave Macmillan, 2002); Parfit, 'Equality or Priority' (n 23); B Williams, 'The Idea of Equality' in L Pojman and R Westmoreland (eds), *Equality: Selected Readings* (Oxford University Press, 1997).

courts. If we are to properly account for the requirements of equality before the law, we must incorporate additional constitutional values to do so. It is only when we adopt a particular ethical stance that we can begin to move beyond the general commitment to moral equality towards particular, concretised conceptions of what must be done to adequately respect the moral equality of persons with an existing tradition and context. In what follows, I will argue that the common law provides a framework of principle that can be used to interpret the requirement of equal concern and respect in a distinctly deontic manner, one which may be attuned to consequences but which must recognise the legal rights of persons and the absolute duties of others. Constitutional principle is the public law equivalent of deontic constraints on consequentialist reasoning. While legal equality could be interpreted as requiring a given distributional scheme, to do so would entail a substantial departure from settled principle and law. The important questions that must be addressed are: first, what rights flow from an obligation to respect moral equality; and second, whether one of those is a right to just distribution. It is therefore argued that legal equality may be compatible with principles of just distribution, but that it is unlikely to necessitate distribution. Within the common law, equality manifests as a deontic principle informing the structure of legal reason and demanding the protection of fundamental juridical rights against various forms of wrongful treatment.

Dworkin is therefore wrong to suggest that appeals to the very notion of equality as a right resolves the clash between distributional and non-distributional equality principles. Indeed, his later writings elide this very distinction and contend that proper respect for deontic equality demands something in the way of just distribution.[49] However, the judiciary is not at liberty to address this question in abstraction; a judge, in her deliberation, must operate within the confines of the rule of law, resolving disputes by reference to legal principle and past practice and not abstract analysis of political morality more suited to the legislature and the executive. It is only when we place equality within an existing framework of common law principles that we can more accurately identify the specific deontic commitments that a constitutional conception of equality must entail. What is more, examining existing principle through the lens of equality assists in the identification of a strong normative underpinning which gives meaning and legitimacy to many aspects of the common law.

IV. LEGAL EQUALITY AND THE LIMITS OF PUBLIC LAW

Within the common law constitutional order, the scope of the judicial power to review the actions and policies of government is not, and should not be, unlimited. This is not to say that there is a concrete list of powers, exercise of

[49] Dworkin, *Sovereign Virtue* (n 24).

which is not amenable to scrutiny by the courts. The House of Lord's attempt, in the *GCHQ* case, to identify governmental powers which are inherently beyond the reach of law must be examined in its proper constitutional context.[50] It is now well established that judicial review of executive action extends to the use of both statutory and prerogative powers; indeed, this was the central thrust of the *GCHQ* decision.[51] However, according to Lord Roskill, significant use of government power is not subject to any legal supervision at all. Prerogative powers concerning the entering and leaving of treaties, the defence of the realm, the granting of mercy or honours, and the dissolution of Parliament, among others, were 'not to be amenable to the judicial process' by virtue of 'their nature and subject-matter'.[52] It was simply not the constitutional role of courts 'to determine whether a treaty should be concluded or the armed forces disposed in a particular manner or Parliament dissolved on one date rather than another'.[53]

However, a central aspect of the rule of law is that the government is equally subject to law and must act within its proper bounds. There is always a question of the scope of a given power, be it statutory or prerogative, and that is always subject to the constraints of constitutional principle and the requirement to respect the fundamental rights of legal subjects: 'the courts have exercised a supervisory jurisdiction over the decisions of the executive for centuries'.[54] As Lord Diplock stresses, government ministers:

> are accountable to Parliament for what they do so far as regards efficiency and policy, and of that Parliament is the only judge; they are responsible to a court of justice for the lawfulness of what they do, and of that the court is the only judge.[55]

It should, therefore, be no surprise that the unanimous judgment of the court in *R (Miller) v The Prime Minister* was that:

> Every prerogative power has its limits, and it is the function of the court to determine, when necessary, where they lie. Since the power is recognised by the common law, and has to be compatible with common law principles, those principles may illuminate where its boundaries lie. In particular, the boundaries … are likely to be illuminated, and indeed determined, by the fundamental principles of our constitutional law.[56]

What, then, are we to make of Lord Roskill's comments in the *GCHQ* case? In particular, given that the scope of judicial review is not, and should not be,

[50] *Council of Civil Service Unions v Minister for the Civil Service* [1984] 3 All ER 935.

[51] See also *R (Miller) v The Prime Minister* [2019] UKSC 41.

[52] *Council of Civil Service Unions v Minister for the Civil Service* (n 50) 956.

[53] ibid.

[54] *R (Miller) v The Prime Minister* (n 51) [31].

[55] *R v Inland Revenue Comrs, ex p National Federation of Self-Employed and Small Businesses Ltd* [1982] AC 617, 644. See also *R v Secretary of State for the Home Department, ex p Fire Brigades Union* [1995] 2 AC 513, 572–73; W Wade and C Forsyth, *Administrative Law*, 7th edn (Oxford University Press, 1994) 34: 'ministerial responsibility is no substitute for judicial review'.

[56] *R (Miller) v The Prime Minister* (n 51) [38].

unlimited, what are the constraints on judicial oversight of government action? The hallmark of justiciability in public law is grounded in the essential nature of judicial review as a check on unlawful misuse of executive power and not on the efficacy or substantive merits of a given governmental policy. It is fundamentally the courts' concern with upholding the principles of the constitution and respecting the rights of legal subjects that undergirds judicial review and not concern for the merits of a given decision or action as a matter of public policy.[57] As such, while it is not for the courts to pass judgment on the merits of entering or leaving an international treaty or of proroguing parliament on one date rather than another, the judiciary is under a constitutional obligation to ensure that a government minister does not step beyond the legal limits of their powers in pursuing public policy goals.[58] Those limits will be set by both constitutional principle and the fundamental rights of subjects which necessarily flow from those principles. Where the exercise of prerogative or statutory power by a public authority threatens to infringe the rights of subjects or to undermine constitutional principle, applicants are entitled to seek judicial review.

Crucially, the legal constraints on governmental power are primarily deontic in nature, informed by consistent application of legal principle. Government ministers are generally free to pursue policy objectives, orientated towards the achievement of a particular end or *telos*. Judicial review ensures that the means chosen to achieve those goals are consistent with the legal obligations and duties that ministers are subject to. It is not for the court to constrain the exercise of government power simply because it is of the view that one policy is better than another or by reference to purely consequentialist reasoning, removed from constitutional principle.[59] Indeed, law by its very nature is committed to a deontic, duty-based stance; one which necessarily entails the existence of both legal duties and legal rights. This is not to say that consequences cannot or do not enter into legal reasoning. It would be absurd to think that. Rather, to claim that law is deontic is merely to point to the fact that legal reasoning cannot take a purely consequentialist approach which ignores legal rules, principles or rights. The role of a court of law is not to further the pursuit of its own policy goals, except when they are bound to do so by statute. It is this reason primarily, and not concerns about democratic legitimacy or expertise, that grounds the obligations upon a court to review on the basis of legal principle and legal principle only.

[57] See P Craig, 'Ultra Vires and the Foundations of Judicial Review' (1998) 57 *Cambridge Law Journal* 63; TRS Allan, *Law, Liberty, and Justice: The Legal Foundations of British Constitutionalism* (Clarendon Press, 1993) 212; TRS Allan, 'The Constitutional Foundations of Judicial Review: Conceptual Conundrum or Interpretative Inquiry' (2002) 61(1) *Cambridge Law Journal* 87.

[58] See *Laker Airways v Department of Trade* [1997] 2 All ER 182; *R v Secretary of State for the Home Department, ex p Fire Brigades Union* [1995] 2 AC 513; *R (Miller) v Secretary of State for Exiting the European Union* [2017] UKSC 5; *R (Miller) v The Prime Minister* (n 51).

[59] See Law LJ in *R v Somerset County Council, ex p Fewings* [1995] 1 All ER 513, 515.

The rule of law operates, in part, by reference to a bifurcated conception of constitutional duty. On the one hand, the executive must not must pursue its goals and policies without throwing off the restraints of legal principle; it must act lawfully and within its proper constitutional bounds, as determined by the common law. On the other hand, the judiciary must uphold its obligation to the constitutional order by ensuring that its own oversight of executive action is guided by legal principle and legal principle alone. Equally, Parliament must uphold the constitutional values which lend it legitimacy and the judiciary is bound to construct statute in a manner which is compatible with these obligations and not by reference to the personal preferences of individual judges. It is, thus, not open to a court to review the merits of, for example, budgetary decisions simply because it is of the view that an egalitarian, or prioritarian, or utilitarian distributional scheme should be preferred. Such assessment is exactly the kind which the court is precluded from engaging in, without express statutory authorisation, by virtue of both the separation of powers and the rule of law.[60]

A fundamental feature of our constitution is that public policy is for elected representatives to pursue; the judiciary may only review that pursuit where there exist strong deontic reasons to do so, informed by considerations of constitutional principle, justice to the individual claimant, and fundamental rights. If there is a well-grounded claim that there has been a breach of constitutional obligation on the part of a public body (such as the infringement of a right or disregard for applicable legal principle), judicial review should generally be available unless there are compelling reasons not to review which are themselves grounded in constitutional principle.

The central question for our purposes pertains to what is justiciable in a court of law as a governmental violation of legal equality. Policy questions relating to resource distribution are historically beyond the scope of what the judiciary is empowered to assess. In a constitutional democracy, respectful of democracy, it is for parliament and the executive to choose policies which will reasonably achieve the public good, subject to the constraints of legal principle and fundamental rights which help to set out the bounds of plausible conceptions of the common good.[61] As Allan notes, 'The executive is subject to the supervisory jurisdiction on grounds of legal principle, which fasten on the applicant's right to fair treatment, rather than political policy.'[62] The right of the legal subject to just governance must ensure that those subject to a public authority enjoy the legal capacity to reasonably respond to a public wrong, if at all possible.[63]

[60] See Ch 6 below where the public sector equality duty is analysed.

[61] TRS Allan, *Constitutional Justice: A Liberal Theory of the Rule of Law* (Oxford University Press 2001) 22–23.

[62] Allan, *Law, Liberty, and Justice: The Legal Foundations of British Constitutionalism* (n 57) 213.

[63] J Weinrib, *Dimensions of Dignity: The Theory and Practice of Modern Constitutional Law* (Cambridge University Press, 2016) 153.

Having said all of this, however, it would be wrong to think that the only duties on legal officials are those correlatively entailed by individual rights. The nature of constitutional principle is such that it often includes undirected duties to act reasonably, fairly, and lawfully. These are best described not as policy goals or purely consequentialist forms of reasoning, but nor are they simply concerned with the protection of individual rights. Rather, they demand that policy choices made by legislatures or governments operate within a plausible range of defensible conceptions of the public good. This may involve a degree of teleological thinking but it should not be confused with pure consequentialism, unmoored from common law principle. This will be explored in greater detail in the final chapter.

Judicial review is not concerned solely with matters of process as distinct from substance. Many aspects of the substance of a decision may be challenged if they fall foul of constitutional principle. The distinction between review and appeal remains, if by review we mean assessment of the compatibility of a given determination with fundamental constitutional principle and not simply an assessment of the procedures by which it came to be.[64] Of course, the court could review the merits of administrative decision-making entirely on the basis of consequentialist grounds, if it is authorised and obligated to do so by statute. Indeed, this is one way of understanding the public sector equality duty contained within the Equality Act 2010.[65]

Judicial review is ultimately justified by reference to principle, not consequence. It is not the fact the judicial review might result in more transparent and accountable governance that explains its role within constitutional adjudication. Rather, it is the fact that it transforms 'the inherent equal human dignity of each person subject to law's authority into a justiciable legal norm'.[66] Transparency and accountability might, hypothetically, flourish under a system with no judicial review. But even if it did, this would not mean that constitutional principle would embrace an abandonment of constitutional rights to challenge the lawfulness of executive conduct.

It follows, then, that the constitutional requirements of legal equality must also attach to legal principle and the rights of legal subjects. Some of these principles have been introduced in the previous chapter: equal subjugation to law, non-discrimination, and *stare decisis*. Others may not immediately be seen as necessarily informed by the value of equality. These could include the rule of law, reasonableness, and parliamentary sovereignty. One of the reasons for the disconnect here might be the mistaken belief that an equality principle must demand equalisation. Once we move beyond that misconception, it

[64] Allan makes a similar point when he argues that we should 'interpret the call for judicial restraint as a reinforcement of the familiar distinction between public policy and legal principle': Allan, *Constitutional Justice: A Liberal Theory of the Rule of Law* (n 61) 189.

[65] See Ch 6 below.

[66] Weinrib (n 63) 172.

becomes increasingly clear that many of the core principles of the common law constitution are informed by a commitment to respect the equal moral status of legal subjects. Equalisation for its own sake is not, properly understood, an aspect of equality before the law. In the next section, it will be shown that even the seemingly most obvious example of constitutional egalitarianism – the principle that like cases should be treated alike – is best understood as an equality-based principle focusing on the demand for justification rather than one which focuses on equalisation.

V. *STARE DECISIS*

It may be tempting to describe the requirements of equality-based constitutional principles by reference to equal distribution of legal benefits and burdens. On this reading, distribution is simply the natural corollary of consistently applied principles. However, it is important to be clear that no legal system would or should equally distribute legal benefits or burdens. One of the primary purposes of a system of law is to adequately tailor and consistently apply political coercion to appropriate cases. What is occurring here is the fair distribution of legal burdens as guided by equality-based principles. While all are informed by a commitment to treating legal subjects as moral equals, only one of these principles appears to be informed by anything that would approximate egalitarianism. Egalitarianism is most commonly associated with distribution. However, there is a well-known and often criticised egalitarian treatment principle which focuses on ensuring that treatment is equalised without necessarily having regard to the distributional outcomes of the treatment itself.[67] Commonly described as a principle the like cases should be treated alike, this principle can be said to embody the ideal of 'formal equality'. Such a principle would be best described as a deontic egalitarian principle: deontic because it focuses on an act irrespective of its consequences; egalitarian because it requires equalisation.

The maxim that like cases should be treated alike occupies a paradoxically ambivalent place within moral and political discussion of equality. On the one hand, it is an essential feature of both justice and fairness that those in similar situations be afforded similar treatment and that differences in treatment be justified.[68] To treat similarly situated persons differently raises a question of justification which would not exist were it not for a commitment to treating persons as moral equals whose similar situation demands appropriately similar treatment. Without moral likeness, like treatment has little grounding as an ethical requirement. On the other hand, equalisation of treatment has been subject

[67] See in particular Holmes (n 18).

[68] See Lord Hoffmann in *Arthur JS Hall v Simons* [2002] 1 AC 615, 688–69, referring to 'the fundamental principle of justice which requires that people should be treated equally and like cases treated alike'.

to significant criticism in recent decades. First, as has been mentioned in the previous chapter, there is the charge of emptiness: that the value of equality does not provide any guidance and that it is the independent legal rules themselves which determine how a court should act. As Thomsen has argued, however, it is clear, at least as it manifests in law, that the doctrine of precedent does place independent constraints on adjudicative bodies to adhere to previously decided precedents, unless there are strong reasons not to.[69] But this only shows us the contingent value of equal treatment and does not exhaust equality principles within the common law constitution.

Second, there is the more general criticism from advocates of telic equality theories that principles of equal treatment do not guarantee or even seek to pursue distributional schemes such as egalitarianism or prioritarianism. The disconnect between act and outcome is usually represented as a conflict between 'formal' and 'substantive' equality, where substantive equality is defined by the desire to bring about certain kinds of distributional change as between particular socially salient groups.[70] This distinction will be addressed in greater detail in Chapter 6. For present purposes, it will suffice to note that this criticism holds, but seems to be premised more on a struggle to seize the rhetorical power of the term 'equality' rather than anything intrinsic to equal treatment. By this I mean that equal treatment can, of course, be critiqued for failing to distribute; but the salience of this critique is diminished when one accounts for the fact that a principle of equal treatment is not teleological or consequentialist in nature. It does not guarantee just distribution because it is simply not concerned with distribution at all. That may be a reason not to value it particularly highly, but it is very similar to a general criticism that equal treatment is not utilitarian or that it cannot guarantee a reduction in torture.

Third, equal treatment as a deontic egalitarian principle can be critiqued in the same way that all egalitarian principles can be critiqued: for an inability to address the levelling-down objection.[71] The core of many criticisms of equality-based philosophical and legal theory is that a requirement of equalisation can be satisfied by treating people equally badly (deontic egalitarianism) or by removing benefits from the advantaged to bring them down to the level of the worst off (telic egalitarianism). To use a well-known example, in the US case of *Palmer v Thompson*,[72] the city of Jackson, Mississippi had segregated its swimming pools on the basis of race. When challenged on the grounds of racial

[69] F Thomsen, 'Concept, Principle, and Norm – Equality Before the Law Reconsidered' [2018] *Legal Theory* 1.

[70] See S Fredman, *Discrimination Law*, 2nd edn (Oxford University Press, 2011) 11–12, 25–32; C Bourn and J Whitmore, *Anti-Discrimination Law in Britain*, 3rd edn (Sweet & Maxwell, 1996) 4–5.

[71] See N Holtug, 'Egalitarianism and the Levelling down Objection' (1998) 58 *Analysis* 166; *cf* Parfit, 'Equality or Priority' (n 23).

[72] *Palmer v Thompson*, 403 US 217 (1970).

discrimination, the city simply closed all of its swimming pools. This clearly alleviated the egalitarian concern for unequal treatment or distribution of benefits. But it was evidently an unjust policy.

The levelling-down objection shows us that equalisation for its own sake is likely to be unconvincing as an intrinsically valuable practice, either because it does not distribute benefits or resources fairly, or because it in some way fails to respect a non-egalitarian, deontic equality principle of equal concern and respect. As such, *any* egalitarian principle, be it deontic or telic, is vulnerable to the levelling-down objection. But what is more, unlike the charge that equal treatment fails to distribute fairly, the distinctly deontic element of the levelling-down objection confronts equal treatment on its own terms and points to something which is wrongful about the act of equalising in certain contexts. As Peters notes, a requirement of equal treatment amounts to the claim that 'sometimes a person should be treated wrongly simply because another, identically situated person has been treated wrongly'.[73]

The levelling-down objection raises a significant challenge to egalitarian thought, including to deontic egalitarianism and the principle of equal treatment.[74] However, it is not entirely clear that it raises an identical challenge to the common law principle of *stare decisis*. At a surface level, the principle that likes should be treated alike and the principle of *stare decisis* are identical. But once we account for the fact that *stare decisis* operates within an institutional and evolving context, the central thrust of Peters' critique falls away. *Stare decisis* does not value equal treatment for its own sake: it demands the justified application of legal rules and principles to pertinent cases, subject to the requirement that departures from previous practice be distinguished appropriately and justified by reference to legal principle. It is thus an equality-based principle which demands equal concern and respect for the interests of subjects, but not an egalitarian principle.

From the perspective of the common law, the fact that one person is known to have been treated wrongly by virtue of a misunderstanding of legal principle raises a strong inference that there is need for a development or reinterpretation of existing legal practice. It is, therefore, important to be clear about what exactly constitutes a precedent and how *stare decisis* operates to respect both moral equality and the rule of law. There are a number of explanations offered to justify the doctrine of *stare decisis*, many of which attach to subtly different conceptions of the doctrine itself, ranging from the value of equal treatment *qua* equal treatment, to Burkean deference to ancestral wisdom.[75] There are also distinctly rule-of-law-based justifications which focus on the importance of

[73] C Peters, 'Equality Revisited' (1997) 110 *Harvard Law Review* 1210, 1212.

[74] Although the levelling down objection has not gone unchallenged by egalitarians. See for example Temkin (1993) (n 21) 255–56; Parfit, 'Equality or Priority' (n 23).

[75] See generally N Duxbury, *The Nature and Authority of Precedent* (Cambridge University Press, 2008); M Gerhardt, *The Power of Precedent* (Oxford University Press, 2008).

congruence, constancy, and generality.[76] Further still, the importance of interpretation through legal principle within common law adjudication can explain why precedents have the force and weight that they do, given the role that judicial decision-making plays in the construction and maintenance of both legal practice and legal principle.[77] This being the case, there are potentially rule of law concerns with a doctrine which itself may sometimes, even if it does not always, seem to result in erroneous or invidious interpretations of law perpetuating through time. As Waldron notes;

> stare decisis is not an absolute, and even in a system of precedent, earlier decisions can be revisited. But stare decisis is supposed to make a difference, and the problem for the rule of law is that the difference it makes is to give a measure of entrenched weight to an earlier decision in a way that might make it more difficult for subsequent generations of judges to apply the law as they understand it.[78]

As such, Waldron stresses that this entrenchment must be justified and proceeds to offer some rule-of-law-based reasons to do so. Our focus is on the equality-based reasons which might explain why entrenched weight may be desirable in this context.[79] In the previous chapter, we encountered Thomsen's argument that equality-based arguments in favour of precedent are not valueless or empty.[80] *Stare decisis* generates reasons for judges to adhere to the decisions of previously decided applicable cases, the strength of these reasons being directly proportional to the proportion of previous cases decided in this manner. Thomsen is correct to conclude that these reasons are of some instrumental value, even if they do not have inherent value in a manner that a deontic egalitarian might claim.

The upshot of this is that there will be times when the entrenched weight attached to previous decisions may not be sufficient to prevent the development of legal principle in a contrary manner. Much like the doctrine of parliamentary sovereignty, the principles and values which lend normative weight to *stare decisis* do not extend support to the ostensible use of *stare decisis* to undermine those very grounding values and principles. The principle cannot be self-defeating. This is not the only circumstance when a precedent can be legitimately departed from, consistent with *stare decisis*, but all instances of departure result from the determination that the provision of justice to the individual case, consistent with legal principle, outweigh the entrenched weight which attaches to a given precedent.

[76] See L Fuller, *The Morality of Law*, rvsd edn (Yale University Press, 1969) Ch 2; J Waldron, 'Stare Decisis and the Rule of Law: A Layered Approach' (2012) 111 *Michigan Law Review* 1.

[77] TRS Allan, 'Principle, Practice, and Precedent: Vindicating Justice, According to Law' (2018) 77 *Cambridge Law Journal* 269.

[78] Waldron, 'Stare Decisis and the Rule of Law: A Layered Approach' (n 76) 7.

[79] This is not to say that the rule of law is not itself in many ways an equality-based principle.

[80] Thomsen (n 69).

The same is true of administrative law principles applicable to the conduct of public bodies. Authorities are not bound to replicate their previous mistakes simply because a new party wishes to be afforded equal treatment: whether an authority should be permitted to depart from a previous mistake 'depends on whether that would give rise to an unfairness amounting to an abuse of power'.[81] Legitimate expectations must be balanced against the injustice of replicating previously wrongful treatment, the overriding concern being to prevent unfairness that would amount to an abuse of power. It is for this reason that the court in *Gallaher* concluded that 'the domestic law of this country does not recognise equal treatment as a distinct principle of administrative law'.[82] It may have been more accurate to stress that there is no concrete *rule* demanding equal treatment, even if there is a general *principle* that is itself informed by a broader principle of legal equality and the values which underpin it.[83] Thus, while 'treating like cases alike and unlike cases differently is a general axiom of rational behaviour … frequently invoked by the courts in proceedings for judicial review as a ground for holding some administrative acts to be irrational', it is not always required.[84] As Lord Bingham, discussing the decision of a public body to award appropriate compensation, notes:

> It is generally desirable that decision-makers, whether administrative or judicial, should act in a broadly consistent manner. If they do, reasonable hopes will not be disappointed. But the assessor's task in this case was to assess fair compensation for each of the appellants. He was not entitled to award more or less than, in his considered judgment, they deserved. He was not bound, and in my opinion was not entitled, to follow a previous decision which he considered erroneous and which would yield what he judged to be an excessive award.[85]

The point here is that, within the common law, equal treatment is not valued simply because treatment is equalised; it is valued because departures from equal treatment raise important normative concerns which must be addressed before they can be justified. In particular, if no rational justification can be offered for the departure, unequal treatment will be prohibited as unreasonable.[86] It is for this reason that Rault J stressed that '[e]quality before the law requires that persons should be uniformly treated, unless there is some valid reason to treat them differently'.[87] The correctness of a decision of this kind is, therefore,

[81] *R v Secretary of State for Education and Employment, ex p Begbie* [2000] 1 WLR 1115, 1127B–D, per Peter Gibson LJ.

[82] *R (on the application of Gallaher Group Ltd and others) v The Competition and Markets Authority* [2018] UKSC 25, [24].

[83] On the distinction between rules and principles, see Dworkin, *Taking Rights Seriously* (n 2) Ch 2. See also Foran, 'The Cornerstone of Our Law: Equality, Consistency, and Judicial Review' (n 1).

[84] *Matadeen v Pointu* [1999] 1 AC 98, [9] (Lord Hoffmann).

[85] *R (O'Brien) v Independent Assessor* [2007] 2 AC 312, [30].

[86] *R (in the application of Gallaher Group Ltd and others) v The Competition and Markets Authority* [2018] UKSC 25, [50]. See also Ch 5 below.

[87] *Police v Rose* [1976] MR 79, 81.

always contingent upon both the institutional history of the practice in question and the strength of the justification for departure from previous decisions.

There is thus an error that Waldron and many others make when assessing the costs involved in adopting the doctrine of *stare decisis*: the presumption that it is ever open to a court or executive body to assess a case 'on its merits' in a manner which ignores their role within the institutional and historical practice of law and the place that individual cases have within the broader context of the common law.[88] To adhere to the doctrine of *stare decisis* is not simply to hold to a previous decision without consideration of the merits of the case before you. While there are evidently some costs involved in adhering to this doctrine as an aspect of judicial reasoning, choosing to follow precedent *instead* of deciding a case on its merits is not one of them. Judges do not and cannot reason in a vacuum any more than Parliament can legislate in a vacuum.[89] It is not open to the court to disregard settled principle and applicable precedent without first accounting for and weighing the importance of both adherence and departure. To decide a case on its merits is fundamentally to decide on the basis of applicable legal principle, including principle derived from past precedents. Judges who take no notice of previous decisions at all and decide cases purely on the basis of their own personal morality flout the rule of law and are in danger of breaching the principle of equality before the law by failing to afford appropriate weight to the interests of similarly situated claimants. To decide cases as if there is no body of established principle to guide deliberation is to abandon the rule of law entirely.

The rule of law, in placing principled constraints on state power, including judicial power, ensures that the correct answer to a legal dispute is never fully removed from its historical context. These principles demand justification for departing from established practice, but they do not demand that established practice never be departed from. There are both instrumental and intrinsic reasons for this and some of the intrinsic arguments are based on the important role that legality places on equality before the law.

Stare decisis is a comparative standard and raises comparative concerns. It is one thing to claim that a departure from previous patterns of treatment has resulted in one experiencing a detriment or having predictability undermined and legitimate expectations frustrated.[90] It is another to complain that the departure must be *justified*, given the equal moral status of persons. The doctrine of precedent is one important factor in deciding how best to provide justice to individual cases. The value of treating like cases alike is an aspect of *stare decisis*, but it

[88] Waldron, 'Stare Decisis and the Rule of Law: A Layered Approach' (n 76) 3, 12, 14–15.

[89] *R v Secretary of State for the Home Department, ex p Pierson* [1998] AC 539 (Lord Steyn).

[90] On the inadequacy of this as an explanation for *stare decisis*, see Waldron, 'Stare Decisis and the Rule of Law: A Layered Approach' (n 76) 12–13; J Waldron, 'The Concept and the Rule of Law' (2008) 29 *Sibley Lecture Series*; J Waldron, 'The Rule of Law and the Importance of Procedure' (2011) 50 *Nomos* 3. See also Dworkin, *Law's Empire* (n 17) 31–43, 130, 157–58.

cannot be assessed in abstraction from the principles which lend it its legitimacy. To the extent that following precedent produces an injustice such as the failure to respect moral equality, *stare decisis* does not and cannot legitimately require adherence to it. The judge who departs from precedent must do so in a way that is legally and constitutionally justified. She must explain, through legal reasoning, why it is that this new interpretation of law is a better way to achieve justice and to do so in a manner which maintains a commitment to the underlying values which inform the doctrine of *stare decisis* in the first place.

It may be argued that the doctrine is breached any time a precedent is departed from or overturned. However, this would leave little distinction between the principled departure from precedent on grounds of developing common law reasoning and departure which is in no way justifiable because justification is not offered or because there has been a mistake. The difference between these two types of departure from precedent must have meaning and weight within the common law. There is necessarily an internal standard that *stare decisis* itself places on how exactly departures from precedent can be justified. *Stare decisis* does not require slavish adherence to *decisions*; it requires respect for legal principle and institutional history.

For these reasons, we can conclude that the doctrine of *stare decisis* is an equality-based principle, but that it is not egalitarian in nature because it does not demand equalisation. Treating like cases alike is a key aspect of *stare decisis*, but it does not exhaust the nuances of the principle, nor does it fully account for the important role that institutional history and practice plays in our interpretation of what is and is not consistent with it. As such, we can conclude that equal treatment itself lacks intrinsic value within the common law and that the principle of equality before the law and, by extension, that of *stare decisis*, must be informed by a more foundational commitment to treating legal subjects as moral equals with equal status under the law. Central to this commitment is a respect for the dignity and rights of persons in a manner which would limit the ends which can legitimately be pursued through law.[91]

[91] M Foran, 'The Rule of Good Law: Form, Substance and Fundamental Rights' (2019) 78 *Cambridge Law Journal* 570.

3

Equal Dignity and the Rule of Law

Any discussion of equality is haunted by the spectre of the levelling down objection. All principles of equalisation are vulnerable to this critique. It is a significant concern that the levelling down objection could also be levied against a Dworkinian principle of equal concern and respect. This principle, like egalitarianism, does seem to demand the equalisation of some things (concern and respect). So, one could feasibly provide others with *equal* concern and respect by refusing to afford *any* concern or respect to them at all. Take the example of the two sick children mentioned in Chapter 1: both need the medicine but only one of them will die if they don't receive it.[1] It is true that treatment as an equal, in this context, would preclude giving half a dose of medicine to each child as this would amount to putting greater weight on the interests of the less ill child. However, it is not, strictly speaking, true that the only other option available is to give one dose of medicine to the most unwell child. Another option is to refuse to give medicine to either of them. Dworkin may thus have been mistaken to assume that treatment as an equal is doing all of the work in his analysis. Indeed, in his later writing, he stressed that it is important to have both respect *and* equal respect.[2]

At first blush, there doesn't seem to be anything within a requirement to treat persons as equals that would lend guidance to a choice between these two options. It would, nevertheless, be a mistake to construe the principle of legal equality as one which is indifferent to this choice. Legal equality demands that legal officials respect the normative upshots of people's status as moral equals in a manner which is consistent with our *other* constitutional norms and values. The constitutional requirements placed on legal officials involve treating legal subjects as moral equals, but not as equally sub-human. Nevertheless, it is not clear at this point whether it is equality or legality which ultimately prevents the state from treating its subjects with no concern or respect at all. That is the focus of this chapter. The suggestion here is that the principle of legal equality is fundamentally a principle of equal *dignity* under the law. As such, it represents the coming together of two important moral concepts which, when analysed in isolation from each other, are vulnerable to powerful critiques. Respect for both

[1] R Dworkin, *Taking Rights Seriously* (Harvard University Press, 1977) 227.
[2] R Dworkin, *Law's Empire* (Harvard University Press, 1986) 200–201.

dignity *and* equality is central to the foundations of our constitutional order and vital for a coherent understanding of the rule of law which affords appropriate weight to the values which underpin the common law itself.[3]

I. DIGNITY AND LEGALITY

The use of human dignity within constitutional and human rights jurisprudence has been subject to sustained critique, even, or perhaps especially, in contexts where dignity has been explicitly invoked by constitutional and human rights instruments as the grounding interpretative lens. It makes some lawyers and philosophers uncomfortable to place such a seemingly empty concept at the heart of judicial reasoning. Dignity has been described as 'impossibly vague',[4] an idea which cannot 'provide a universalistic, principled basis for judicial decision-making'.[5] It is seen to be, at best, a noble ideal which has retained its normative purchase precisely because it is a 'vacuous concept'[6] which varies 'radically with the time, place, and beholder'.[7] Ultimately, the concept is decried as relying on rhetorical argument that 'masks a great deal of disagreement and sheer confusion'.[8]

Many of these criticisms will be quite familiar, seeing as they have been levied, in almost exactly the same manner, against the concept of moral equality as well.[9] It seems that the issue here is not one that is confined to the concept of dignity, but which is faced by any attempt to recognise the existence of values, principles or standards within the legal canon. Anything which cannot be identified fully in abstraction from moral interpretation is perceived as providing no guidance at all. Thus, dignity is empty, justice is empty, equality is empty, and, notably for the public lawyer, reasonableness is empty.[10] But no legal standard,

[3] TRS Allan, *The Sovereignty of Law: Freedom, Constitution, and Common Law* (Oxford University Press, 2013) Ch 3. See also R Dworkin, *Is Democracy Possible Here?* (Princeton University Press, 2006) 9–21; J Laws, *The Common Law Constitution* (Cambridge University Press, 2014).

[4] C McCrudden, 'Human Dignity and Judicial Interpretation of Human Rights' (2008) 19 *European Journal of International Law* 655, 723.

[5] ibid 655.

[6] M Bagaric and J Allan, 'The Vacuous Concept of Dignity' (2006) 5 *Journal of Human Rights* 257, 269.

[7] S Pinker, 'The Stupidity of Dignity' (*The New Republic*, 2008).

[8] M Rosen, *Dignity: Its History and Meaning* (Harvard University Press, 2012) 67.

[9] P Westen, 'The Empty Idea of Equality' (1982) 95 *Harvard Law Review* 537; C Peters, 'Foolish Consistency: On Equality, Integrity, and Justice in Stare Decisis' (1996) 105 *Yale Law Journal* 2031; C Peters, 'Equality Revisited' (1997) 110 *Harvard Law Review* 1210; C Peters, 'Slouching Towards Equality' (1999) 84 *Iowa Law Review* 801; F Thomsen, 'Concept, Principle, and Norm – Equality Before the Law Reconsidered' [2018] *Legal Theory* 1.

[10] See Lord Carnwath, 'From Judicial Outrage to Sliding Scales – Where Next for Wednesbury?' ALBL Annual Lecture (2013), www.supremecourt.uk/docs/speech-131112-lord-carnwath.pdf; *cf* RG Wright, 'Arbitrariness: Why the Most Important Idea in Administrative Law Can't Be Defined, and What This Means for the Law in General' (2010) 44 *University of Richmond Law Review* 839.

not even the seemingly clearest rule, can be identified without interpretation.[11] We should not confuse the potential for disagreement with emptiness. The fact that there are multiple ways of interpreting a concept does not mean that the concept has no meaning at all.

As a constitutional principle, operative within an evolving practice and always interpreted as one part of a wider corpus of principles, legal equality must account for the important role that legality itself plays in ensuring that governance is respectful of the demands of human dignity.[12] In the decades since the end of the Second World War, human dignity has come to represent an organising ideal within public law, invoked as a specific right or as an underlying value which grounds many of the core obligations on public authorities.[13] The concept of dignity has, in many ways, come to occupy an exalted place within the legal sphere. Much of our commitment to human dignity involves a concerted effort to embrace a concept which can serve a useful function in a post-holocaust world. In many instances, codified constitutional documents, written or amended in the latter half of the twentieth century, incorporate some reference to inviolable human dignity.[14] From here, analysis of the role of dignity within public law can begin.

However, that cannot be the approach of the public lawyer attempting to locate human dignity within the United Kingdom, to say nothing about expounding what may be required to respect it. It will not suffice to point to the constitutions of other jurisdictions, nor even to international treaties that the United Kingdom has agreed to be bound by. If dignity is to be found within this constitution, it is to the principles of the common law that we must turn. In particular, the core constitutional principle of legality is revelatory. Weinrib

[11] See L Fuller, 'Positivism and Fidelity to Law – A Reply to Professor Hart' (1958) 71 *Harvard Law Review* 630; Dworkin, *Law's Empire* (n 2); TRS Allan, 'Principle, Practice, and Precedent: Vindicating Justice, According to Law' (2018) 77 *Cambridge Law Journal* 269.

[12] See J Waldron, 'How Law Protects Dignity' (2012) 71 *Cambridge Law Journal* 200; J Waldron, *Dignity, Rank, and Rights* (Oxford University Press, 2012) 47–73; L Fuller, *The Morality of Law*, rvsd edn (Yale University Press, 1969) 162–67.

[13] J Weinrib, *Dimensions of Dignity: The Theory and Practice of Modern Constitutional Law* (Cambridge University Press, 2016); A Chaskalson, 'Human Dignity as a Foundational Value of Our Constitutional Order' (2000) 16 *South African Journal of Human Rights* 193; R Berkowitz, 'Dignity Jurisprudence: Building a New Law on Earth' in D Cornell (ed), *The Dignity Jurisprudence of the Constitutional Court of South Africa* (Fordham University Press, 2013) 65; C Byk, 'Is Human Dignity a Useless Concept? Legal Perspectives' in M Düwell (ed), *The Cambridge Handbook of Human Dignity: Interdisciplinary Perspectives* (Cambridge University Press, 2014) 362; C Dupré, 'Human Dignity in Europe: A Foundational Constitutional Principle' (2013) 19 *European Public Law* 319.

[14] Basic Law of the Federal Republic of Germany, 1949, Art 1; Constitution of the Republic of Armenia, 1995, Art 3; Constitution of the Republic of Bulgaria, 1991, Art 4(2); Constitution of the Dominican Republic, 2015, Art 38; Constitution of Greece, 1975, Art 2(1): 'respect and protection of the value of the human being constitute the primary obligations of the State'; Constitution of Peru, 1993, Art 1; Constitution of the Republic of Poland, 1997, Art 30; Constitution of Sweden, 1974, Art 2: 'Public power shall be exercised with respect for the equal worth of all and the liberty and dignity of the individual'.

is quite right to stress the need to ground a constitutional theory of dignity *within* the practice itself.[15] It is, thus, incumbent upon constitutional theorists to ground their analysis within a distinctly legal framework, attentive to the demands of the rule of law. From the internal perspective of the citizen and judge, the rule of law demands that legal officials respect the fact that legal subjects are independent moral agents who are equally entitled to be respected as such.[16]

If we are to understand the concept of dignity within the common law, we must look to the sources of common law, including the classical legal tradition which formed the basis of common law. According to this tradition, dignity signifies something's goodness on account of itself, its intrinsic value.[17] Humans all share this same intrinsic value by virtue of us all being human persons.[18] Other beings can and do possess their own kind of dignity, by virtue of their being the thing that they are. Thus, we can speak of the dignity of the lion or the mouse or even the river. But humans have our own kind of dignity which connotes the intrinsic value of our shared humanity, manifest equally within each and every individual person.

This view is in direct contrast to that of Aristotle, who argued not only that slavery can be morally defended but that it can be defended on the ground that some humans are naturally inferior to others. In response to unnamed adversaries[19] who claimed that slavery is contrary to the natural law, Aristotle advances a theory of natural slavery. He begins by setting out his opponents' position:

> But other thinkers consider ruling slaves on the part of an owner to be against nature. They think that the differentiation between owner and slave obtains merely by convention, whereas by nature there is no difference between the two. The relationship between an owner and a slave is grounded in force/violence; therefore, it is not based on justice.[20]

In response to this, Aristotle maintained what he deemed to be the 'evident' distinction, found in nature, between those who rule people and those who are ruled: 'some people are free and others slaves by nature'.[21] He denied the personhood of barbarians because – he asserts – they lack 'the deliberative faculty of the soul in the least'.[22] A similar argument is advanced to justify the subordination

[15] Weinrib (n 13) 2.

[16] Allan, *The Sovereignty of Law* (n 3) 90–91. See also T Bingham, *The Rule of Law* (Allen Lane, 2010) 55.

[17] Aquinas, *In* III *Sent.*, d. 35, q. 1, a. 4, qla 1, corp. See also Rosen (n 8) 16–17.

[18] See T Wu, 'Aquinas on Human Personhood and Dignity' (2021) 85 *The Thomist* 377.

[19] There are good reasons to think that these adversaries were (at least some of) the Sophists who very probably elaborated a criticism of the institution of slavery as against nature. See I Ramelli, *Social Justice and the Legitimacy of Slavery: The Role of Philosophical Asceticism from Ancient Judaism to Late Antiquity* (Oxford University Press, 2016) 26–27.

[20] *Pol* 1253b20–25.

[21] *Pol* 1255a1–2.

[22] *Pol* 1260a10–12.

of women, recognising their personhood or humanity in the form of a soul, 'but without full authority'.[23]

In contrast, the Stoics rejected this theory of natural slavery and the natural inferiority of women because they rejected the grounding of human value upon a variable characteristic such as deliberative faculty. Instead, they argued that all human beings have 'a share in the logos'.[24] Thus, while some may be better able to actualise their participation within the logos by fostering wisdom and virtue, all humans share a common nature as rational beings, *logikai*.

This understanding of all humans as rational beings developed to become a central tenant of natural law theorising of dignity, emphasising a shared nature united by reference to the kind of being that humans are, rather than any actual abilities possessed.[25] It is the radical, from *radix* – root – capacity of all humans to flourish as persons by directing our rational mind towards the good that grounds our dignity. This capacity is actual in that it exists even if the potentialities it involves are not yet activated.[26] It is on this basis that Rawls argues that 'the capacity for moral personality is a sufficient condition for being entitled to equal justice'.[27] Human dignity signifies our ontological unity and radical moral equality. It forms the basis of moral claims that all persons can make against others. Any conception of human rights which seeks to live up to their foundational vision as universal moral claims grounded in humanity must account for what it is about humanity which is of moral worth and why this worth does not and cannot vary between persons. The classical natural law tradition has, over more than two thousand years, developed an account for this value. The insights that the early Stoics and Sophists gave us, by grounding human value in human nature, remain pertinent today in the face of new challenges to human dignity.

Dignity, on this account, becomes a juridical concept, one which is informed by 'the moral possibility and purpose of public law conceived of as a relationship between rulers and ruled'.[28] It forms the foundation of concrete legal principles such as the common law rejection of slavery while also constituting a background presumption of legal reasoning itself, presuming as it does that the claims that one can bring within law pertain to rights and duties equally shared without unreasonable or unjustified distinction. Dignity is thus embodied in the legal recognition of the intrinsic moral worth of persons, something possessed to the same extent by all persons.[29] This understanding of dignity

[23] *Pol* 1260a12–13.
[24] Ramelli (n 19) 46.
[25] See P Lee and R George, 'The Nature and Basis of Human Dignity' (2008) 21 *Ratio Juris* 173.
[26] J Finnis, 'Equality and Differences' (2012) 2 *Solidarity* 1, 2.
[27] J Rawls, *A Theory of Justice* (Clarendon Press, 1972) 504.
[28] Weinrib (n 13) 10.
[29] This might be referred to as the *concept* of dignity, rather than a *conception* of dignity. See ibid 4; Rawls (n 27) 5–10. However, if we are to add meat to the bones of this concept, it is to the ideal of legality that we must turn. The conception of dignity embraced by law, therefore, is one which must be attentive to the distinct ways in which legality respects and upholds the agency and moral equality of persons.

demands the appropriate payment of respect to certain moral facts about the legal subject, embraced by the common law. When conceived in this way, the rule of law becomes 'a form of governance in which the duty of government to respect, protect, and fulfil the dignity of all who are subject to it forms a justiciable condition of the valid exercise of public authority'.[30] The next few chapters will focus on how dignity can be respected and protected. The final chapter will explore how it might be fulfilled.

Governance in accordance with the rule of law serves to protect legal subjects from arbitrary abuses of power. The principles of the rule of law do more than just this, however. They also constitute a framework of principle which endows the legal subject with a distinctive normative status. The obligation on the state to act only on the basis of legal authority, to refrain from arbitrary arrest and detention, or to publish legal rules prior to their enforcement, is meaningless if no moral wrong is done by legal officials when they ignore these requirements, imprison persons without trial, or enforce retroactive criminal statutes. As Fuller notes:

> Every departure from the principles of the law's inner morality is an affront to man's dignity as a responsible agent. To judge his actions by unpublished or retrospective laws, or to order him to do an act that is impossible, is to convey to him your indifference to his powers of self-determination. Conversely, when the view is accepted that man is incapable of responsible action, legal morality loses its reason for being. To judge his action by unpublished or retrospective laws is no longer an affront, for there is nothing left to affront – indeed, even the verb 'to judge' becomes itself incongruous in this context; we no longer judge a man, we act upon him.[31]

The wrongfulness of retroactive criminal prosecution or arbitrary detention without trial, therefore, cannot be reduced to the immediate misery which is entailed: there is an additional wrong that is done by profoundly disrespecting the moral agency, autonomy, and dignity of the individual. To be a legal subject is not merely to be a member of 'a subservient populace ready to do what they are told to do'.[32] Rather, members of a legal community are participants in a relationship of reciprocity wherein one is respected as an agent. This relationship, and the respect that is necessary to constitute and sustain it, arises from normative commitments latent within the rule of law and the principles of legality. In particular, these commitments reflect the way in which a legal order presupposes and tacitly endorses certain claims about the moral status of individuals – what Fuller describes as the view of man implicit in legality. Waldron is entirely correct to draw a connection between law and dignity: 'Dignity seems at home in law: law is its natural habitat.'[33] The rule of law, by respecting the

[30] Weinrib (n 13) 20.
[31] Fuller, *The Morality of Law* (n 12) 162–63.
[32] Undated and untitled document, The Papers of Lon L Fuller, Harvard Law School Library, Box 12, Folder 1 (notes for 'Reply to Critics'), cited in K Rundle, *Forms Liberate: Reclaiming the Jurisprudence of Lon L Fuller* (Hart Publishing, 2012).
[33] Waldron, *Dignity, Rank, and Rights* (n 12) 13.

demands of dignity, serves to direct public authority and coercion towards respecting the intrinsic value of all persons and facilitating the actualisation of human potential.

In contrast, Hart stressed that legality presupposes no such conception of the legal subject. As an institutional framework for instrumental activity, pursued by those with lawgiving authority, a governmental system can be compatible with the rule of law even if it conceives of the legal subject as no more an agent than a sheep on its way to the slaughterhouse.[34] Hart may (or may not) be correct in this assessment of law *qua* law, but he would be entirely mistaken if he sought to apply such an argument to the conception of the rule of law embraced by the common law.

The common law recognises the legal subject as a moral agent, not only capable of guiding their own conduct in accordance with legal rules, but also capable and entitled to make their own claims and representations before a court. To be a legal subject under the common law is to possess the capacity to enter into juridical relationships, to alter the normative and legal landscape through one's actions, and to demand that others, including legal officials, respect and respond appropriately to this change in circumstance. The legal subject does not *request* the court to find in their favour because that would be a nice thing to do; she *demands* that her legal rights be respected and, in affording her claims this status, the law endows her with 'the dignity of the rights-bearer'.[35] Indeed, there is a deep and intimate connection between dignity and rights, 'as the ground of rights, the content of certain rights, and perhaps even the form and structure of rights'.[36] As such, Gewirth argues that the fundamental purpose of rights:

> is to secure for each person a certain fundamental moral status: that of having rational autonomy and dignity in the sense of being a self-controlling, self-developing agent who can relate to other persons on a basis of mutual respect and cooperation, in contrast to being a dependent, passive recipient of the agency of others.[37]

To have a right under the common law is to possess 'the dignity of a recognised claimant entitled to push his case before us and demand that it be considered'.[38] And, in this consideration, the rule of law demands impartiality: a fair trial, respectful of the demands of due process and natural justice.[39]

[34] HLA Hart, *The Concept of Law*, 2nd edn (Oxford University Press, 1994) 117.
[35] Waldron, 'How Law Protects Dignity' (n 12) 205. See also Dworkin, *Taking Rights Seriously* (n 1).
[36] Waldron, *Dignity, Rank, and Rights* (n 12) 14.
[37] A Gewirth, 'Rights and Virtues' (1985) 38 *Review of Metaphysics* 739, 743; see also Waldron, *Dignity, Rank, and Rights* (n 12) 50.
[38] Waldron, 'How Law Protects Dignity' (n 12) 204; Waldron, *Dignity, Rank, and Rights* (n 12) 50; see also J Feinberg, 'The Nature and Value of Rights' (1970) 4 *Journal of Value Inquiry* 243.
[39] J Waldron, 'The Rule of Law and the Importance of Procedure' (2011) 50 *Nomos* 3; L Fuller, 'The Forms and Limits of Adjudication' in K Winston (ed), *The Principles of Social Order: Selected Essays of Lon L. Fuller*, rvsd edn (Hart Publishing, 2001).

To act with fidelity to the rule of law is necessarily to be committed to the view that man is, or can become, a responsible agent: a self-determining centre of action, capable of understanding and following rules.[40] But, what is more, it is to afford appropriate recognition and respect for this moral status, by respecting the rights which are necessarily entailed by this.[41] These rights include the right to a fair trial, to be free from arbitrary arrest and detention, and to have other legal rights respected and enforced. Dignity can, thus, inform the content of some rights. However, it may be more illuminating to speak not of a right to dignity, but of a general right to have one's dignity appropriately respected.[42] Disrespect for someone's dignity by, for example, punishing them under a secret law, does not mean that they have no dignity. Rather, it means that their dignity has not been adequately accounted for in the actions of legal officials. It is the intrinsic moral worth of persons, not contingent in any way, that informs and gives weight to the limits which any state must respect if it is to maintain its legitimacy.

A system of law is a system not just of rules but also of duties and corresponding rights. As a bulwark against any assertion of arbitrary power, the rule of law demands the principled application of legal rules to pertinent cases that ensure that legal rights and obligations are adequately respected. It requires not merely that legal rules be strictly enforced, according to their true meaning, but also that the content of these rules should adhere to basic requirements of justice.[43] For example, a 'bill of attainder' which purports to authorise the particularised punishment or detention of a specified individual or group is the most flagrant affront to the principle of legality. In subjecting someone to a bill of attainder, one removes the ordinary protection of law and the right to a fair trial, conducted by an independent judiciary concerning only breaches of the general law applicable to all. Such a bill constitutes the antithesis of equality before the law, a plain denial of the principle of equal subjection to law, and an abandonment of 'even the pretence of even-handedness or impartiality'.[44]

While the law is often seen as a system of constraints on individual liberty, it is better conceived as also ensuring and protecting a degree of freedom from arbitrary interference from others.[45] The rule of law, by enforcing legal obligations and protecting legal rights, guarantees to the legal subject governance by law and thus the enjoyment of a degree of independence from the will of others.[46] This guarantee has two aspects to it: the preservation of independence

[40] Fuller, *The Morality of Law* (n 12) 162.

[41] M Foran, 'The Rule of Good Law: Form, Substance and Fundamental Rights' (2019) 78 *Cambridge Law Journal* 570, 580–85.

[42] Waldron, *Dignity, Rank, and Rights* (n 12) 17: 'Dignity is what some of our rights are rights to; but dignity is also what grounds all of our rights.'

[43] Foran (n 41) 592–94.

[44] Allan, *The Sovereignty of Law* (n 3) 94.

[45] N Simmonds, *Law as a Moral Idea* (Oxford University Press, 2008) 99–104; Allan, *The Sovereignty of Law* (n 3) 95–96.

[46] J Raz, 'The Rule of Law and Its Virtue' in *The Authority of Law: Essays on Law and Morality*, 2nd edn (Oxford University Press, 2009) 220.

such that interference with our autonomy occurs only where permitted by law; and the entailed capacity that we will then have to pursue independent lives as full moral agents. The importance of this for our present purpose is exemplified by the analogy with slavery mentioned above: the slave is denied the dignity of the free man by being cast out from the system of juridical relationships protected by the rule of law and treated, not as a dignified moral agent, but as an object of property rights.[47]

The rule of law should not be conceived of as a mere hodgepodge of disparate principles, but rather as a normatively grounded, coherent *doctrine*.[48] It obtains when a particular state of affairs is established: for Raz in his early writing, this is one where legal subjects are capable of guiding their conduct in accordance with legal rules.[49] As such, he stresses that 'in the final analysis the doctrine rests on its basic idea that the law should be capable of providing effective guidance. The principles do not stand on their own. They must be consistently interpreted in light of the basic idea.'[50] For Fuller, and, I suggest, the common law, this occurs where legal subjects are respected as dignified moral agents. Of course, on this conception, the importance of action-guidance remains salient. However, it is not the ultimate standard; rather, action-guidance is derived from a more foundational commitment to dignity and reciprocity. It is this fundamental normative underpinning which constitutes the 'spirit of the doctrine', as Raz describes it.[51]

The inadequacy of an entirely guidance-based account, and the necessity of a deeper understanding is shown starkly when considering Raz's analysis of how the rule of law respects dignity. To Raz, adherence to the rule of law is necessary if law is to protect human dignity.[52] Responding appropriately to a legal subject's autonomous agency is essential to respecting their dignity, and respect for the rule of law is necessary for this. To fail to adhere to the rule of law would be to insult the dignity of the individual by implying or expressing 'a denial that he is an autonomous person or that he deserved to be treated as one'.[53] We can see similarities between this idea of an insult to dignity and the expression of indifference described by Fuller.[54] The importance of that expression will be discussed in greater detail below when we address the expressive wrong that

[47] See Allan, *The Sovereignty of Law* (n 3) 96; P Pettit, *Republicanism: A Theory of Freedom and Government* (Clarendon Press, 1997) 36–37; Q Skinner, *Liberty Before Liberalism* (Cambridge University Press, 1998) 70; Simmonds (n 45) 101–102.

[48] J Raz, 'The Law's Own Virtue' (2019) 39 *Oxford Journal of Legal Studies* 1, 3; Raz, 'The Rule of Law and Its Virtue' (n 46) 215–18.

[49] Raz, 'The Rule of Law and Its Virtue' (n 46) 214.

[50] ibid 218.

[51] Raz, 'The Law's Own Virtue' (n 48) 3.

[52] Raz, 'The Rule of Law and Its Virtue' (n 46) 221. Note that Raz draws a distinction between governance under law and governance under the rule of law.

[53] ibid.

[54] Fuller, *The Morality of Law* (n 12) 162–63.

discrimination may engender.[55] For now, it is important to stress that failure to adhere to the rule of law amounts to the adoption of an attitude of profound disrespect towards the legal subject.

Fidelity to the rule of law thus entails the adoption of a particular attitude, one which includes 'showing' the legal subject respect.[56] However, to Raz (at least in his early writing), while conforming to the rule of law is necessary for the law to respect dignity, there is no requirement that legal officials adopt an appropriate attitude of respect. Since action-guidance is the ultimate normative grounding for the doctrine, on his early account, respect for human dignity is not necessary. It is for this reason that he claims that the rule of law is compatible with slavery; one can effectively guide conduct in the implementation and enforcement of slavery and so the rule of law, being primarily about guiding action, in no way conflicts with state-implemented slavery.[57] Indeed, Raz must conclude this. For, if he did not, he would have to accept that the rule of law affects the ends which might be pursued through law. To him, 'rule of law principles are not about the content of the law, but about its mode of generation and application'.[58] If we accept that the rule of law, in fact, does affect the content of law by precluding bills of attainder, retroactive criminal statutes, or acts which attempt to use public means for private ends (all of which Raz concedes as incompatible with the rule of law), then we must also accept that the rule of law sees no sharp distinction between procedure and substance.[59]

The rule of law is not simply about form or procedure. Nor is it solely concerned with action guidance. Indeed, Raz himself has recently recognised that it was a mistake to focus on action guidance as the bedrock normative grounding for the rule of law:

> people can plan and organise their affairs on the basis of partial information, and in the face of risk. Indeed, given that the application of law would inevitably be imperfect, the law itself … generates uncertainties and risk. On occasion, the law deliberately adopts rules that generate risk. We must conclude that, while the law aims to guide, its ability to do so is much less securely connected with the rule of law principles I enumerated that is often assumed.[60]

All legal rules require interpretation in one manner or another and the common law method of doing so reveals a tension between predictability and principle. It is a central feature of the common law that unclear cases be decided by a court with reference to general principles internal to the legal order. The implication

[55] See Ch 4 below.
[56] On the importance of expressive meaning and showing respect, see L Green, 'Two Worries about Respect for Persons' (2010) 120 *Ethics* 212, 214.
[57] Raz, 'The Rule of Law and Its Virtue' (n 46) 221.
[58] Raz, 'The Law's Own Virtue' (n 48) 2. See also Raz, 'The Rule of Law and Its Virtue' (n 46).
[59] See Foran (n 41) 575–80; J Gardner, 'The Supposed Formality of the Rule of Law' in *Law as a Leap of Faith: Essays on Law in General* (Oxford University Press, 2012).
[60] Raz, 'The Law's Own Virtue' (n 48) 4–5.

of this is that 'many of the general principles on which the conclusions depend will be only implicit in the body of formulated law and will have to be discovered by the courts'.[61] So, if the rule of law is informed ultimately by an ideal of predictability or action-guidance, there would seemingly be no room for principled interpretation, nor for the development and evolution of the common law. Indeed, often the law does not operate through the use of determinative, fixed rules; rather, it identifies and demands adherence to *standards* such as reasonableness or the requirement to act with 'due regard' to some pertinent factors in one's deliberation. In such instances, legal subjects 'recognize a norm, they apprehend its bearing on their conduct, and they make a determination and act on it'.[62] No legal system can provide guidance which does not need to be interpreted, either by a legal official or by a legal subject in their determination of how a given legal rule or standard might apply to their conduct.

There is good reason to think that the rule of law does not prohibit such central aspects of the common law system. Interpretation in accordance with legal principle does not fundamentally conflict with the ideal of action-guidance; rather, it demands that the court:

> tread a delicate line between adherence to the 'letter of the law', when such strict adherence is essential to the law's stability and predictability, and a more fluid and flexible invocation of deeper principles or underlying standards, when such principles or standards reflect wider shared expectations or assumptions about the requirements of justice.[63]

In practice this will require an attention to context with certain settings, such as the criminal law, requiring a stricter adherence to the ideal of predictability than others. Nevertheless, it is clear that the rule of law cannot be exhausted by recourse to action-guidance alone. In his recent work, Raz has advanced the argument that the rationale for the rule of law, its normative underpinning and virtue is best conceived as ensuring that government act 'with a manifest intention to protect and advance the interests of the governed'.[64] A key aspect of this is that 'the interests of all the governed should be given their proper significance and importance'.[65] Raz does not give much guidance as to what those interests are; however, it seems that we can reasonably conclude that it would not include a hierarchy of moral worth or status as between legal subjects. Proper respect for moral equality is, therefore, essential for any understanding of what it would mean to give the interests of the governed their proper significance and importance. If this is true, it seems that Raz cannot maintain both that the rule of law manifests a requirement that government afford appropriate weight to

[61] F von Hayek, *The Constitution of Liberty* (Routledge & Kegan Paul, 1960) 209.
[62] Waldron, *Dignity, Rank, and Rights* (n 12) 53.
[63] Allan, *The Sovereignty of Law* (n 3) 99.
[64] Raz, 'The Law's Own Virtue' (n 48) 13.
[65] ibid 7.

the interests of the governed and also that it would be compatible with slavery. To act as a custodian, as Raz terms it, governments must become guardians of the public interest, manifesting an intention to respect and promote the interests of all legal subjects. It is simply not possible to do this while maintaining a system of slavery, of apartheid, or of institutional discrimination, except by undermining the very notion of 'public' interest by focusing only on the interests of some and ignoring or inappropriately weighing the interests of others.[66]

The rule of law thus envisages a very particular conception of the legal official which complements the very particular conception of the legal subject mentioned above. To be a legal official is to act in the *public* interest and not one's own private interest. It is for this reason that the rule of law precludes the use of public means for private ends.[67] The legal official is consequently required to act in accordance with and only on the authority of law, to respect the rights of legal subjects, and to show appropriate respect for her status as a dignified moral agent by acting reasonably in accordance with legal principle and eschewing bias or the perception of bias. There is, therefore, an important connection between the legal official and the legal subject, one which demands what Fuller described as a relationship of reciprocity.[68]

Initially, this notion of reciprocity is presented as something akin to a quid pro quo arrangement; where the government expects legal subjects to follow specific rules and assures legal subjects that, if they do, they will only be subject to those rules.[69] We can see parallels between this account and the guidance-based understanding of the rule of law that Raz initially advanced. However, this is quickly supplemented by a deeper understanding of what reciprocity must necessarily imply when it exists between governor and governed. First, the notion of equal subjugation to law and an understanding of the equal value in reciprocal performance:

> The bond of reciprocity unites men, not simply *in spite* of their differences, but *because* of their differences. When, therefore, we seek equality in a relation of reciprocity what we require is some measure of value that can be applied to things that are different in kind.[70]

The public role of the legal official is not and cannot be identical to that of the private citizen. Yet, when conceived of as connected by the bonds of reciprocity, it becomes clear that the rule of law demands an equality of status between both parties. The legal official may perform a public function, but this does not place them above the legal subject, in law or in morals. Indeed, the public nature of their role necessarily demands that they act in the interests of subjects and not

[66] This will be explored in greater detail in Ch 7.
[67] Raz, 'The Rule of Law and Its Virtue' (n 46) 220; Raz, 'The Law's Own Virtue' (n 48) 7–8.
[68] Fuller, *The Morality of Law* (n 12) 19–27, 61–62, 137–40.
[69] ibid 39–40.
[70] ibid 23.

their own. If anything, the legal official, when acting as such, is a public *servant* and is, thus, expected to place the interests of others above their own.

Second, because the rule of law, and by extension, the legitimacy of governance, is dependent upon a relationship of reciprocity, the authority of law can be withdrawn from the actions of officials who abuse it.[71] Fuller conjures the notion of a social contract to explain this. On this account, the validity of law 'is made to depend on the state's fidelity to a contract between itself and the citizen'.[72] The central thrust of this argument can be summarised as demanding that state action proceed from the presumption that the citizen is, at least, an equal party to the relationship of governance. On this conception, the rule of law is properly understood as a commitment to the protection of human dignity and the rights associated with that dignity.

From this we can conclude that the role of the legal official is not one which countenances a 'one-way projection of authority, emanating from an authorized source and imposing itself on the citizen'.[73] Rather, it constitutes a distinctive role which has its own internal standards and limits. A doctor who murders his patient can be critiqued for not only committing an evil act, but also for the wickedness which arises from the fact that he was a *doctor*, charged with furthering the interests of his patients. Murdering a patient is simply not equivalent to murdering a stranger for it has the additional wrong-making feature of breaching an internal moral standard. So too does a legal official who attempts to abuse their powers open themselves up for additional condemnation. It is bad enough if you attempt to steal, but to steal from the public funds by abusing your position as a legal official is to commit a wrong that arises precisely because you have a special fiduciary role within our society.[74] As Weinrib notes, 'if the right of government to exercise public authority rests on the dignity of all who are subject to it, then public authority contains its own internal standard of moral adequacy'.[75]

Raz seemed to implicitly recognise this when describing the rule of law as a negative value, designed only to minimise the danger created by the law itself.[76] He is correct to note that there are some wrongs that can only occur through the abuse of governmental power. However, he fails to account for the important upshot of this: a system of law may create instances where power can be abused, but the abuse of this power amounts to a *betrayal* of the office of legal official, not a valid exercise which can only be critiqued from an external perspective. Just as we would declare a doctor who murders his patients as no true doctor, so too must we declare the legal official who abuses their office as no true official.

[71] ibid 61–62, 137–38.
[72] ibid 62.
[73] ibid 192.
[74] ibid 193.
[75] Weinrib (n 13) 15.
[76] Raz, 'The Rule of Law and Its Virtue' (n 46) 224.

They act *ultra vires*, beyond their powers in more than a mere source-based way: such abuse is incompatible with the nature of the office itself. Just as we would recognise that murder is not healthcare, so too must we view breaches of the rule of law as lacking legal validity, or at the very least as being extremely defective as law. Officials, like medical professionals, are charged with furthering the interests of those in their charge; it is central to their role that they account for and advance the interests of the governed. On this, we can agree with Raz. However, although his more recent writing is a welcome departure from his earlier analysis, there remains a tension within this framework. It seems that Raz has begun to embrace a conception of the rule of law which is no longer the virtue of the sharp knife, but of the conscientious custodian who adopts an appropriate attitude of respect for the interests of the legal subject. As such, many of his previous claims concerning the compatibility of the rule of law with injustice are in need of reassessment.

We can, thus, conclude that the rule of law is fundamentally informed by a commitment to respecting the dignity of the legal subject. However, this commitment would be meaningless if it did not also entail a commitment to respecting the moral equality of legal subjects. In the remainder of this chapter, we will explore the connection between moral equality and dignity. In particular, it will be shown that the value of equality does not collapse into what we could call 'independent' dignity concerns and that the rule of law demands respect for both dignity and equality simultaneously.

II. DIGNITY AND EQUALITY

It was mentioned previously that equality has been subject to a powerful critique of emptiness and circularity. Our focus at that point was on the claim that treating like cases alike demands only that a given legal rule be enforced according to its terms, since likeness is determined by reference to the rule itself.[77] It was suggested that this critique falls away once likeness is seen to include moral likeness, similar to the notion of equal worth or equal status. However, an additional critique has been levied within this general corpus of arguments that equality is an empty ideal. This argument, advanced by Raz, operates against the background critique of circularity and emptiness mentioned above and which Raz mostly agrees with. His task, therefore, is to identify 'a sense of "principles of equality" which is not merely formal and empty'.[78] He does this by embracing a conception of an equality principle which is consequentialist and distributional in nature, demanding the equal distribution of goods on grounds of an existing inequality in the distribution of that good.

[77] Westen (n 9); Peters, 'Foolish Consistency' (n 9).
[78] J Raz, *The Morality of Freedom* (Clarendon Press, 1988) 217.

While this account is quite similar to that which was advanced in the previous chapter regarding egalitarianism, it differs in one key respect: to Raz, there are no other equality-based principles beyond egalitarian distribution principles. He follows Westen in his conclusion that sufficiently general or universal principles which are applied according to their terms are not, properly or directly, equality based: 'Generality implies equality of application to a class. Adding "equally" to the statement of the conditions or consequences of a principle does not necessarily turn it into one which has more to do with equality'.[79] However, it is a mistake to refer to any other equality-based principle as merely rhetorical in nature on the ground that 'they are not claims designed to promote equality but rather to promote the cause of those who qualify under independently valid principles'.[80]

Raz's reliance on the fact that such principles do not or are not intended to *promote* equality is revealing. The focus on equality as an end or telos to be pursued and promoted precludes from the outset any deeper commitment to the moral equality of persons that is premised on deontic respect. There are two key presumptions underpinning this claim that non-egalitarian equality principles are merely rhetorical in nature. The first is the idea that the only equality-based aspect of such principles manifests in what he refers to as 'closure principles':

> F is a ground for a right to G and nothing overrides it. For example, 'Every human being is equally entitled to education' may imply that no quality but that of being human is relevant to a right to education. Every moral and every political theory which claims either that it is a complete theory, or even merely that it is complete regarding some issue, contains a principle of equality in this sense. That is, it contains a closure principle stating that nothing else counts for the justification of moral or political action, or for action over education, etc.[81]

Thus, if Fs are equally entitled to G, this means that nothing other than being an F should count towards one's entitlement to G. But it also means that we can remove 'equally' from this sentence without changing its meaning.[82] Raz, Westen, and Peters are all correct in their contention that there is little that the value of equality is doing in this context, even if equality might tell us something about what should count as G and who should count as F. Nevertheless, the mistake that Raz makes is to assume that all non-egalitarian equality principles are simply rhetorical in this manner. He stresses that his claim that these principles are merely rhetorical is not meant to be derogatory. Rather, it is that these principles often invoke equality 'to gain from the good name that "equality" has in our culture … if their resort to fashionable egalitarian formulations makes

[79] ibid 221.
[80] ibid 228.
[81] ibid 220.
[82] See Westen (n 9); Peters, 'Foolish Consistency' (n 9); Peters, 'Equality Revisited' (n 9).

them more attractive, so much the better. The price we pay is in intellectual confusion'.[83]

However, there are strong reasons to doubt Raz's claim that non-distributional equality principles are in no meaningful way connected to the value of equality. In particular, his critique of Dworkin's concept of equal concern and respect is in need of close scrutiny. Raz claims that a principle requiring the state to treat its legal subjects with equal concern and respect is really just an independent principle of concern and respect which contains a closure principle:

> principles of equal respect or concern, etc., often amount to little more than an assertion that all human beings are moral subjects, to an assertion of humanism. Such principles can be expressed with equal ease without invoking equality. They are not designed to increase equality but to encourage recognition that the well-being of all human beings counts.[84]

Again, we see a focus on increasing equality rather than respecting the equal moral status of persons. There is a further problem with this argument, however. Without a focus on *equal* concern and respect, there is nothing to explain the moral inequity of principles which recognise that the well-being of all counts, but which contend that the well-being of some should count for more than others. I have in mind here, not arguments in favour of special moral obligations one may have, but rather the belief that, for example, women are moral subjects but, in some sense, inferior moral subjects to men, that their interests and well-being exists and counts but not equally to that of men. We cannot ignore the philosophical defence of sexism or racism which relied precisely on the argument that the well-being of all human beings count, but that some people simply count for less by virtue of the colour of their skin or their sex.

If a principle of equal concern and respect collapses into nothing more than a principle of concern and respect, then we are faced with explaining the moral inequity of cast systems or apartheid, or other systems which recognise the interests and well-being of all but simply do not afford them equal weight. Even a system of slavery may afford some protections for the interests of slaves and thus in some sense recognise that their well-being counts. Indeed, if this is what Raz has in mind when thinking of government as a custodian, then he could maintain that the rule of law may obtain even for the victims of slavery. However, this would demand a very particular, indeed a twisted, conception of stewardship akin to the guardian who abused those they have sworn to protect. At best this is a failed steward; at worst, no steward at all.

It could be that what Raz really means here is that *proper* or *appropriate* recognition of a person's well-being or humanity would exclude treating them as an inferior in this manner. But if this were true, it would mean that respect for someone's humanity or dignity actually *would* be meaningfully connected to the

[83] Raz, *The Morality of Freedom* (n 78) 228.
[84] ibid.

value of equality and would not simply be relying on the language of equality to advance rhetorical claims which have nothing to do with equality. Nevertheless, it seems that what Raz means when he says that 'Being human is in itself sufficient ground for respect' is that the only claims that matter (or even exist), in this context, are non-comparative ones.[85] This is the second presumption underpinning this claim that non-distributional equality principles are merely rhetorical: all non-distributional equality claims are rhetorical because they necessarily collapse into independent, non-comparative, claims to, for example, respect.

What of a principle that the state must afford our interests equal weight and treat us with equal concern and respect? Is this really just a principle that the state affords our interests *some* weight which has been applied universally or which contains a closure element? Surely, even if it was a principle that the state affords our interests *appropriate* weight, it would have to reject any attempt to implement an unjustified hierarchy of weightings, would it not? Yes, under a principle of appropriate weighing of interests, one may have a non-comparative claim to respect. But there will also exist a comparative claim to the same respect afforded to others. Take, for example, Dworkin's example of the parent with two sick children mentioned above.[86] In this example, one child will die without medicine and one will only be mildly ill without medicine. What should the parent do when they only have one dose of medicine? What wrong is done when the parent does not give medicine to the most ill child? Raz says that the real claim here is an independent claim to the medicine:

> the wrong is the same as where a parent has only one child ... to whom he denies the medicine when he is sick ... To accuse him of unequal treatment, however, is not to identify the nature of the wrong: it could be any wrong and it is definitely not the wrong of creating or perpetuating inequalities ... The same wrong can exist in situations involving no inequality.[87]

However, there are two claims at play here: an independent claim to medicine, and also a comparative claim to being treated as a moral equal to the other child. The child who would die without medicine is entitled to be given the whole dose because to deny them medicine would be an affront to their dignity. But, it would also be wrong to split the dose in two and give half to each child. Raz is incorrect to assume that the issue here is that the children be treated equally, for it is precisely *unequal* treatment that respect for moral equality requires. To do anything other than give the full dose to the most unwell child would be to profoundly disrespect the dignity of that child by weighing their interests inappropriately as against the interests of their sibling. The wrongness of this is not simply in the denial of medicine; it is also in the fact that, by giving

[85] ibid.
[86] See Dworkin, *Taking Rights Seriously* (n 1) 227.
[87] Raz, *The Morality of Freedom* (n 78) 228–29.

half a dose to each child, even if and, indeed, precisely *because* this would be to treat them equally, one manifests an attitude which considers the death of one child to be equivalent to the mild illness of another. The comparative wrong done here is not due to an inequality in treatment or distribution of medicine, but to what an equal distribution represents and manifests in terms of the attitude of the parent. It is for this reason that an account of human dignity which is conceived in terms of the right of each person to equal freedom must necessarily also include a right to be treated as a moral equal, even where freedom is equalised.[88]

If affording proper weight to one's interests includes affording weight to an interest in being treated as a moral equal to others, then there is necessarily a connection between humanity (or dignity) and moral equality.[89] We could follow Raz and argue that the driving obligation here is simply to respect dignity or humanity, independent of how I am treated relative to others. Within a constitutional context, this would amount to the claim that, where I am disrespected, I have a non-comparative claim against the state. But there is a good reason to think that I also have a comparative claim grounded in moral equality, for two reasons.

First, where I am treated with a complete lack of respect, say because I have been enslaved, I do, of course, have an independent, non-comparative claim that I have not been treated as a dignified agent or that my independent rights have been violated. But, should I be enslaved, and others not be enslaved, I have an *additional* claim that my interests have not been afforded the same weight as others. This claim is central to a proper understanding of human dignity. It is likely the case that both of these claims are ultimately explained as affronts to one's dignity. While the concept of dignity includes respect for the moral equality of persons, it is not exhausted by that commitment. There is no reason why dignity cannot give rise to different claims which reference different aspects of the concept. Respect for autonomy and independence may explain why slavery *qua* slavery is an affront to dignity, but it does not fully explain why the enslavement of one person or group *and not another* is as wrongful as it is. To fully account for the wickedness of, for example, race-based slavery, it is necessary to account for the additional claim that arises from the disrespect for moral equality that it engenders. As Sangiovanni argues, 'essential to any adequate explanation of the wrongness of genocide – and also any adequate explanation of the wrongness of invidious racial discrimination – is the way that mass murder in one case and comparative disadvantage in the other are used to stigmatize and dehumanize'.[90] On his account, stigmatisation,

[88] On dignity as a right to equal freedom, see Weinrib (n 13) 3.

[89] Note that some would reject the idea of dignity and instead focus solely on humanity: see A Sangiovanni, *Humanity without Dignity: Moral Equality, Respect, and Human Rights* (Harvard University Press, 2017).

[90] ibid 5.

dehumanisation, infantilisation, instrumentalisation, and objectification all instantiate a disrespect for the moral equality of persons.[91]

There are, thus, certain practices which are wrongful in ways which can only be fully explained by reference to disrespect for moral equality. Of course, this does not mean that the totality of the wrong-making features here relate to equality concerns: 'the worst of what the Nazi state did to the Jews was not the humiliation of herding them into cattle trucks and forcing them to live in conditions of unimaginable squalor; it was to murder them'.[92] Dignity can be infringed in ways that are only tangentially related to moral equality, if they are related at all. But it should not be forgotten that victims of crimes against humanity have both comparative and non-comparative wrongs done to them and that being treated as less than human constitutes both.

Second, there will be circumstances where moral equality grounds a comparative claim but does not ground an independent claim. If the state funds ballet classes for one ethnic group but refuses to fund classes for other ethnic groups, there is a failure to respect moral equality, not because failing to fund ballet classes violates dignity, but because the choice to fund classes for one racial group but not others could only be justified if the interests of members of one racial group counted for more than the interests of other racial groups. As such, the policy in question is wrong comparatively, because it treats some as less than fully equal to others and not because it violates a non-comparative, independent claim. Now, there could be what Raz calls a strictly egalitarian principle at play here. However, a focus on distributions would be impoverished. The fundamental principle is one of equal dignity; equalisation is derivative.

It is for this reason that equalisation of treatment or distribution in the medicine example would be a violation of moral equality rather than required by it. Put another way, respect for moral equality recognises that the obligation to respect dignity cannot be exhausted simply by focusing on the relationship between legal officials and individual citizens; one must also examine how the state has treated the individual legal subject or a group of subjects in comparison to how it treats other legal subjects. This analysis cannot be comprehensively done by simply demanding equalisation: in many instances, respect for moral equality will demand *unequal* treatment. This chapter defends the position that, properly understood, equality and dignity are mutually dependent concepts. As such, a constitutional commitment to respecting moral equality must necessarily be interpreted with reference to other constitutional principles, including the rule of law and its commitment to human dignity.

[91] ibid 2.

[92] M Rosen, 'Dignity Past and Present' in M Dan-Cohen (ed), *Jeremy Waldron, Dignity, Rank, and Rights* (Oxford University Press, 2012) 97.

III. HIERARCHY: DIGNITY IMPLIES EQUALITY

It is now generally accepted that, if dignity is a meaningful moral concept, then it is one which should be universal in scope and applied equally to all by virtue of our humanity. Dignity provides the normative touchstone for many international human rights documents. For example, the Universal Declaration of Human Rights states that 'All human beings are born free and equal in dignity and rights.'[93] The International Covenant on Civil and Political Rights similarly declares that 'All persons deprived of their liberty shall be treated with humanity and with recognition for the inherent dignity of the human person.'[94] The concept of dignity as something which we all share equally is expressly recognised within many constitutional texts, most notably those of post-atrocity states such as modern Germany ('Human dignity shall be inviolable. To respect and protect it shall be the duty of all state authority'),[95] and South Africa ('Everyone has inherent dignity and the right to have their dignity respected and protected').[96] It should be no surprise that those countries with a history of violently denying the moral equality of persons would, in their attempt to rectify the atrocities of the past, look to a concept of dignity which is inherent in all persons and which explicitly rejects subordination of persons or groups.

It should not be forgotten, however, that dignity can be and was invoked to explain and justify these very atrocities. This concept of dignity not only embraced hierarchy in status; it necessitated it. In many ways the dignity of the nobleman depended on the fact that the peasant did not have the same kind of dignity, if they had any dignity at all. As Herzog notes, 'at the heart of the dignity enjoyed by aristocrats was the claim, "I don't have to answer to the likes of you"'.[97] This conception of dignity is reserved for the privileged and, like privilege, it cannot exist without an excluded, underprivileged, or disfavoured underclass. Without a commitment to moral equality, a commitment to dignity as a moral or legal concept gives rise to a serious problem of hierarchy. At the core of these hierarchies lie comparative claims that one person is intrinsically superior to another in some morally salient way and should be treated accordingly. In what follows, it is argued that conceptions of dignity which deny or are grounded in the denial of moral equality are mistaken. To properly respect the dignity of persons, one must respect the moral equality of persons; dignity and moral equality, when correctly understood, are fundamentally interdependent.[98] It is for this reason that the Constitutional Court of South Africa has explicitly

[93] UDHR, Art 1.
[94] ICCPR, Art 10(1).
[95] Basic Law (*Grundgesetz*), for the Federal Republic of Germany, Art 1(1).
[96] Constitution of South Africa, Art 10.
[97] D Herzog, 'Aristocratic Dignity?' in M Dan-Cohen (ed), *J Waldron, Dignity, Rank, and Rights* (Oxford University Press, 2012) 101.
[98] See Waldron, *Dignity, Rank, and Rights* (n 12) 55–57; Chaskalson (n 13).

drawn a connection between dignity and the prohibition of invidious discrimination, noting that 'the purpose of [South Africa's] new constitutional and democratic order is the establishment of a society in which all human beings will be accorded equal dignity and respect regardless of their membership of particular groups'.[99] Central to this is the importance of comparative claims that can be made that one not be treated as an inferior to others.

There are two broad categories of dignity theories: worth-based accounts and rank- or status-based accounts. Worth-based accounts focus on a universal, equally distributed value that we all share.[100] In contrast, rank- or status-based accounts are associated with social meaning and derive from one's social position and the norms and attitudes which define it.[101] It is here where we find references to composing one's self with dignity or being dignified in defeat. These social norms associate dignity with a certain bearing: a presence or self-possession which reflects the dignity of restraint and resilience and which manifests in both one's attitude and one's conduct.[102]

Unlike worth-based accounts, rank is typically hierarchical, informed by and intended to cement social stratification. Indeed, it is sometimes argued that worth-based accounts of dignity should be preferred precisely because they embrace the moral equality of persons in a manner that is not done by rank-based accounts.[103] However, this seems quite odd, given that worth-based conceptions of dignity could also embrace a hierarchy *in moral worth*. In fact, one need only cast one's gaze back a hundred years to find philosophical defence of the unequal worth of certain persons based in large part on naturalistic assertions of autonomy and rationality: 'Individuals or races with higher capacities … have a right to more than merely equal consideration as compared to those of lower capacities'.[104] In many ways, it was a belief in the unequal worth of persons, informed in part by their seemingly unequal capacities, that justified differences in status or rank in the first place. These differences necessarily manifested in both individual and comparative claims that those at the top of the hierarchy could make. It was not just that different groups or individuals were entitled to make different claims; it mattered that

[99] *President of the Republic of South Africa and Another v Hugo*, 1997 (4) SA (CC), 1997 (6) BCLR 708, §92.

[100] See I Kant, 'Groundwork of the Methaphysics of Morals' in M Gregor (ed), *Immanuel Kant, Practical Philosophy* (Cambridge University Press, 1996) 84–85; S Darwall, *The Second-Person Standpoint* (Harvard University Press, 2006); J Griffin, *On Human Rights* (Oxford University Press, 2008).

[101] M Dan-Cohen, 'Dignity and Its (Dis)Content' in Dan-Cohen (ed) (n 97) 4.

[102] Waldron, *Dignity, Rank, and Rights* (n 12) 21–22; A Kolani, 'Dignity' (1976) 51 *Philosophy* 251, 253–54.

[103] Dan-Cohen (n 101).

[104] H Rashdall, *The Theory of Good and Evil: A Treaties on Moral Philosophy*, 2nd edn (Oxford University Press, 1924) 242; *cf* Waldron, *Dignity, Rank, and Rights* (n 12) 68–69; J Waldron, *One Another's Equals: The Basis of Human Equality* (The Belknap Press of Harvard University Press, 2017).

some were entitled to make *better* claims than others. In fact, that was the whole point. These privileges arose from a deep belief in the superiority of some over others. We cannot fully understand the significance of that without exploring the very real comparative element.

Furthermore rank-based conceptions could themselves embrace moral equality. Waldron defends a status-based account of dignity which is explicitly committed to the moral equality of persons: he presents 'an account of dignity as a high-ranking status, comparable to a rank of nobility – only a rank assigned now to every human person, equally without discrimination: dignity as nobility for the common man',[105] and stresses that 'the modern notion of human dignity involves an upwards equalization of rank, so that we now try to accord to every human being something of the dignity, rank, and expectation of respect that was formerly accorded to nobility'.[106] In so doing, Waldron operates against the backdrop of what we might call an 'expanding circle' view of dignity which 'was originally applied to a relatively narrow class of beings' but which 'has come to be extended over time until it is, to all intents and purposes, universal'.[107] Remember, however, that what has been universalised here is not an independent conception of dignity, but rather a comparative conception of *equal* dignity. It is not simply that we are all recognised as dignified persons: we are also recognised as dignified persons whose dignity is of equal weight and whose social or legal status reflects this underlying equality of worth. Waldron emphasises that, when discussing differentiations in rank, 'It is often a striking implication of this sort of ranking that *within* each rank, everything is equal'.[108]

This account has particular appeal to the constitutional lawyer, given its explicit embrace of both the rule of law and the generally juridical nature of the concept as Waldron defines it.[109] Indeed, many of the hallmarks of this high rank are legal rights and privileges we now consider to be essential to constitutional governance but which were once reserved only for the aristocrat and often even then only for the aristocratic man. For example, those of a certain high dignity were once entitled to be tried according to an entirely separate legal system: nobles were given the privilege of trial by their peers or by the House of Lords rather than a common jury. Even Magna Carta, the seemingly great foundation of civil liberties, contained reference to this hierarchy: 'Earls and barons shall not be amerced except through their peers'.[110] What is more, the dignity of the aristocrat granted them certain immunities, usually against suit from the common man.[111] Other entitlements which were once reserved only for nobles

[105] Waldron, *Dignity, Rank, and Rights* (n 12) 22; see also Waldron, *One Another's Equals: The Basis of Human Equality* (n 104).

[106] Waldron, *Dignity, Rank, and Rights* (n 12) 33.

[107] Rosen (n 92) 79.

[108] Waldron, *Dignity, Rank, and Rights* (n 12) 32.

[109] ibid 47–70; Waldron, 'How Law Protects Dignity' (n 12).

[110] Magna Carta (1215), Art 21.

[111] See the example contained within Waldron, *Dignity, Rank, and Rights* (n 12) 56–57.

are now considered essential to constitutional governance in accordance with the rule of law – most notably, a fair trial where one's innocence is presumed, where guilt must be proven adequately and where one is entitled to make representations and to have those representations afforded appropriate weight. These entitlements have historically been associated with the dignity of the aristocrat or the free man (as opposed to the slave or the woman), but are now, as Waldron argues, extended to all such that we live within a 'single-status society'.[112] The rule of law, properly understood to entail appropriate respect for the dignity of the legal subject, demands nothing less.

However, we would be wise to challenge Waldron on the neatness of this account of an expanding circle of *aristocratic* dignity.[113] In particular, a focus on dignity as a rank or status unmoored from the concept of moral worth is in danger of not fully accounting for the ways in which historically high statuses necessitated those of low status being subordinated in much the same way that shadow needs a source of light to differentiate it from complete darkness. It must be asked whether we can really draw such sharp distinctions between status-based and worth-based accounts of dignity? It seems that no amount of equalisation of rank or status would be completely compatible with a commitment to the unequal worth of persons. Likewise, it would be, at the very least, difficult to maintain a society based on certain forms of social hierarchy once we have embraced a fundamental commitment to moral equality. Just as the belief in the unequal worth of some justifies an inequality in social status and rank, so too must a rejection of that belief necessitate a dismantling of legally or socially enshrined hierarchies which might flow from such inequality.

A class- or race-based society may explain the superior status of the aristocrat or the white man primarily by reference to honour or rank, but it could just as easily do so by reference to differences in moral worth. Indeed, the two often go hand in hand, supporting each other and entrenching the unjust hierarchy which permeates them both. It is thus of crucial importance that the *comparative* disrespect for dignity embraced by such societies not be forgotten. An unjust hierarchy of rank or status must rest on, for example, 'comparative indifference to the welfare of the black races, when it collides with the higher well-being of a much smaller European population'.[114] It could equally be grounded in a comparative indifference to the welfare of the poor as compared to the nobility or to the well-being of one sex over another. This indifference necessarily expresses an attitude supportive of differences in moral worth just as much as it does in status or rank. As the Constitutional Court of South Africa notes, the history of apartheid has shown that wrongful discrimination

[112] ibid 57. See also G Vlastos, 'Justice and Equality' in L Pojman and R Westmoreland (eds), *Equality: Selected Readings* (Oxford University Press, 1984).

[113] See Herzog (n 97).

[114] Rashdall (n 104) 241.

> proceeds on [an] assumption that the disfavoured group is inferior to other groups. And this is an assault on the human dignity of the disfavoured group … Equality as enshrined in our Constitution does not tolerate distinctions that treat other people as 'second class citizens.'[115]

Ultimately, any account of a constitutional requirement to respect dignity which does not also respect moral equality is suspect; not simply because it is incompatible with equality, but because it is premised upon the *denial* of the dignity of those at the bottom of the hierarchy. The dignity of the aristocrat is partially defined by reference to the *lack* of dignity of the peasant; the worth of the white man by reference to the incivility of the Black man or the irrationality of the woman. We are left with the impression that 'high' status cannot exist without an excluded underclass from which to draw a distinction.

Waldron can thus be challenged for the simplicity of his account: as admirable as the underlying commitment to the expanding circle view is, it is better conceived as a broadening in recognition of equal moral *worth* as necessary for a proper understanding of dignity. From here, the legal and moral obligations necessary to respect that worth manifest themselves by demanding recognition of a form of status, 'something that travels with you everywhere you go, not just a role you occupy now and again'.[116] Of course, Waldron is correct to associate dignity with more than simply respect for moral equality: the aristocratic privileges he identifies as now being universalised manifest independent claims to live under the rule of law, to be afforded a fair trial, and to generally be treated as an autonomous agent whose interests matter. But they also manifest comparative claims and not all aristocratic privileges have been included in this expansion of high status. Specifically, any privilege which would set one person above another in worth or rank is rejected. So, instead of embracing a concept of dignity which is premised upon universalising the peak of an unjust hierarchy of both worth and status, we should instead focus on a conception of human dignity which rejects inequalities of this kind in the first place. This conception would align with Waldron's contention that equality and dignity are 'fundamentally interdependent' but would remove any particular reliance on notions of high status, in favour of a focus on the high *demands* expected to fully respect equal dignity.[117] Herzog is, thus, quite right to stress that 'too much of what aristocrats had, in law and society, is stuff we want to abolish, not extend to everyone'.[118]

On a charitable reading, this is not all that different from Waldron's own account. Indeed, he stresses that 'simple universalization is not sufficient to characterize what had to go into this new world of levelled-up dignity'.[119] This we can agree on. However, it is not the expansion of a fixed high status

[115] *Minister of Finance v Van Heerden*, 2004 (11) BCLR 1125, §116.
[116] Herzog (n 97) 114.
[117] Waldron, *Dignity, Rank, and Rights* (n 12) 55.
[118] Herzog (n 97) 114.
[119] Waldron, *Dignity, Rank, and Rights* (n 12) 146.

to previously disenfranchised groups or individuals which provides the central normative thrust of this reconceptualisation of dignity; it is the importance of comparative claims. The objectionable facets of aristocratic dignity, which Waldron accepts must be abandoned, arise from instances where those of high rank make *comparative* claims that they be treated in some way better than those of a lower rank. It is only when these claims are replaced with claims to be treated as moral equals that the dignity of all is properly respected. There can be disagreement over whether a given social role embodies dignity in itself. But a role which is explicitly premised on being a comparative inferior cannot be fully respectful of human dignity.

Equally so, the traditional privileges reserved for aristocrats of immunity from legal responsibility are incompatible with a fully inclusive account of dignity and also with the rule of law, given its commitment to both dignity and equality. The rule of law presupposes a relationship of reciprocity between legal official and legal subject, but within the realm of juridical relations *between* citizens, there is a presumption of moral equality as well.[120] The legal subject, when making representations before the court, is entitled to be heard, to have their grievance taken seriously, and to have their rights adequately enforced. Equally, the respondent is expected to take the charge against them seriously (for the court does), to respond adequately to the claims that have been made, and to respect the outcome of the decision, even if it might place them at a severe inconvenience. This is true under the rule of law, even if one party is a noble and the other a pauper.

Returning to Dicey's conception of legal equality, it is clear that legality in many ways nullifies the potency of rank: legal equality means 'not only that no man is above the law, but (which is a different thing) that here, every man, whatever be his rank or condition, is subject to the ordinary laws of the realm and amenable to the jurisdiction of the ordinary tribunals'.[121] It is not simply the case that all are presumed to be aristocrats, with all the entailed privileges and immunities. Rather, the rule of law succeeds in ensuring that status of this kind loses the legal sting in the tail. All are equal in the eyes of the law; the rule of law demands a blindness to many facts which might be entirely relevant in other social situations, but which would render any legal decision grounded in them arbitrary.[122] It is no surprise, then, to find that it was for precisely this reason that the nobility resisted the rule of law so fiercely:

> law was already a realm for the give-and-take of reasons and arguments, justifications and criticisms, among dignified equals … that is precisely why the nobility often

[120] TRS Allan, 'The Rule of Law as the Rule of Private Law' in L Austin and D Klimchuk (eds), *Private Law and the Rule of Law* (Oxford University Press, 2014); Fuller, 'The Forms and Limits of Adjudication' (n 39).

[121] AV Dicey, *An Introduction to the Study of the Law of the Constitution* (JWF Allison ed, Oxford University Press, 2013) 193.

[122] Herzog (n 97) 112. See also Ch 5 below.

> wanted nothing to do with it. How unseemly to be shoved into a position where you had to answer to the base underlings![123]

Thus, while Waldron has captured an important insight when he identifies dignity with a particular kind of status, recognised in law, what he fails to account for is not just that this status is usually associated with unjust hierarchies that it is difficult to avoid, but that it is usually tied to something distinct from one's intrinsic worth. As far back as the earliest natural law defence of equal dignity we have seen claims that a person's worth should be tied to some variable characteristic that they possess rather than to their intrinsic worth as human persons. Specifically, in response to the idea of equal dignity, there is often a contention that one's worth or dignity depends upon the possession of a variable characteristic which serves as the source for value. Aristotle justified the category of natural slaves on the basis that natural slaves are deficient in their deliberative faculty, something one can possess to greater or lesser degrees. Slaves are said to be similar to animals or even a kind of living tool, precisely because they lack deliberative faculties in their entirety: a natural slave 'participates in reason only to the point of apprehending it, but not to the point of possessing it'.[124] Similarly, women are portrayed as superior to slaves but inferior to free men because, while they can make decisions, they cannot do this on their own, dependent as they are upon their adult male relatives.[125]

In response to this we must reject the locating of worth within a variable characteristic such as intelligence, wealth, or social standing, and tie dignity not to rank but to intrinsic worth that itself grounds the kinds of comparative claims set out above. The worth-based conception of dignity, when universalised, necessarily implies the moral equality of all but could fail to account for important comparative claims. Indeed, the universalisation of dignity seems to have broader implications than the universalisation of a general moral principle. When a principle is universalised, all that is done is an expansion of whatever was required under the principle to cover everyone. When a concept like dignity-as-worth is universalised, the result is a recognition that we all possess dignity equally and that conclusion necessarily has implications for how we are to interact with each other and how we are to treat people relative to how we treat others. So, the dignity-as-worth account already arguably presupposes not only the moral equality of persons, but also the existence of comparative claims as well.

The rank or status account is compatible with injustice should it not embrace moral equality. Waldron is attempting to put forward an account of dignity as rank, but one which would be coupled with a commitment to moral equality. However, in so doing, he is in danger of glossing over the importance of these comparative claims and the significance of high social rank being premised

[123] ibid 102.
[124] *Pol* 1254b22–3.
[125] Aristotle, *Gen an* 1.728a; 1.82f; *Pol* 1254b10–14.

upon the lower rank of others. The concept of dignity that we must focus on here is that which is implied by the rule of law: a legal dignity. This conception must necessarily reject any neat distinction between worth and rank. Dignity as rank should be praised for paying appropriate attention to social meaning and the importance of being seen or understood to have dignity. Central to this is the importance of being seen and understood to be a moral equal to others. The moral wrong that is done to someone by placing them at the bottom of an unjust hierarchy cannot be fully understood without reference to comparative injustice. This injustice is an affront to both social constructions of equal rank as well as the equal moral worth intrinsic to us all. Dignity is thus partly a relational concept which gives rise to comparative claims, grounded in the value of equality. If human dignity constitutes a justiciable legal principle that can constrain the actions of public authorities, it does this through the doctrines of the common law constitution by delineating itself into a set of fundamental constitutional rights.[126] Equality-based rights are simply those which arise from dignity's commitment to the moral equality of persons.

IV. LEVELLING DOWN: EQUALITY NEEDS DIGNITY

We have established that dignity, properly understood, must necessarily entail *equal* dignity. It is not so clear that adequate respect for moral equality demands independent respect for dignity in much the same manner. Indeed, this is the great foil that any equality-based moral or legal principle must address before it can be taken seriously. Equality, even if we move beyond a principle of equalisation towards one of equal concern and respect, seems to be entirely compatible with the kind of universal indifference mentioned at the beginning of this chapter. However, I suggest that the levelling down objection actually highlights the value of a key aspect of moral equality: it forces one to choose between treating everyone with appropriate respect or treating no one with respect.

Most of the accounts of equality mentioned in the previous chapter would reject the idea that the demands of moral equality are satisfied by treating people with *no* concern or respect. Perhaps, then, it is not precisely *equal* concern and respect that we are focused on – the equalisation of concern and respect strictly speaking. It is respect for an important aspect of someone's moral status – something we all have equally. Respect for moral equality is, therefore, not simply respect for the fact that people are equally worthy of no respect: it is recognition that people all possess an intrinsic worth that we can call dignity. But what is more, constitutionalism likely requires more than simply a minimum amount of respect: the rule of law and its connected principles demand the adoption of an appropriate attitude of respect towards the legal subject, an attitude which

[126] See Weinrib (n 13) 21.

includes but is not exhausted by a commitment to respecting the moral equality of persons.

Given this, the demands of equality within our constitutional order must be read alongside the demands of dignity. The common law operates in such a manner that constitutional principle can never be fully explicated in isolation from other constitutional principles or values. The value of equality is partly that it often forces the levelling down choice. The state must choose between providing, for example, a fair trial to all or removing that privilege from the favoured few. In many instances, levelling down is avoided because our existing constitutional obligations force the state to choose between treating a disfavoured minority with appropriate respect or removing all privileges from those at the upper ends of a given hierarchy. There is value in forcing that choice, even if it can be resolved by reference to independent constitutional claims without recourse to comparative claims. This does not mean that the comparative claim does not obtain. The disenfranchised are entitled to make two constitutional challenges: one against the breach of their independent common law rights; and one against their unjustified comparative disadvantage relative to other legal subjects who are expected to be treated as moral equals.

It was precisely this idea that formed the backdrop of the Belmarsh case.[127] The United Kingdom knew that it would not be justified in legislating to permit the arrest and indefinite detention of citizens who were merely suspected of being terrorists. So instead, legislation was passed with permitted this only for foreign suspected terrorists. The value of a constitutional principle of equality before the law for a case such as this is to first demand adequate justification for the distinction that was drawn between domestic and foreign suspected terrorists. Second, once no adequate justification is offered, is to demand that foreign suspected terrorists be afforded the same protections as domestic citizens have.

In other instances, levelling down occurs but can be justified as preferable to an unjustly discriminatory policy. Take the ballet classes example mentioned above or, better yet, the example of *Palmer v Thomsen*, where the state was forced to choose between desegregating its swimming pools and closing them.[128] The state chose to close them. Now, we may have moral qualms about that choice, and there may even be a legal challenge should the closure generate a sufficiently serious perception of bias on the part of legal officials.[129] Nevertheless, there is generally no constitutional challenge that can be made in these instances, given the limits of public law and the general duty on the judiciary not to dictate budgetary decisions. All that can be demanded as a point of constitutional law is that the failure to respect the principle of legal equality be rectified. Nevertheless, there is also value in forcing the state to choose between levelling down and

[127] *A v Secretary of State for the Home Department* [2004] UKHL 56.
[128] *Palmer v Thomsen*, 403 US 217 (1970).
[129] See Ch 5 below.

expanding privileges. As undesirable as the closure of swimming pools might be, maintaining racial segregation would be far worse. The value of legal equality in these instances is in its capacity to prevent the continuance of exactly this kind of comparative injustice.

Just as legal cases cannot be assessed on their merits in a manner which fails to account for existing legal rules and principles, neither can moral questions be fully answered in isolation from our existing moral commitments. If confronted with someone who believes that slavery is morally permissible, the levelling down objection results in the extension of slavery to more cases than previously countenanced. In such instances, we can reject the desirability of levelling down and conclude that inconsistent wickedness is better that consistent wickedness. We would rather there be as few instances of slavery as possible. But our problem is ultimately with slavery, not equality. Legal equality does not see value in equalisation for its own sake; it is always contingent upon other normative commitments such as the commitment to respecting the dignity of persons. Concern for equality will force the state to choose between enslaving everyone or enslaving no one. Of course, the state *could* then enslave everyone, but respect for dignity and the rule of law will prevent that.

The fundamental point is that, where equal *dignity* is fundamental, the levelling down objection is avoided because the guiding principle is not to equalise at all costs: we must be treated as dignified equals and that will sometimes require equalisation and sometimes it won't. As such, the claim here is not that legal equality itself exhausts the demands of dignity. Rather it is that, given an existing commitment to dignity within the constitution and the connection between dignity and moral equality, legal equality demands the extension of this to all. Dignity certainly gives rise to independent claims: many common law rights can be explained by reference to dignity without any recourse to moral equality. However, there are also comparative concerns present. It is, thus, important to stress that, while the levelling down objection might indicate that some forms of equalisation are undesirable, it doesn't mean that existing inequalities are therefore justified and acceptable. While it may be true that a requirement of equal concern and respect could, superficially, be satisfied by treating people with no respect at all, the requirement clearly could not be satisfied by treating some with respect and others with no respect. Thus, to the extent that we accept that the state is under an obligation to treat legal subjects with *any* degree of respect, then legal equality mandates that we must all be treated with *the same* degree of respect.

It could be argued that all equality principles are necessarily egalitarian principles in the sense that they mandate the equalisation of concern and respect. However, this is misguided. Respect for moral equality is not a resource to be distributed; it is not a benefit or burden which must be allocated fairly as might be the case when speaking of the requirements of equality of treatment, or equality of outcomes. Rather, it amounts to a commitment to recognising and respecting an important aspect of our moral status. It entails properly accounting for the normative upshots of this reality in our deliberation of how to act and our determinations of what we owe to one another.

The rule of law and the conception of man inherent within legality have a general affinity towards a particular deontological conception of the moral status of the legal subject. Legal equality is therefore a particular account of how one is to best respect the equal moral status of legal subjects. The affinity between the common law and deontology suggests that legal equality is primarily concerned with the principled articulation of the moral and legal principles which accrue by virtue of the foundational commitment to equal dignity that helps give meaning to our constitutional order. This conception of legal equality is not just compatible with the common law constitution; it is arguably the foundation upon which the pillars of British public law rest; the fountain from which other principles spring. Properly understood, principles of democracy, parliamentary sovereignty, and the rule of law are all fundamentally committed to a particular conception of the moral equality of legal subjects. Dworkin is quite right to stress that this is a foundational commitment and that principles of equalisation are merely derivative. What is more, a number of constitutional principles can be derived from this commitment which do not require the equalisation of anything. Indeed, there is a strong case to be made that principles of non-discrimination are exactly such kinds of principles. That will be the focus of the next chapter.

4

Discrimination: The Concept

IN 1954 THE United States Supreme Court ruled that racially segregated schools were constitutionally prohibited under the Equal Protection Clause of the Fourteenth Amendment, even if the schools in question were otherwise equal in quality.[1] In so holding, the court endorsed the position that in order for the state to adequately respect the principle of equality before the law, it must not wrongfully discriminate among classes of persons. The Equal Protection Clause is now understood to guarantee the protection of equal laws, and not merely the equal application of laws regardless of their content. Although it had historically been interpreted to give 'the same protection to all for the preservation of life, liberty and property, and the pursuit of happiness',[2] *Brown* signified a vital step towards ensuring that the ideal set out in earlier cases could become a reality for those who have faced wrongful discrimination at the hands of the state.

Within British public law, there is similarly a general principle of judicial review that people are to be treated in a non-discriminatory manner.[3] A line of cases tracing back at least a century indicates that discriminatory decisions will be classed as arbitrary and unreasonable in certain situations.[4] The connection between moral equality and legally prohibited arbitrariness will be explored in greater detail in the next chapter. Our present focus concerns the nature of wrongful discrimination and its relationship with principles of legal equality.

The principle of non-discrimination within the common law is grounded within a broader principle of reasonableness and is intimately connected to the common law commitment to legal equality. However, before we can adequately situate non-discrimination within the superior courts' power to judicially review executive action, we must first have a good understanding of what constitutes discrimination. It is only when conceptual clarity is achieved that we can begin to identify those instances of discrimination which are wrongful; and only when we have done that can we identify instances of discrimination which are constitutionally prohibited by a principle of equality before the law. Within that framework, all instances of wrongful discrimination may be prohibited by a

[1] *Brown v Board of Education of Topeka*, 347 US 483 (1954).
[2] *Slaughter House Case*, 83 US (16 Wall) 36, 127 (1873) (Swayne J).
[3] See J Jowell, 'Is Equality a Constitutional Principle?' (1994) 7 *Current Legal Problems* 1.
[4] See Ch 5 below.

principle of reasonableness. However, there is a separate and uniquely wicked form of discrimination which directly violates our core commitment to moral equality. This form of discrimination, demeaning discrimination, is an affront to the very spirit of rule of law compliant governance.

Discrimination is fundamentally relational in character. The concept itself, independent of any moral evaluation, necessarily entails comparatively less favourable treatment. As such, when discrimination is wrongful, the comparative nature of the concept will necessarily ground an equality-based claim. Demeaning discrimination occurs where the primary, direct wrong of an instance of wrongful discrimination is that is treats a person or group as inferior in some way. Other forms of wrongful discrimination, including wrongful indirect discrimination, still disrespect moral equality, but in a more oblique way. The primary wrong of these forms of discrimination could be grounded in many other considerations, including consequentialist considerations of harm or violations of liberty, autonomy, or individuality. Nevertheless, because they are necessarily comparative wrongs, the value of equality can be usefully engaged as a unifying core to underpin all instances of wrongful discrimination.

There is currently some disagreement among equality-based theorists as to the role of social meaning in our analysis of wrongful discrimination. Scholars such as Deborah Hellman have argued that social meaning is central to determining whether an act of discrimination disrespects moral equality.[5] In contrast, Benjamin Eidelson has presented a powerful critique arguing that social meaning is merely contingently related to equality-violating discrimination and that attention would be better focused on the fact that such acts amount to deliberative failures which manifest an attitude of disrespect for moral equality, independent of the social meaning which attaches to them.[6] This chapter will attempt to reconcile these approaches. Both Hellman and Eidelson have identified important aspects of equality-violating discrimination and there is no reason why, with suitable modification, these two accounts cannot come together to give a more complete depiction of when and why certain forms of discrimination disrespect moral equality. Eidelson's focus on deliberative failures as an explanation of why wrongful discrimination is wrongful is essential to make sense of the traditional place of non-discrimination within the administrative law doctrine of rationality, and Hellman's focus on social meaning is necessary if we are to account for the important role that the perception of non-bias has within the administrative law principles of natural justice and procedural fairness. It is only when read together that we can give a comprehensive account of a constitutional principle of non-discrimination as it manifests within existing doctrine.

In recent years, legal theorists have suggested that there is an important distinction which can be drawn between equality-based and liberty-based

[5] D Hellman, *When Is Discrimination Wrong?* (Harvard University Press, 2011).
[6] B Eidelson, *Discrimination and Disrespect* (Oxford University Press, 2015).

conceptions of wrongful discrimination.[7] A theory is equality-based if it explains the wrong of wrongful discrimination by reference to acts which treat persons as less than equals. A theory is liberty-based if the primary wrong of wrongful discrimination is the infringement of a person's right to have certain freedoms, such as the freedom to marry, without being unjustly hindered by virtue of certain traits which they possess.[8] This chapter will offer a defence of the equality-based view by appealing to the fundamentally relational nature of discrimination. In addition, some aspects of Hellman's defence of an equality-based account of discrimination will be challenged. According to Hellman, one reason for preferring equality-based accounts over liberty-based accounts is that equality-based accounts manifest 'thinner' constitutional principles than liberty-based accounts.[9] Specifically, she argues that equality-based accounts raise fewer and less controversial questions which must be answered within the interpretative process. It will be shown that, while an equality-based account should be preferred, this is not because of anything to do with the questions it raises: equality should be seen as the grounding for constitutionally prohibited discrimination because of the central role that this value plays within the constitutional order and because an appeal to moral equality allows us to adequately account for the reasons discrimination is wrong when it is wrong.

I. CLARIFYING THE CONCEPT

The interpretation of a constitutional principle of non-discrimination is heavily dependent on particular conceptions of discrimination: their normative foundations, justifications, and the ends to which they are directed. Within the United Kingdom, contemporary anti-discrimination protection operates primarily through the Equality Act 2010. In this context, British scholars have advanced various conceptions of wrongful discrimination, informed by familiar values of equality,[10] liberty,[11] and social inclusion.[12] However, very little work has

[7] D Hellman, 'Equality and Unconstitutional Discrimination' in D Hellman and S Moreau (eds), *Philosophical Foundations of Discrimination Law* (Oxford University Press, 2013); S Moreau, 'In Defense of a Liberty-Based Account of Discrimination' in Hellman and Moreau (ibid); T Khaitan, *A Theory of Discrimination Law* (Oxford University Press, 2015).

[8] Moreau, 'In Defense of a Liberty-Based Account of Discrimination' (n 7) 71.

[9] Hellman, 'Equality and Unconstitutional Discrimination' (n 7) 51–53.

[10] See S Fredman, *Discrimination Law,* 2nd edn (Oxford University Press, 2011); B Hepple, 'The Aims of Equality Law' (2008) 61 *Current Legal Problems* 1; B Hepple, *Equality: The Legal Framework*, 2nd edn (Hart Publishing, 2014); S Fredman, 'Breaking the Mold: Equality as a Proactive Duty' (2012) 60 *The American Journal of Comparative Law* 265; S Fredman, 'Substantive Equality Revisited' (2016) 14 *International Journal of Constitutional Law* 712.

[11] See Khaitan (n 7); H Collins and T Khaitan, 'Indirect Discrimination Law: Controversies and Critical Questions' in H Collins and T Khaitan (eds), *Foundations of Indirect Discrimination Law* (Hart Publishing, 2018); T Khaitan and S Steel, 'Wrongs, Group Disadvantage and the Legitimacy of Indirect Discrimination Law' in Collins and Khaitan (eds) (ibid).

[12] H Collins, 'Discrimination, Equality and Social Inclusion' (2003) 66 *Modern Law Review* 16.

been done to offer a coherent account of the concept of non-discrimination as it operates within the common law.[13] In contrast, constitutional theory in the US has a long history of addressing questions concerning the precise nature of constitutionally prohibited discrimination. Fourteenth Amendment jurisprudence is informed by two competing accounts of wrongful discrimination.[14] On one reading, principles prohibiting discrimination are seen as grounded in comparative justice, where wrongful discrimination is conceived of as a violation of moral equality.[15] On another, they are seen as grounded in non-comparative justice, where a prohibition on wrongful discrimination arises from fidelity to the value of liberty.[16]

Within the common law, a principle of non-discrimination, as informed by the principle of equality before the law, will necessarily be grounded in an equality-based, deontic account which prohibits comparative wrongdoing. But what is more, a liberty-based conception of wrongful discrimination is also fundamentally informed by the value of equality. At their core, liberty-based claims to non-discrimination are claims to *equal* liberty. There are two key levels of analysis: one concerned with what discrimination is; the other with why it is wrongful when it is wrongful. Sometimes scholars elide this distinction.

When discussing anti-discrimination rights, the term 'discrimination' often carries with it a negative connotation and can be contrasted with a neutral interpretation which leaves open the question whether it is bad or morally blameworthy.[17] It is understandable how this might occur: legal and political scholars are usually interested in, for example, legitimate (or illegitimate use of) governmental discretion and not so much with discretion as a philosophical concept. Nevertheless, it hardly needs saying that it is quite difficult to comprehensively account for the morally salient aspects of a concept without first coming to terms with the concept itself. In this regard, philosophical theories

[13] Although there has been some work on the related topic of equality as a constitutional principle. See Jowell (n 3); TRS Allan, *Law, Liberty, and Justice: The Legal Foundations of British Constitutionalism* (Clarendon Press, 1993) Ch 7; J Stanton-Ife, 'Should Equality Be a Constitutional Principle?' (2000) 11 *King's Law Journal* 133; C O'Cinneide, 'Equality: A Core Common Law Principle, or 'Mere' Rationality?' in M Elliott and K Hughes (eds), *Common Law Constitutional Rights* (Hart Publishing, 2020); C O'Cinneide, 'Equality: A Constitutional Principle?' (*UKCLA Blog*, 2011) www.ukconstitutionallaw.org/2011/09/14/colm-ocinneide-equality-a-constitutional-principle/.

[14] D Hellman, 'Two Concepts of Discrimination' (2016) 102 *Virginia Law Review* 895.

[15] See R Dworkin, *A Matter of Principle* (Clarendon Press, 1986); R Dworkin, *Sovereign Virtue: The Theory and Practice of Equality* (Harvard University Press, 2000); K Simons, 'The Logic of Egalitarian Norms' (2000) 80 *Boston University Law Review* 693; Hellman, *When Is Discrimination Wrong?* (n 5); Hellman, 'Equality and Unconstitutional Discrimination' (n 7).

[16] See P Westen, 'The Empty Idea of Equality' (1982) 95 *Harvard Law Review* 537; S Moreau, 'What Is Discrimination?' (2010) 38 *Philosophy & Public Affairs* 143; S Moreau, 'Discrimination as Negligence' (2010) 40 *Canadian Journal of Philosophy* 123.

[17] P Singer, 'Is Racial Discrimination Arbitrary?' (1978) 8 *Moral Matters* 185, 186. See also K Lippert-Rasmussen, 'The Badness of Discrimination' (2006) 9 *Ethical Theory and Moral Practice* 167, 167–68; K Lippert-Rasmussen, *Born Free and Equal: A Philosophical Inquiry into the Nature of Discrimination* (Oxford University Press, 2013) 1–2; Hellman, *When Is Discrimination Wrong?* (n 5) 2–3, 13.

of discrimination are unfortunately in short supply. Despite the importance of anti-discrimination norms for both the legitimacy of governance and the morality of one's private conduct, remarkably little has been written about this topic from a philosophical perspective. As Eidelson notes, 'Since the idea of wrongful discrimination is expected to do so much work in our social and political lives, it is something of a philosophical embarrassment that so little has been done to explore or account for it'.[18] Nevertheless, Eidelson himself does provide an excellent account and his work has gone a long way towards filling this gap. Discrimination *qua* discrimination can be defined as follows:

> To discriminate against X, one must treat X less favourably than one does or would treat Y on the basis of property P.[19]

In this form, discrimination remains morally neutral. Thus, we can describe having discriminating taste in one's choice of wine, music, or company as virtuous without contradiction. Discrimination is necessarily responsive to differences along some dimension. As Eidelson notes, 'one can discriminate on the basis of religion, or on the basis of eye colour, and so on, but one cannot discriminate on no basis at all'.[20]

The type of discrimination that is relevant for our purpose pertains to wrongful discrimination by legal officials wielding public power.[21] As Hellman notes, within this context, 'to call something "discrimination" is to criticize it, to assert that it is wrong'.[22] Not all differentiation in treatment is wrongful. Thus, the state is not prohibited from any and all unequal distributions of benefits or burdens. Nor is it the case that all unjustified governmental policies violate moral equality: according to a principle of equality before the law, a policy is unjustified *because* it is wrongfully discriminatory in a particular way – it is not discriminatory simply because it is unjustified. The difficult question that must therefore be answered is thus: what exactly amounts to constitutionally prohibited discrimination?[23] Some forms of discrimination are inherently unjustifiable and always wrongful. Others are not but can be contingently wrongful dependent on various factors, including the harm caused or the underlying reason for the discrimination. It will be shown in the next chapter that discrimination may be wrongful and thus unjustified if it falls foul of the general principles of judicial review, including requirements of legality, procedural fairness, and reasonableness. In addition to this, discrimination may be wrongful if it directly violates the moral equality of persons.[24]

[18] Eidelson (n 6) 3. See also Hellman and Moreau (eds) (n 7) 1; Lippert-Rasmussen, *Born Free and Equal: A Philosophical Inquiry into the Nature of Discrimination* (n 17) 4.

[19] Eidelson (n 6) 17.

[20] ibid 15–16.

[21] Hellman, *When Is Discrimination Wrong?* (n 5) 2–3.

[22] ibid 2.

[23] Hellman refers to this as 'the discrimination puzzle': the task of identifying when it is impermissible for the state to draw distinctions between citizens: ibid 1–13.

[24] Whether this should be covered within existing grounds of review or classed under its own ground will be discussed in the next chapter.

Often, when we speak of the state wrongfully discriminating against its legal subjects, we imagine the enactment of prejudicial legislation or the application of neutral laws in a biased manner. This is evidently an important aspect of unlawful discrimination prohibited by a principle of equality before the law. However, particularly within modern contexts, the State is also an employer, a provider of goods and services, and a landlord. While equality before the law pertains only to the relationship between the State and its legal subjects, the principle of non-discrimination advanced below is in many ways similar to that which arises at the legislative level and which concerns itself with the interaction between private citizens. It could be argued that discrimination which is regulated in the private sphere is done so by reference to act types which could be wrongful for a number of reasons.[25] While many acts of wrongful discrimination fail to adequately respect moral equality, it is argued that some may not. Eidelson provides the example of discriminatory acts which fail to treat persons as *individuals* even if they do not disrespect one's standing as a moral equal to others.[26] For example, repeatedly recommending the company basketball club to a Black employee and ignoring their stated interest in another activity where you would listen and respond to a white employee's declaration of lack of interest.[27] As such, even though some forms of discrimination are wrongful because they directly violate our commitment to moral equality, others may be wrongful primarily because they fail to adequately respect liberty or individual autonomy. This framework is set out in Figure 1.

Discrimination	The act of treating X less (or more) favourably than one does or would treat Y, on the basis of property P.
Wrongful discrimination	Discrimination which is morally impermissible for any reason. This could include deontological wrongdoing, consequentialist considerations of harm, disrespect for liberty, equality, individuality, autonomy and so on.
Demeaning discrimination	Discrimination which is morally impermissible because it directly disrespects moral equality and treats individuals or groups as inferiors.

However, because all forms of discrimination entail comparative treatment, all forms of wrongful discrimination disrespect moral equality in some way, even if only indirectly. Demeaning discrimination is a uniquely wrongful form of discrimination that directly violates moral equality by manifesting an attitude

[25] For example, Eidelson points to discrimination which may be wrongful not because it disrespects moral equality but because it disrespects individuality. Eidelson (n 6) Ch 5; B Eidelson, 'Treating People as Individuals' in Hellman and Moreau (eds), *Philosophical Foundations of Discrimination* (n 7).

[26] Eidelson (n 6) Ch 5; Eidelson (n 25).

[27] Eidelson (n 25) 205–206.

Figure 1 Discrimination Venn Diagram

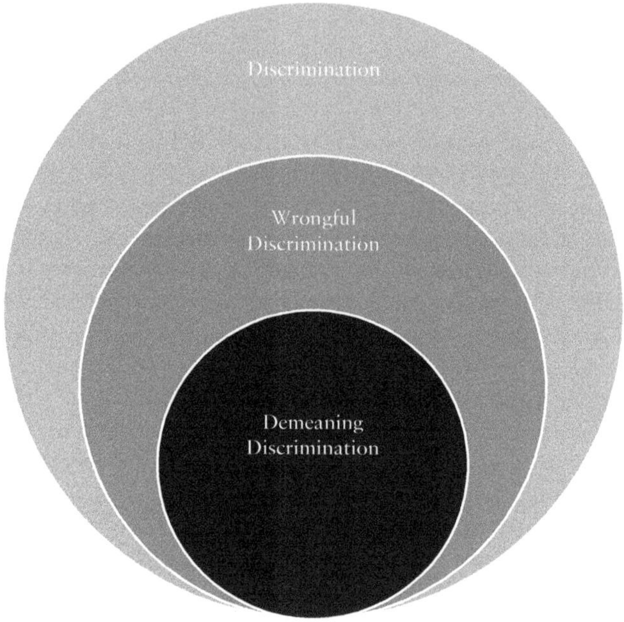

that an individual or group is an inferior.[28] Thus, while some forms of wrongful discrimination may not reach the threshold needed to warrant legal intervention, demeaning discrimination cannot be countenanced. Equally, while some forms of wrongful discrimination may be justified by reference to countervailing consequentialist reasoning, demeaning discrimination cannot. Thus, it may be permissible for the state to fail to respect individuality in some circumstances, particularly when regulating for general classes of persons, by virtue of the overriding need to regulate in the first place. Nevertheless, to the extent that state action directly demeans, it can never be justified.

Demeaning discrimination is partly a social concept, dependent on socially prevalent attitudes; the general concept must be worked out within a given social and cultural context.[29] Consequently, a definitive and conclusive determination of what amounts to wrongfully demeaning discrimination is quite difficult to provide given its cultural and historical variability.[30] Nevertheless, the mere fact that social meaning is an important aspect of constitutionally prohibited

[28] This account joins Deborah Hellman, Benjamin Eidelson and Andrea Sangiovanni in claiming that the core of wrongful discrimination is disrespectful or demeaning treatment. See Hellman, *When Is Discrimination Wrong?* (n 5); Eidelson (n 6); A Sangiovanni, *Humanity without Dignity: Moral Equality, Respect, and Human Rights* (Harvard University Press, 2017).

[29] Hellman, *When Is Discrimination Wrong?* (n 5) 27–29.

[30] L Alexander, 'What Makes Wrongful Discrimination Wrong? Biases, Preferences, Stereotypes, and Proxies' (1992) 141 *University of Pennsylvania Law Review* 149, 219.

discrimination is not reason enough to disregard this account. Many aspects of constitutional and administrative law are fundamentally informed by a commitment to ensure that justice is not only done, but that it is seen to be done.[31] The legitimacy of governance is secured only when it occurs in a manner which immunises the state from charges of bias: even if there is no actual threat of bias, it is a longstanding administrative law principle that perceptions of bias are just as important as bias itself. The same is true of constitutional principles of non-discrimination. It is not enough for the state to operate with respect for moral equality, abstracted from social reality. Essential to proper respect is an attunement to the social meaning of actions and a commitment to being seen not to be prejudiced or biased.

II. DISCRIMINATION AS A RELATIONAL CONCEPT

This section will argue that discrimination against someone entails comparatively negative or less favourable treatment. On this account, comparative treatment, an inherently relational standard, is a necessary feature of discrimination.[32] However, before we examine this aspect of discrimination, some ground-clearing is warranted. It is sometimes assumed that equality-based accounts of wrongful discrimination necessarily entail comparative tests and that liberty-based accounts necessarily entail non-comparative tests.[33] However, as Moreau notes, it is important to be clear about which level of analysis we are working on. If we are talking about what makes discrimination wrongful when it is wrongful, we can account for violations of liberty, or equality, or many other values; if we are talking about what discrimination *is*, we can describe either comparative treatment or non-comparative treatment.

Thus, Khaitan is right to stress that prohibitions on discrimination can be grounded within the value of equality even while discrimination itself amounts to a non-comparative form of treatment.[34] Indeed, this is the basis of Moreau's claim that comparison can occur at two levels: one at the foundational level, explaining why we are entitled to be treated as equals; another at the action-regarding level, when determining what treatment as an equal consists of.[35]

[31] See *Davidson v Scottish Ministers* [2004] UKHL 34, [7] (Lord Bingham); *Re Medicaments (No 2)* [2001] EWCA Civ 1217, [67]; *R v Cowle* (1759) 2 Burr 834, 861.

[32] Lippert-Rasmussen, 'The Badness of Discrimination' (n 17) 168–69, 173.

[33] See Hellman, 'Equality and Unconstitutional Discrimination' (n 7); Hellman, 'Two Concepts of Discrimination' (n 14).

[34] Khaitan (n 7) 132.

[35] Moreau, 'In Defense of a Liberty-Based Account of Discrimination' (n 7) 73–74. See also S Moreau, *Faces of Inequality: A Theory of Wrongful Discrimination* (Oxford University Press, 2020), where Moreau advances an account of wrongful discrimination which, while including harms that are done to one's deliberative freedom, is ultimately informed by a commitment to respecting moral equality.

Equally, it is entirely possible for one to conclude that discrimination is fundamentally comparative treatment and also that this is wrongful, when it is wrongful, because of the harm that is done to a person's liberty interests. It could also be true that constitutional prohibitions on discrimination which arise from the principle of equality before the law are distinct from legislative prohibitions on discrimination and that constitutional prohibitions embrace a comparative conception while legislative prohibitions do not. Indeed, it is very likely the case that legislative prohibitions on discrimination embrace multiple normative foundations, capturing many instances of discrimination which are impermissible for both consequentialist and deontic reasons.[36] Still, it is no surprise that equality-based theorists frequently adopt a comparative conception of discrimination and that liberty-based theorists tend to adopt a non-comparative, grounds-based conception. What follows is a defence of a comparative conception of discrimination.

Most legal and philosophical accounts of discrimination include some reference to comparatively disadvantageous treatment. Lippert-Rasmussen argues that discrimination occurs *iff* someone is treated disadvantageously (or is believed by the discriminator to have been treated disadvantageously) on the basis of their membership within a socially salient group.[37] Similarly, Eidelson argues that discrimination against someone occurs when the following two conditions are satisfied:

(1) X treats Y less favourably in some respect than Z;
(2) and there is a difference in how X regards Y and Z with regard to a certain property, P, and this difference figures in the explanation of this disadvantageous treatment.[38]

It should be noted that the concept itself can include comparatively advantageous treatment.[39] However, this would not amount to discrimination *against* a person or group and would rather amount to discrimination *in favour* of that person or group. Nevertheless, even favourable discrimination would necessarily entail discrimination against a person or group, by virtue of the comparative nature of the concept. It is usually this disadvantageous discrimination which is prohibited at law, though wrongfully discriminating in favour of a group or individual may be prohibited under constitutional or administrative law as an example of the misuse of public power. At the legislative level, many common

[36] See C O'Cinneide, 'The Uncertain Foundations of Contemporary Anti-Discrimination Law' (2011) 11 *International Journal of Discrimination and the Law* 7; C O'Cinneide, 'Justifying Discrimination Law' (2016) 36 *Oxford Journal of Legal Studies* 909; P Shin, 'Is There a Unitary Concept of Discrimination?' in Hellman and Moreau (eds) (n 7).

[37] Lippert-Rasmussen, 'The Badness of Discrimination' (n 17) 168. See also Sangiovanni (n 28) 116.

[38] Eidelson (n 6) 17.

[39] See ibid 2.

law jurisdictions have defined prohibited discrimination with some reference to disadvantageous treatment on the basis of a protected characteristic. In the British context, protected characteristics are drawn primarily from the Equality Act 2010. There appears to be no fixed list of protected characteristics at common law, indicating that a complete focus on grounds may be of little use in an attempt to explain the principles of non-discrimination at this level.[40]

Still, the statutory framework in most common law jurisdictions, while varying with regard to the characteristics they protect, are unified in their reliance on a relational conception of discrimination. For example, the UK's Equality Act 2010 defines unlawful discrimination as occurring where, 'because of a protected characteristic, A treats B less favourably than A treats or would treat others'.[41] The Irish Equal Status Act takes unlawful discrimination to occur where, on the basis of a protected characteristic, 'a person is treated less favourably than another person is, has been or would be treated'.[42] Canada's Human Rights Act outlaws certain practices which 'differentiate adversely' on the basis of a prohibited ground of discrimination.[43] Under the Australian Sex Discrimination Act, a person discriminates on the basis of sex if they treat the aggrieved person 'less favourably than, in circumstances that are the same or are not materially different, the discriminator treats or would treat a person of a different sex'.[44]

This chapter does not purport to provide a comprehensive analysis of anti-discrimination law within each of these jurisdictions except to note that many of them include some reference to disadvantageous treatment within their anti-discrimination norms and that this corresponds with some prominent philosophical accounts of discrimination. Thus, there appears to be a degree of consensus among both legal frameworks and philosophical writing in this area that comparatively less favourable treatment is an important aspect of discrimination.

However, the comparative approach has been subject to significant criticism by discrimination lawyers in recent years. In particular, the use of a 'comparator test', whereby a necessary step in determining whether discrimination has occurred involves comparing how the claimant has been treated to how another similarly situated person (be they real or hypothetical) who does not share the protected characteristic in question has been treated, has been challenged. For example, if a man claimed that he had been denied single-parent welfare benefits because of

[40] In the US context certain characteristics operate at the constitutional level to indicate heightened degrees of judicial scrutiny. This will be addressed in greater detail in the next chapter.

[41] Equality Act 2010, s 13. See also the UK's Sex Discrimination Act 1975, s 1: 'In any circumstances relevant for the purposes of any provision of this Act … a person discriminates against a woman if – (a) on the ground of her sex he treats her less favourably than he treats or would treat a man …'.

[42] Equal Status Act 2000, s 3(1)(a).

[43] Canadian Human Rights Act 1985, ss 5(b), 6(b), 7(b).

[44] Sex Discrimination Act 1984, s 5(1).

his sex, we would need to compare how a similarly situated woman has been or would be treated to determine whether this treatment was actually afforded on the grounds of sex. Importantly, all we have done here is establish that discrimination has occurred: X (the claimant) has been treated less favourably than Y (a similarly situated woman) on the basis of P (sex). We have not established whether this instance of discrimination was wrongful, nor for what reason.

Some legal scholars have argued that the standard of less favourable treatment is misguided and that a non-comparative account which looks to whether someone has been treated *un*favourably on the basis of a protected characteristic rather than *less* favourably should be preferred.[45] This raises a number of important questions regarding what precisely the comparator test is seeking to identify. Is it not simply an attempt to determine whether the treatment in question was actually done *on the basis of* a protected characteristic? On this account, the comparator test used within legal and philosophical analysis of wrongful discrimination is described as heuristic: a means of deciding a question of causation.[46] Further, some argue that comparative treatment should not be necessary because reliance on comparative tests has prevented the recognition of certain forms of wrongful discrimination. However, it is important to distinguish the test from what it is that is being tested for. Those in favour of a non-comparative account of discrimination rightfully point to circumstances where a comparator test is inappropriate as a guide for determining whether there has been wrongful discrimination.[47]

The most notably example is pregnancy discrimination.[48] It is difficult to imagine a male equivalent of a pregnant woman.[49] This has led some courts to attempt to compare a pregnant woman with a sick or unwell man.[50] Such an approach indicates that the use of a comparator test to determine if a pregnant woman has been discriminated against on the basis of her sex is inappropriate.[51]

[45] See in particular; Khaitan (n 7) 71–73, 132–33. See also D Réaume, 'Dignity, Equality, and Comparison' in Hellman and Moreau (eds) (n 7).

[46] Khaitan (n 7) 71–75; E Holmes, 'Anti-Discrimination Rights without Equality' (2005) 68 *Modern Law Review* 175, 186; Réaume (n 45).

[47] Note that tests for indirect discrimination are evidently comparative in nature where harm is determined by reference to the impact that a facially neutral provision, criterion, or practice has on those who share a protected characteristic such that they are put at a particular or disproportionate disadvantage in comparison to persons who do not share that characteristic. See Equality Act 2010, s 19; *Griggs v Duke Power Co*, 401 US 424 (1971).

[48] A McColgan, 'Cracking the Comparator Problem: Discrimination, "Equal Treatment" and the Role of Comparisons' (2006) 6 *European Human Rights Law Review* 650; P Lewis, 'Pregnant Workers and Sex Discrimination: The Limits of Purposive Non-Comparative Methodology' (2000) 16 *International Journal of Comparative Labour Law and Industrial Relations* 55; S Goldberg, 'Discrimination by Comparison' (2011) 120 *Yale Law Journal* 728.

[49] See *Turley v Allders Department Stores Ltd* [1980] ICR 66, 70; *Gedulig v Aiello*, 417 US 484 (1974).

[50] *Hayes v Malleable Working Men's Club* [1985] ICR 703, 708.

[51] As a result, the Equality Act includes free-standing provisions for pregnancy discrimination: Equality Act 2010, ss 17, 18. However, if pregnancy discrimination was an outlier and not paradigmatic, then Khaitan would be wrong to rely on it to conclude that the core instances of

Other instances where a typical comparator test might be inappropriate are cases of intersectional discrimination where someone is treated less favourably because of a combination of grounds.[52] Atrey argues that in these cases a contextualised comparator test may be the most appropriate way of determining discrimination.[53] Still, for those who favour a non-comparative conception of discrimination, pointing to potential comparator tests which can be conducted does not do much to address their more foundational argument that comparator tests are simply methods of determining causation and that the wrong itself is non-comparative. As such, it should be stressed that even when we use a non-comparative test we are still seeking to determine whether, for example, women have been treated less favourably than men are or would be treated.

There is arguably no appropriate comparator to a pregnant woman; relying on the treatment that would be afforded to a hypothetical man may not be particularly illuminating. The alternative is to adopt another test, one which does not attempt to imagine how a hypothetical comparator might be treated. Instead, this new, non-comparative test looks to whether the people who are negatively affected by a policy all share a protected characteristic such as sex. In these instances, we can conclude that those affected have been directly wronged because of that characteristic in question.[54] But we have also shown that they have been wronged in a way that people who do not share that characteristic (male employees, for example) have not been. If *all* the people who suffer a detriment are or would be women, then it is necessarily the case that these women have been treated less favourably than their male colleagues. The comparator test *is* heuristic; it is a good indicator that can help us to identify whether the property claimed to be the ground for less favourable treatment actually was the basis of the treatment in question. But the non-comparator test is *also* heuristic. Both are testing for a comparative wrong, just in different ways. It would be wrong to assume from the fact that we sometimes rely on non-comparator tests that the wrong we are testing for when identifying wrongful discrimination is non-comparative. Even when we do not use a comparator test, we are still testing for comparative treatment. Crucially, the choice between comparative or non-comparative tests for discrimination concerns how best to *identify the ground of treatment*, not whether the treatment itself is comparative or non-comparative. Both of these tests, should they be satisfied, will indicate that X has been treated less favourably than Y on the basis of whatever property has been established through use of the test. Choosing to use a non-comparative test

discrimination are non-comparative. It seems that Khaitan must be committed to the idea that paradigmatic cases of discrimination result in non-comparative harm and that, consequently, pregnancy discrimination is not an exception.

[52] S Atrey, 'Comparison in Intersectional Discrimination' (2018) 38 *Legal Studies* 379.

[53] ibid 390–93.

[54] See *James v Eastleigh Borough Council* [1990] 2 AC 751; *Bull v Hall* [2013] UKSC 73, [29]; *Brooks v Canada Safeway Ltd* [1989] 1 SCR 1219, [41], [47]; (C-73/08) *Bressol v Gouvernment de la Commaunité Française* [2010] 3 CMLR 559, [56].

to identify the ground of treatment does not rob discrimination of its relational nature.

Comparison is central to any conception of wrongful discrimination which is grounded within an equality-based framework: one cannot explain how certain forms of discrimination disrespect moral equality without first explaining how it is that discrimination could impact upon our normative or material standing relative to one another. Liberty-based accounts explain why discrimination is wrongful, when it is wrongful, by reference to violations to a person's capacities or freedom and often claim that equality is an empty vessel that acts as a rhetorical proxy for deeper liberty concerns.[55] The result is that liberty-based conceptions tend to also adopt a non-comparative conception of what discrimination *is*. Discrimination, on this account, occurs when someone is treated unfavourably on the basis of certain characteristics independent of how others are treated. The drawing of such conclusions collapses the concept of discrimination into an action which is defined not by anything particular to the action itself but by the grounds on which the action is made.

Analysis such as this gives little attention to the concept of discrimination, abstracted from instances when it may be morally impermissible. This problem of focusing exclusively on unjustified discrimination is not unique to the liberty-based conception, however. This is a danger that is just as real for those of us in the equality-based camp. However, I suggest that equality-based accounts of wrongful discrimination often correctly adopt a comparative conception of discrimination *qua* discrimination and so even when such accounts fail to give adequate attention to the concept in its neutral form, they are more likely to be accurate, even if only accidentally.

Non-comparative conceptions must necessarily place great emphasis on expounding and defending a theory which can explain why it is that certain grounds of discrimination (and not others) are prohibited at law because what defines discrimination is the ground, not the act.[56] We can determine whether you have been treated unfavourably because of your race if we use a comparator test to see how other, similarly situated persons who do not share your race, have been or would be treated. On this account, comparison is not necessary to establish discrimination; it is simply a proxy for identifying free-standing, non-comparative treatment: a tool for identifying the ground for the action in question. What is important is that you have been subject to a detriment because of, for example, your sex; it would not matter if other people who did not share your sex were also subject to that same detriment. So long as we can identify sex

[55] See in particular, Westen (n 16); C Peters, 'Foolish Consistency: On Equality, Integrity, and Justice in Stare Decisis' (1996) 105 *Yale Law Journal* 2031; C Peters, 'Equality Revisited' (1997) 110 *Harvard Law Review* 1210; F Thomsen, 'Concept, Principle, and Norm – Equality Before the Law Reconsidered' (2018) *Legal Theory* 1.

[56] On grounding generally, see M Foran, 'Grounding Unlawful Discrimination' (2022) 28 *Legal Theory* 3.

as the ground for the treatment in question, you have been subject to sex-based discrimination.[57]

This focus on grounds without much attempt to explain the concept abstracted from particular instantiations makes it difficult to define discrimination *qua* discrimination: when we examine the tests in isolation from the underlying justifications offered to explain why discrimination is wrong when it is, it is unclear what differentiates discriminatory treatment from other forms of treatment. If racial discrimination is detrimental treatment afforded on the basis of race, then discrimination itself could simply be detrimental treatment. Discrimination, whether morally permissible or not, could be nothing more than the act of treating someone badly for some reason. However, such a conclusion would be mistaken. If I hurl insults at a passer-by, I may offend and deeply insult them. I will have subjected them to a detriment and treated them badly. I have not discriminated against them. To have discriminating taste in wine, I must pick and choose; I must pass over some and seek out others on the basis of quality. To discriminate, one necessarily compares. When separated from questions of impermissibility, a non-comparative conception of discrimination becomes elusive.

This, of course, does not mean that treating someone badly on the basis of a characteristic such as race, where there is no comparative wrongdoing, is always morally permissible. On the contrary, it is usually highly immoral. But it is not discriminatory. If I walk into a room and proceed to hurl sex-based insults at those present, I treat everyone badly on the basis of their race. However, far from discriminating, I am insulting *indiscriminately*. I would only be discriminating in this context if I refused to insult men but insulted women or vice versa. It is the comparatively disadvantageous treatment which makes my conduct discriminatory, not the fact that it is done on the basis of sex. As Jay J stresses, the issue 'is not the identification of the ground but proof of less favourable treatment'.[58]

Finally, this account of discrimination includes less favourable or disadvantageous treatment but does not ground the wrong of wrongful discrimination within consequentialism. It is not, strictly speaking, the fact that someone has been *harmed* that makes discrimination wrongful. Rather, it is the fact that someone has been treated in a manner which disrespects them. Lippert-Rasmussen has argued that we can distinguish disadvantageous treatment from treatment that causes harm.[59] For example, he argues that refusing to hire an

[57] See, for example, *HM Chief Inspector of Education, Children's Services and Skills v The Interim Executive Board of Al-Hijrah School & others* [2017] EWCA Civ 1426, [48]–[51]; *cf The Interim Executive Board of X School v Her Majesty's Chief Inspector of Education, Children's Services and Skills* [2016] EWHC 2813 (Admin), [147]–[148].

[58] *The Interim Executive Board of X School v Her Majesty's Chief Inspector of Education, Children's Services and Skills* [2016] EWHC 2813 (Admin), [147].

[59] Lippert-Rasmussen, *Born Free and Equal: A Philosophical Inquiry into the Nature of Discrimination* (n 17) 18.

applicant who is better qualified treats them disadvantageously even if, as a result of this rejection, she is successful in obtaining a better job.[60] Another prominent example would be the racially discriminatory denial of an airline ticket which is wrongful, even if the plane then crashes and the discriminatee therefore benefits overall from the refusal.[61] Conversely, you can treat someone advantageously while overall harming them if, by hiring them, despite a more qualified candidate applying, they unknowingly lose out on getting a much better job as a result.[62] Thus, Lippert-Rasmussen argues that one can experience disadvantageous treatment in relation to the distribution of particular goods even if, overall, one has not been harmed or may even benefit from the treatment itself.[63] So when we speak of comparative wrong being a necessary feature of wrongful discrimination, it is the treatment itself that is wrongful, independent of the consequences which might arise from such treatment. As Hellman notes, the wrongness of discrimination is not reducible to the harm that one may inflict in discriminating, even though discrimination often does considerable harm.[64]

Like egalitarianism, wrongful discrimination is relational in nature: what matters is not simply that X has been disadvantaged, it is that X has been disadvantaged in a way that Y has not been. For the egalitarian, unequal distributions of benefits or burdens have something bad that equal distributions do not have.[65] What matters here is not how one is situated absolutely, but how one is situated relative to how others are situated.[66] Principles of non-discrimination are similarly concerned with relative treatment as opposed to absolute treatment because discrimination is essentially a comparative form of treatment. The ground for discrimination goes a long way towards explaining when acts of discrimination may be wrongful, but the ground itself does not define the action. We can coherently speak of discrimination without specifying the ground because the term 'discrimination' names an action independent from its basis, ground, motivation, and so on.

In light of the above, we can conclude that a necessary feature of discrimination is disadvantageous treatment, not simply unfavourable treatment. However, not all disadvantageous treatment amounts to demeaning, or even wrongful, discrimination. Only some kinds of discrimination are wrongful

[60] ibid.

[61] J Woodward, 'The Non-Identity Problem' (1986) 96 *Ethics* 804, 811.

[62] Lippert-Rasmussen, *Born Free and Equal: A Philosophical Inquiry into the Nature of Discrimination* (n 17) 18.

[63] ibid. See also J Gardner, 'Discrimination as Injustice' (1996) 16 *Oxford Journal of Legal Studies* 353.

[64] Hellman, *When Is Discrimination Wrong?* (n 5) 26–27. See also Eidelson (n 6) 3.

[65] M Fleurbaey, 'Equality versus Priority: How Relevant Is the Distinction?' (2015) 31 *Economics and Philosophy* 203, 205.

[66] This is in contrast with, for example, a prioritarian position. See D Parfit, 'Equality or Priority' in M Clayton and A Williams (eds), *The Ideal of Equality* (Palgrave Macmillan, 2000); N Holtug, 'Theories of Value Aggregation: Utilitarianism, Egalitarianism, Prioritarianism' in I Hirose and J Olson (eds), *The Oxford Handbook of Value Theory* (Oxford University Press, 2015).

and only some kinds of wrongful discrimination are wrongful because they demean persons by directly disrespecting their moral equality. Nevertheless, the comparative nature of discrimination means that, where it is wrongful, it is always at least partly violative of moral equality. In the next section, the precise nature of demeaning discrimination will be elaborated. It will be shown that proper respect for the moral equality of persons precludes forms of discrimination which express disrespect for the moral equality of persons, including those which do so by virtue of the social meaning which attaches to action. From here we will explore indirectly-equality-violating discrimination and the question of justification.

III. DEMEANING DISCRIMINATION, DISRESPECT, AND SOCIAL MEANING

Discrimination *qua* discrimination, abstracted from moral judgement, occurs when one treats X less favourably than one does or would treat Y on the basis of property P. We have established that this is necessarily a relational concept. What must now be addressed is the question of what makes wrongful discrimination wrongful. I suggest that the core justification for constitutional intervention to prevent wrongful discrimination on the part of the state is the obligation to respect the moral equality of persons. It is not a mistake to conceive of wrongful discrimination as a prime violation of the principle of equality before the law. Demeaning discrimination is an affront to the core values of constitutionalism, democracy, and the rule of law. Central to this is an awareness of social meaning but also, crucially, a grounding within the administrative law principle of rationality. Before that grounding can be fully understood, we must first account for discrimination as a form of deliberative failure to respect important moral truths such as the equal dignity of persons. It is only when we account for both rationality and social meaning that we can begin to describe the concept of demeaning discrimination that I wish to advance and which I argue is prohibited under administrative law doctrine.

Deborah Hellman argues that a law or policy wrongfully discriminates when it demeans: when it 'fails to treat the people affected as equals'.[67] This definition mirrors the definition of a violation of legal equality that I have advanced.[68] What matters for determining whether a particular policy treats people as less than equals (ie demeans them), according to Hellman, is the social meaning which attaches to the act rather than anything specific to the act itself. As such, 'it is morally wrong to draw distinctions among people and treat them differently as a result when doing so demeans any of those affected'.[69] It is not

[67] Hellman, 'Equality and Unconstitutional Discrimination' (n 7) 53. See also Hellman, *When Is Discrimination Wrong?* (n 5) 13–34.

[68] See Ch 2 above.

[69] Hellman, *When Is Discrimination Wrong?* (n 5) 33.

necessary that the demeaned *feels* demeaned, however.[70] To demean is 'partly an expressive act': '[i]t is our common history and culture and its conventions and social understanding that determine which actions express a rejection of the equal humanity of others'.[71] It is for this reason, and not the feelings which might arise, that spitting on someone or segregating a bus on the basis of race demean. Whatever we think about abstract, speculative morality, law is grounded within a social, historical and cultural context. Its requirements are worked out within that context, constituting a shared tradition with common standards and customs.

Accounting for social meaning allows us to understand exactly why it is wrongful for the state to implement policies which express disrespect for moral equality, without having to account for the harm that they might engender. It moves us away from a liberal preoccupation with harm at the expense of richer moral concepts.[72] Within certain forms of liberal constitutionalism, virtually all actionable wrongs must cause harm before they can be legally prohibited.[73] The difficulty is that often discrimination is wrongful even if it does not cause meaningful harm. When this happens, those of a liberal disposition may be inclined to speculate about extremely amorphous harms in order to justify prohibiting the discrimination in question. A strength of Hellman's account is that it does not need to identify these harms in order to explain the wrong of wrongful discrimination.

This is not to say that government-enforced segregation in mid-century America did not indirectly harm Blacks through the knock-on effect of the perpetuation of prejudice and bias. Rather, on Hellman's account, one can explain why such policies are unconstitutional even if these consequences do not obtain. The result is that there is no requirement to prove that these intangible, immeasurable kinds of harm have obtained before one can successfully mount an equal protection claim. The importance of this can be seen when one examines the historical background of *Brown v Board of Education*, where a key question was whether separate educational facilities were equal in quality.[74] Even the *Brown* decision itself, which explicitly sidestepped the claim that segregated educational facilities for Black children were of inferior quality, focused on other harmful consequences of segregation. Specifically, the Court held that segregation violates the Fourteenth Amendment because it 'generates a feeling of inferiority [among Black children] as to their status in the community that may affect their hearts and minds in a way unlikely to ever be undone'.[75] That may be true, but is it necessary to conclude that racial segregation violates legal equality? If it is necessary, how might this be evidenced?

[70] ibid 30.
[71] ibid 35–36.
[72] See A MacIntyre, *After Virtue* (University of Notre Dame Press, 1981).
[73] See J Gardner, 'Liberals and Unlawful Discrimination' (1989) 9 *Oxford Journal of Legal Studies* 1.
[74] See *Plessy v Ferguson*, 163 US 537 (1896).
[75] *Brown v Board of Education of Topeka* (n 1) 494.

A reliance on social meaning allows us to account for the equality violation here without having to reference the feelings which may or may not be generated. If, for example, Black children were exceptionally resilient such that segregation generated a feeling of righteous anger and resistance, spurring them to excel in their later lives, would the segregation be constitutional? No. The reason for this is that racial segregation violates moral equality *regardless* of the consequences. A focus on social meaning ensures that we have the tools to explain this.

However, Hellman's explanation for when discrimination is wrongful suffers from a similar problem to Ronald Dworkin's in that an appeal to treatment as an equal raises more interpretive questions than it resolves due to the myriad of competing accounts of what that standard may require. For example, consequentialist or utilitarian interpretations of the requirement that legal subjects be treated with equal concern and respect are not accounted for within this conception; nor are requirements of non-arbitrariness.[76] The claim here is not that these interpretations are correct. Rather, it is that reliance on the notion of treatment as an equal does not resolve interpretive conflicts between competing accounts of how best to treat people as equals. Nevertheless, Hellman is operating within the correct theoretical framework: constitutional prohibitions on discriminatory conduct arise from a commitment to treating legal subjects as moral equals. This being the case, however, Hellman's account of a principle of non-discrimination encounters problems when one examines its conceptual indistinctiveness from the broader principle of equality before the law. Under this definition of discrimination, any violation of legal equality amounts to wrongful discrimination. However, if we were to conceive of non-discrimination as an example of – but not synonymous with – the principle of equality before the law, we can account for circumstances where the state does not discriminate but where it nevertheless acts in violation of legal equality.

Treatment as an equal can mean a great many things and can give rise to both positive and negative duties. Hellman's defence of a demeaning-based account of discrimination is partly that adopting such an account will leave fewer contentious questions for courts to decide: all that must be asked to determine if there has been unconstitutional discrimination is whether someone has been treated as an inferior.[77] However, such an approach presupposes that legal equality and non-discrimination are singular, unitary concepts.[78] In reality, the determination as to the correct way to treat legal subjects as equals is a matter

[76] For example, Hellman argues that the arbitrary exclusion of persons whose last name begins with the letter A is not discriminatory because it does not violate the principle of equal moral worth: Hellman, *When Is Discrimination Wrong?* (n 5) 14, 18–20, 114–37. However, it will be argued in the next chapter that arbitrary action on the part of the State does in fact violate the principle of equality before the law and the principle of equal moral worth which informs it.

[77] Hellman, 'Equality and Unconstitutional Discrimination' (n 7).

[78] See Shin (n 36); O'Cinneide, 'The Uncertain Foundations of Contemporary Anti-Discrimination Law' (n 36).

of value, not logic.[79] It is for this reason that appeals to the concept of equality independent of additional values are not capable of resolving conflicts regarding how best to respect the equal moral status of legal subjects.

Hellman argues that the equality-based account of discrimination manifests 'thinner' constitutional principles than liberty-based accounts.[80] By this she means that liberty-based accounts require courts to decide what liberties citizens are entitled to and to assess the legitimacy of particular institutions or laws in light of those liberties.[81] This results in liberty-based conceptions of wrongful discrimination, grounded in non-comparative justice, requiring the court to 'constitutionalize normative judgments about the nature or aim of important social institutions, like marriage'.[82] In contrast, Hellman argues that equality-based accounts, grounded in comparative justice and the notion that the state should treat citizens as legal and moral equals, do not require the Court to decide contentious normative questions. Rather, the questions judges will be tasked with deciding:

> will be factual questions (Was the legislature that adopted the law motivated by animus toward a particular group?) or interpretive questions that rely on social facts (is the best way to understand the meaning of this law as denigrating that group?) or other questions of this sort.[83]

While Hellman is certainly correct to locate a constitutional principle of non-discrimination within a broader principle of legal equality, she is mistaken to think that an equality-based account raises questions that are less normatively contentious than a liberty-based account or that it may raise fewer of them. The principle of equality before the law cannot be properly interpreted without first settling a number of extremely contentious normative questions. A liberty-based account may ask if we are entitled to have access to the institution of marriage, independent of how others are treated. But an equality-based account must also ask if denial of access to this institution on an equal footing with others fails to respect moral equality. Both questions will require one to inspect the nature or aim of social institutions. The difference is simply that one approach asks whether there are independent reasons to include, and the other asks whether there are comparative reasons, given the nature of the institution itself. Excluding those under the age of 65 from certain benefits might be wrongful discrimination and it might not. Regardless of whether one is asking whether under-65s are independently or comparatively entitled to the benefit, one cannot avoid asking what the purpose of the benefit scheme is and whether exclusion of under-65s is justified given that purpose. Moreau is thus correct to argue that

[79] Fredman, *Discrimination Law* (n 10) 2.
[80] Hellman, 'Equality and Unconstitutional Discrimination' (n 7) 51–53.
[81] ibid 55–57.
[82] ibid 61.
[83] ibid 60–61.

many of these questions will be identical to those questions which are entailed by a liberty-based conception of discrimination, notably resulting in exactly the same constitutionalising of controversial normative judgements regarding the nature or aim of social institutions.[84]

However, equality-based accounts also raise additional normative questions that must be answered before we can even begin to analyse social institutions. While the liberty-based account must decide what liberties individuals are entitled to, the equality-based account must decide how the state must act in order to properly respect the moral equality of legal subjects. This raises just as many controversial questions as the liberty-based account. At a very basic level there can be a conflict between utilitarian, or broadly consequentialist accounts of treatment as an equal, and deontological accounts of treatment as an equal, as mentioned in previous chapters.

The conflict between deontological and consequentialist accounts of equality is not new.[85] Reliance on requirements of equal concern and respect on its own evidently cannot answer these questions. Indeed, even *within* a deontological framework, there are several contentious normative questions which must be answered before one can be sure what precisely a constitutional principle of non-discrimination may require. For example, Eidelson identifies a central wrong of impermissible discrimination within this broadly deontological approach: all instances of wrongful discrimination disrespect persons in a profound way.[86] To him, 'one disrespects someone as a person if one fails to recognize and afford the appropriate weight' to either of these two moral facts: (1) that 'persons are of value in themselves, and equally so'; and (2) that 'persons are autonomous: they possess a faculty of self-control through which they can make their lives, in significant part, their own'.[87]

Thus, there is an important distinction between Eidelson's account and Hellman's account: Eidelson does not focus on the social meaning of actions and argues that this makes it implausible that an expressive kind of disrespect is intrinsically, as opposed to contingently, wrongful, 'since the conventional meaning of an act, in itself, does not seem to be of any intrinsic moral significance'.[88] Rather, he looks to whether an agent manifests a deliberative failure to give appropriate weight and recognition to important aspects of a person's dignity.[89] Deliberative failures are thus instances where one has acted on improper reasoning or failed to account for relevant moral or factual truths.

[84] Moreau, 'In Defense of a Liberty-Based Account of Discrimination' (n 7) 76–80.

[85] See A Sangiovanni, 'On the Relation Between Moral and Distributive Equality' in G Brock (ed), *Cosmopolitanism versus Non-Cosmopolitanism* (Oxford University Press, 2013); T Nagel, 'Equality' in Clayton and Williams (eds) (n 66); Parfit (n 66); B Williams, 'The Idea of Equality' in L Pojman and R Westmoreland (eds), *Equality: Selected Readings* (Oxford University Press, 1997).

[86] Eidelson (n 6).

[87] ibid 79.

[88] ibid 74.

[89] ibid 76.

Eidelson's account is of particular value for our purposes because he offers a way of explaining the connection between discrimination and arbitrariness such that we can give meaning to the connection between legal equality and administrative law doctrine.

Both Hellman and Eidelson agree that discriminatory motive is not the decisive factor here. They diverge because Hellman thinks the salient feature is the social meaning of the act while Eidelson argues that what matters is the act 'thickly described' – wherein judgement attaches to the complexity of the act and the reasoning behind it.[90] It is not simply the psychological motive behind the act, however. It is the attitude that one holds and the ways in which holding certain attitudes affect the kinds of decisions one might make.[91] Attitudes give us reasons to deliberate and act in certain ways: '[t]o express an attitude through action is to act on the reasons that attitude gives us'.[92] As such, Eidelson argues that one acts disrespectfully 'by failing to act on the reasons that would be given by recognition respect'.[93]

Crucially, this does not mean that adopting an attitude is the same as adopting a mental state on a par with love or envy. As Eidelson notes, '[s]chematically, respect and disrespect for persons are states of mind that consist in taking (or failing to take) certain considerations as reasons for or against certain actions'.[94] Similarly, Raz argues that 'respecting people is … neither a feeling, nor an emotion, nor a belief … It is a way of conducting oneself, and more indirectly, of being disposed to conduct oneself towards the object of respect'.[95] As such, we can describe bias as an attitude, but prejudice as a subjective mental state in the sense that one can be biased without being prejudiced. Pre-judging a case that one is required to adjudicate is generally prohibited by the principles of natural justice. However, certain forms of prejudice are also wrongful if they are informed by biases related to moral inequality. Bias can occur as a result of failures to hold or give appropriate weight to moral truths, even where there exist no positive beliefs regarding the object of bias. In contrast, prejudice requires something in the way of a positive commitment or preconceived opinion that can affect the decision-making process. In a sentence: bias is an attitude, but it need not be a belief. Thus, if I sincerely believe that men and women are moral equals but nevertheless wrongfully discriminate against women, I am biased but not prejudiced.

An attitude, in this sense, is determined by reference to morality, not psychological motivation. It is for this reason that an employer who, motivated

[90] ibid 77. See also R Arneson, 'What Is Wrongful Discrimination?' (2006) 43 *San Diego Law Review* 775, 782.

[91] Eidelson (n 6) 78–79.

[92] ibid 78. See also E Anderson and R Pildes, 'Expressive Theories of Law: A General Restatement' (2000) 148 *University of Pennsylvania Law Review* 1503, 1509–11.

[93] Eidelson (n 6) 78.

[94] ibid 79.

[95] J Raz, *Value, Respect, and Attachment* (Cambridge University Press, 2001) 138.

by profit and not sexism, refuses to hire women between the ages of 20 and 40, nevertheless disrespects female applicants: 'her deliberation is rendered morally defective not simply by the presence of some positive factor of animus or defamatory belief, but by the *absence* of appropriate recognition of [moral equality]'.[96] The reasoning here is that, if this employer had properly taken into account the moral equality of persons, she would not have implemented the policy in question. This hints towards a value that we all have simply by virtue of being persons, a value which we necessarily have equally.[97] A failure to recognise or give proper weight to this moral status in one's deliberations or actions is therefore wrongful: '[t]o respect a person's equal value relative to other persons one must value their interests equally with those of other persons, absent good reason for discounting them'.[98] Disrespect, in this sense, does not necessitate a hostile or contemptuous mindset, nor the positive belief that someone is an inferior. Rather, one may disrespect out of sheer neglect, by failing, for whatever reason, to properly account for the 'normative upshots' of the moral status of persons.[99] One is prejudiced where deliberation fails to adequately respect moral equality, regardless of whether the failure is the result of bias or the result of negligence.

In contrast, but still operating within a disrespect-based framework, Alexander argues that X discriminates against Y when they treat Y worse than they would treat a different person Z on the basis of their false belief that Z has a higher moral status than Y.[100] While these accounts are similar to Hellman's they are by no means identical and they evidently raise as many contentious questions as the liberty-based account does – if not more. Indeed, Hellman's account arguably raises more controversial questions than many other deontic, equality-based, accounts do because we must decide in every case what the social meaning of a given action is in addition to its non-expressive significance. Nevertheless, it would be wrong to say that Hellman offers nothing that could assist in this endeavour. Her expressivist account is not simply a claim that discrimination occurs where persons are treated as less that equals, even if that is her starting point. Hellman's account is an attempt to settle these contentious normative questions relating to how the state might fail to treat its citizens with equal concern and respect by appealing to the notion of treatment which is socially understood to demean. She leaves open the possibility that one can be wrongfully discriminated against even when one has not been demeaned but argues that her account is nevertheless the best way to explain when discrimination is wrong.[101]

[96] Eidelson (n 6) 75.
[97] ibid 79; J Raz, 'On Respect, Authority, and Neutrality: A Response' (2010) 120 *Ethics* 279, 284–85.
[98] Eidelson (n 6) 97.
[99] ibid 74–75.
[100] Alexander (n 30).
[101] Hellman, *When Is Discrimination Wrong?* (n 5) 31.

However, the result is that her account, far from avoiding contentious questions, requires the concept of treatment as an equal to do a lot of heavy theoretical lifting. The test used by courts in determining whether a particular policy or form of conduct is unconstitutional should not simply be to ask, 'does this conduct demean?'. This is for exactly the same reasons that we would reject legal standards which required administrative bodies to 'do what justice requires'. The rule of law manifestly rejects such standards as irredeemably vague, precisely because they require that a number of contentious ethical questions be answered before they can guide conduct.[102] Even if the underlying aim of law is to do justice and even if the underlying aim of anti-discrimination law is to prevent people from being demeaned, more concrete doctrinal rules and principles are needed if these standards are to be effectively enforced. At the risk of being uncharitable, while the account that Hellman advances successfully identifies conduct which always violates moral equality, the test itself is simply a requirement not to act in a manner which might be socially understood to violate moral equality. More precise tests are needed if people (including legal officials) are to be able to reasonably guide their conduct in accordance with a constitutional principle of non-discrimination. This could be provided by recourse to general principles of the common law. However, that would require situating this analysis within a particular constitutional framework and institutional history.

Hellman has focused almost exclusively on why some forms of discrimination are wrongful while offering very little in the way of explaining what discrimination is as a concept. She views the act of discrimination to be simply the drawing of a distinction of some kind. Even if one is analysing a moralised conception of discrimination, it is still necessary to identify which properties that are distinct to discrimination besides simply those which make it wrongful.[103]

Despite these difficulties, Hellman has provided a much-needed realignment within discrimination law theory by emphasising the importance of social meaning to wrongful discrimination. However, the central focus on conventionality results in many important aspects of wrongful discrimination going under-examined. Eidelson is equally to be applauded for his focus on recognition respect, even if his rejection of social meaning is misguided. Thus, it seems that Hellman and Eidelson have independently captured two sides of the same coin. As such, I am not convinced that their accounts cannot be reconciled. Specifically, it is not clear why due respect for the moral equality of persons would not also preclude expressing denigration as Hellman understands it. Eidelson argues that:

> acts of discrimination are intrinsically wrong when and because they manifest a failure to show the discriminatees the respect that is due to them as persons. Thus

[102] See L Fuller, *The Morality of Law*, rvsd edn (Yale University Press, 1969) 35–36, 63–65; F von Hayek, *The Road to Serfdom* (Routledge, 1944) 78.
[103] Eidelson (n 6) 14.

> discrimination is sometimes morally objectionable not because of anything that it causes, but because of what it itself manifests by virtue of how it comes about.[104]

Surely an appropriate responsiveness to someone's moral status would give us reasons to refrain from acting in a way that would *signify* that someone is an inferior, would it not? Indeed, Eidelson recognises that a conventionally disrespectful act, assessed by reference to social meaning, can ground a 'significant but contingent moral reason not to perform it'.[105] What is more, he concludes that awareness of conventional meaning might make a choice to act intrinsically disrespectful, in the sense that there has been a deliberative failing on the part of the actor.[106] Thus, for example, if I am aware of the social meaning attached to spitting on someone and do it anyway, not because I wish to express denigration but because I don't care how my acts are perceived, my actions express disrespect and also manifest sincere disrespect in my subjective deliberation. Eidelson argues that in these cases, it is not the convention that determines whether an act is basically disrespectful, it is the disregard for the harm that an act might cause *in light of* the convention.[107]

However, even where there is no conscious disregard for the social meaning of action, can there not still be a deliberative failure? Can we not say that this action still disrespects in the sense that properly taking into account moral equality would, all things considered, prevent us from acting in a way that would be conventionally understood as demeaning? The normative status of our actions cannot be assessed within a vacuum; social context is an important component of our duties to one another. Essential to a full account of the moral character of a given action is the unique role that expression plays.[108] Here, the expressive nature of an action is not determined by reference to consequences, but to the *meaning* that is expressed and which can be determined with some measure of objectivity.[109] It seems uncontroversial to suggest that the act of burning a nation's flag or a religion's holy book, or spitting on someone expresses meaning.[110] It is also clear that these expressions can matter morally in-and-of themselves. Once we accept that the meaning which is expressed by an act has moral salience, expressive wrongdoing becomes indispensable to any analysis of respect-based moral obligation, including Eidelson's account of wrongful discrimination. As Anderson and Pildes stress: 'Expressive theories tell actors … to act in ways that express appropriate attitudes towards various substantive values.'[111]

[104] ibid 73.
[105] ibid 85.
[106] ibid.
[107] ibid. 85 See also ibid 101–102; Raz (n 95) 171–72.
[108] See A Wood, *Kant's Ethical Thought* (Cambridge University Press, 1999) 141.
[109] T Khaitan, 'Dignity as an Expressive Norm: Neither Vacuous Nor a Panacea' (2012) 32 *Oxford Journal of Legal Studies* 1, 4. See also C Sunstein, 'On the Expressive Function of Law' (1996) 144 *University of Pennsylvania Law Review* 2021; Anderson and Pildes (n 92); D Hellman, 'The Expressive Dimension of Equal Protection' (2000) 85 *Minnesota Law Review* 1.
[110] Khaitan (n 109) 9; Sunstein (n 109) 2023.
[111] Anderson and Pildes (n 92) 1504.

But how exactly are we to determine what is expressed by a given action or government policy? The answer to that question is by no means easy to determine, particularly when dealing with individual cases. Nevertheless, an appeal to speech-act theory may provide some guidance. JL Austin argued that all language is action with the following core aspects:

(1) locution: the act of saying something;[112]
(2) illocution: the 'performance of an act *in* saying something as opposed to performance of an act *of* saying something';[113]
(3) perlocution: the production of 'certain consequential effects upon feelings, thoughts, or actions of the audience, or of the speaker, or of other persons'.[114]

An example of this in action may be illuminating. Suppose Anthony and Anna are in the middle of an amorous exchange and Anthony begins to unbutton Anna's shirt. The following occurs:

(1) locution: Anna says 'no';
(2) illocution: in saying 'no', Anna expresses refusal;
(3) perlocution: Anna persuades Anthony to cease unbuttoning her shirt.

It is the illocutionary force of an act which grounds its expressive meaning.[115] Thus, perlocutionary consequences are not of central concern when discussing the expressive meaning of an act.[116] Furthermore, expressive meaning need not be confined to speech acts: non-speech acts may also carry expressive meaning. Khaitan provides a poignant example:

> Take for example the act of requiring black passengers to sit at the back of the bus. The locutionary equivalent in this case would be the driver saying 'Sit at the back!' to a black passenger, or his gesturing towards the back of the bus when a black passenger gets on it, or an Act of Parliament that says 'Black passengers shall sit at the back of public buses'. Its illocutionary force, in certain contexts, may be in insulting, demeaning or humiliating black people. It may also have perlocutionary force because of its consequences, for example, by persuading black passengers to sit at the back of the bus, generating in them a feeling of shame and anger, diminishing their self-respect, causing psychological harm, or entrenching/perpetuating prejudice against black people.[117]

If what matters here is not mental states but actions which fail to properly account for the normative upshots of moral equality, why does this bus driver who unknowingly acts in a way that conventionally expresses disrespect not also

[112] J Austin, *How to Do Things with Words* (Clarendon Press, 1962) 95.
[113] ibid 99.
[114] ibid 101.
[115] Khaitan (n 109) 11.
[116] Anderson and Pildes (n 92) 1573.
[117] Khaitan (n 109) 10–11.

manifest a deliberative failure? Eidelson rightly argues that one 'may manifest disrespect for ... equal value even if he makes no direct judgement about [someone's] value at all'.[118] What matters is that one affords proper weight to a person's interests; a failure to recognise an interest at all would evidently be disrespectful. I see no reason why we would not have an interest in avoiding being treated in a way that would be conventionally understood as demeaning and degrading. Indeed, I would suggest that to be treated in such a manner *is* one way to be demeaned and degraded.

So, failing to recognise that someone has an interest in not being conventionally disrespected is also basically and intrinsically disrespectful. The cultural context may change such that certain acts might be disrespectful in some contexts and not others. However, the point here is simply that acting in a way that is socially understood to be disrespectful is disrespectful because respect cannot be assessed in a vacuum. Different acts may fall in or out of the category of 'conventionally disrespectful' depending on the cultural context, but the category itself remains firmly within the realm of intrinsically disrespectful conduct. The contingent aspect here is simply that certain acts may or may not be conventionally disrespectful depending on the context. Should an act be determined to be conventionally disrespectful to moral equality, its wrongfulness is not dependent upon perlocutionary consequences. The wrong accrues by virtue of the failure to afford appropriate weight to one's interest in not being conventionally treated as an inferior.

Eidelson accepts that knowingly disregarding social convention may be intrinsically disrespectful. But what if our hypothetical employer recognises that her employees have an interest in not being conventionally disrespected but she simply does not think that her actions are disrespectful? Eidelson himself provides us guidance on this point, in fact. He notes that 'one cannot bring about the satisfaction of someone's interests without knowing what they are, and valuing a person's interests ... means taking their satisfaction as a goal, a reason for action'.[119] If this is true, Eidelson argues that 'one may act disrespectfully by failing to make a serious effort to ascertain a person's interests accurately, at least where one knows one's choice is liable to affect him'.[120] Indeed, he stresses that:

> [t]he interest thesis implies that respecting someone as a being of equal value also entails *responding to* her status as a bearer of interests with presumptively equal normative weight. And to act consistently with what that presumption requires – to actually succeed in respecting it – it is not enough to reason in good faith. Your deliberation and action must actually track the relative normative facts.[121]

[118] Eidelson (n 6) 97.
[119] ibid 101.
[120] ibid.
[121] ibid 103.

Thus, it seems perfectly reasonable to conclude that legal officials are under a positive obligation to ensure not only that they treat legal subjects with appropriate respect, but also that they are seen to treat them with respect. A failure to recognise an interest in not being conventionally disrespected is itself disrespectful. But what is more, having recognised such an interest, it would be disrespectful to take no steps to comprehend what might be conventionally disrespectful. Legal officials acting in accordance with a principle of equality before the law must therefore make appropriate efforts to be attuned to the social meaning that their actions may carry and to avoid acting in ways that express prejudice or denigration. As Green explains, 'Part of what it is to respect people is to *show* them respect. Respect is to be offered, and to be seen and understood to be offered'.[122] He is right to advise caution when assessing the normative upshots of recognising this aspect of respect: 'This step into the symbolic world, raising the question of what count as proper signs of respect, brings new issues and new hazards. Signs are context dependent and can be both uncertain and unstable.'[123] Nevertheless, this is a challenge which must be faced if officials are to act with due regard for the moral equality of persons.

For these reasons, we can conclude that conventional disrespect is, in fact, intrinsically disrespectful, even though our identification of what counts as disrespect is premised upon the social meaning of actions. To be intrinsically wrongful, the wrong must obtain irrespective of the consequences of action. In the case of conventional disrespect, the wrong is in the failure to account for a person's interests or the failure to respond appropriately to one's knowledge of those interests. In contrast, Eidelson views conventional disrespect as wrongful by virtue of its perlocutionary consequences – the material and psychological harm that it gives rise to.[124] Spitting on someone may be wrongful, according to Eidelson, should it cause the victim 'psychological or material harm, either directly or by influencing the way others treat him'.[125] As such, it 'plays a role, indirectly, in determining whether it is compatible with basic respect, since … basic respect normally requires us to count the risk of harm … against the act'.[126] But, surely, we could also see acts of conventional disrespect as wrongful not because of any consequences but simply by virtue of the illocutionary meaning of the act, even if our understanding of what is expressed is contingent upon social convention. Yes, forcing Black passengers to the back of the bus is likely to produce psychological and material harm, reinforcing prevailing notions of inferiority and compounding institutional and cultural disadvantage. But it would be wrong even if it did not produce that harm. Just as with racially segregated schools, if segregation actually produced righteous anger and resilience such

[122] L Green, 'Two Worries about Respect for Persons' (2010) 120 *Ethics* 212, 214.
[123] ibid.
[124] Eidelson (n 6) 85.
[125] ibid.
[126] ibid 87.

that Blacks mobilised a movement for civil rights that ultimately benefited them, this would not negate the wrongfulness of segregating buses. To repeat, it is not the perlocutionary consequences of segregation that ultimately ground the wrong, it is the illocutionary meaning which attaches to the act.

In this sense, there is not much that distinguishes conventional from non-conventional disrespect except that one relies on social meaning and the other does not. Conventional disrespect is still intrinsically wrongful because it is wrongful in-and-of itself, even if these harmful consequences do not obtain. The fact that conventional disrespect itself cannot be identified without reference to social meaning does not mean that the illocutionary expression is not intrinsically wrongful *should it obtain*. As Hellman notes, the fact that such a conclusion would rely on the social meaning of action does not in any way alter its wrongfulness, nor is it wrongful simply because of the consequences it might produce.[127] Eidelson is thus wrong to say that the conventional meaning of an act carries with it no intrinsic moral significance.

Eidelson argues that conventional disrespect can be predicated on thinly described acts: where there is no deliberative failure.[128] In principle, the act of spitting on someone need not be motivated by contempt or malice. There may simply be someone standing in the most convenient place to spit. This, according to Eidelson, means that the act of spitting on someone is not basically or intrinsically disrespectful. However, this analysis ignores what Eidelson himself has rightly said about basic or intrinsic disrespect obtaining where there has been a *negligent* deliberative failure. To disrespect someone is, according to Eidelson, to fail to account for the normative upshots of some facet of her moral standing; 'it is just not up to a culture to decide what constitutes such a failure'.[129] It is true that disrespect should not be solely determined by reference to social meaning. However, should the social meaning attached to an act express prejudice, failing to respond appropriately to that would be intrinsically disrespectful and therefore wrongful, even if there are no harmful consequences. Were someone to spit on another, simply because they were in the most convenient place to spit, there *has* been a deliberative failure – a negligent failure to be sure, but a failure, nonetheless. If the person being spat on was unaware that they had been spat on there would be no psychological harm. Still, the act of spitting on someone expresses profound disrespect in certain cultures and a failure to recognise that and refrain from spitting manifests a sincere deliberative failure to properly account for and give appropriate weight to the equal moral status of others, even if it only obtains within a particular cultural context.

It seems that the point of conflict between Hellman and Eidelson is more related to the necessity of reliance on social meaning or convention in our identification of situations where someone is treated as less than an equal. At root,

[127] Hellman, *When Is Discrimination Wrong?* (n 5) 26–27.
[128] Eidelson (n 6) 84.
[129] ibid 86.

this conflict may be between speculative moral theory, abstracted from cultural or social context and a more richly embedded morality which finds its meaning partially by reference to that context. It should come as no surprise that the common law favours the later. As mentioned above, Hellman stresses that '[i]t is our common history and culture and its conventions and social understanding that determine which actions express a rejection of the equal humanity of others'.[130] Eidelson rejects the central nature of social meaning in his account but does see it as having a role to play in the identification of some forms of disrespectful conduct. He is mistaken to conclude that conventional disrespect is wrongful simply in virtue of its consequences, but he is correct when he argues that social meaning is not a necessary feature of demeaning or degrading conduct.

This being said, a charitable reading of Hellman's theory would come to the same conclusion. She argues that demeaning discrimination occurs where the state acts with intent to harm a person or group,[131] where the state disregards the interests of a person or group or fails to take them as seriously as it takes the interests of others,[132] or where the state expresses denigration towards persons or groups.[133] While she primarily focuses on social meaning, she does mention that demeaning treatment is 'partly' an expressive act, indicating that there are likely non-expressive ways to demean. Hellman's account is somewhat underdefined and glosses over these important (and contentious) normative questions which all must be answered before a coherent interpretation of constitutionally prohibited discrimination can be successfully advanced.[134] Still, drawing on both Hellman and Eidelson gets us a very long way towards doing exactly that.

IV. INDIRECTLY-EQUALITY-VIOLATING DISCRIMINATION

In light of the above, we can conclude that equality-based conceptions of wrongful discrimination should not be favoured simply because they raise less contentious normative questions. Rather, wrongful discrimination is only intelligible as a moral wrong when we recognise that differences in certain characteristics do not impact upon the equal moral worth of individuals. Now, Moreau may be correct in her argument that liberty-based accounts and equality-based accounts are both premised upon this commitment.[135] There are arguably many

[130] Hellman, *When Is Discrimination Wrong?* (n 5) 35–36.
[131] Hellman, 'Two Concepts of Discrimination' (n 14) 903–904.
[132] ibid 905.
[133] ibid 905–906.
[134] Indeed, Hellman has, in her more recent scholarship, suggested that an additional element of wrongful discrimination occurs where acts of discrimination compound previous injustice. See D Hellman, 'Indirect Discrimination and the Duty to Avoid Compounding Injustice' in Collins and Khaitan (eds) (n 11).
[135] Moreau, 'In Defense of a Liberty-Based Account of Discrimination' (n 7) 72–73.

instances of wrongful discrimination which are wrongful primarily because they fail to recognise and afford appropriate respect to other important aspects of one's moral status such as autonomy or individuality.[136] However, these failures ultimately do, in fact, amount to violations of legal equality. An individual complainant may have an intrinsic claim that a given act of discrimination disrespected their autonomy and individuality, but this claim may expand to include an equality-based claim should it come to light that others have not been or would not be treated in this disrespectful manner. Indeed, this is inevitable given the comparative nature of discrimination.

Nevertheless, Eidelson is right to stress that the primary claim of someone who is wrongfully *advantaged* by virtue of a stereotypical assumption that Asians are musically gifted is not that they have been treated as an inferior. Rather, their claim is that they have been not been properly treated as an individual.[137] As a method of explaining the claim that one can reasonably make, this is perfectly sound. However, as a standard by which we are to assess the justifiability of government action, it is too narrowly focused on the experiences of one individual. Yes, our hypothetical Asian applicant may have no explicit equality-based claim, but the person who was disadvantaged by this decision certainly does. As such, wrongfully discriminatory actions, by virtue of the comparative nature of discrimination, will necessarily be an affront to moral equality at some level and so will fall foul of administrative law requirements of reasonableness.[138]

Liberty-based accounts tend to ground the impermissibility of impermissible discrimination within a broadly consequentialist framework, focusing on 'the badness of its contingent effects'.[139] These effects could include not only particularised harm to an individual but also harm that is done to social groups and the effect that this has on the social distribution of resources or opportunities.[140] As such, a harm-based account implies that wrongful discrimination is never intrinsically bad but always merely contingently bad such that there would be no wrongdoing were these harmful effects not to obtain.[141] While these harms are evidently salient within an equality-based account, the core wrong that is done is the failure to properly respect the equal moral status of persons.

This is equally true for indirect- or disparate-impact discrimination. The concept of indirect discrimination arises as a result of a grounds-orientated account of discrimination, where the ground in question is essential to

[136] Eidelson (n 25).

[137] ibid 205–207.

[138] There may, however, be instances of discrimination which are morally bad because they produce undesirable consequences but do not wrong individuals in any way that is independent of such harm. In such cases, it is feasibly the case that the act is morally impermissible but not a violation of moral equality. Nevertheless, such forms of discrimination would be beyond the reach of judicial review as the court must point to a breach of legal principle for review to be successful.

[139] Eidelson (n 6) 72.

[140] See Khaitan and Steel (n 11); Khaitan (n 7).

[141] Lippert-Rasmussen, 'The Badness of Discrimination' (n 17) 174.

determining whether the act of discrimination is impermissible. In this context, an act of discrimination is prima facie neutral and permissible if it does not occur on the basis of a finite list of protected characteristics. A seemingly neutral act of discrimination may be unlawful should it produce consequences which put those who share a protected characteristic at a particular disadvantage. Thus, if a protected ground is sex, a policy which treats those below a certain height less favourably by excluding them from being fire-fighters may be unlawful because it would place female applicants at a particular disadvantage relative to male applicants. Crucially, the consequences alone are not enough to determine the justifiability of the policy in question. All that is done by a finding of disparate impact is the removal of a presumption of permissibility. These consequences usually indicate that there is an intimate connection between the actual ground for the decision and a protected characteristic such that we might say, for example, that height is a proxy for sex in this context.[142] Should no compelling justification be offered, the act in question will be classed as unjustifiably discriminatory.[143]

Statutory frameworks may need lists of protected grounds to ensure that legislation is adequately capable of guiding conduct and to provide a framework of stability to duty-bearers.[144] This is unnecessary under common law as there is no need for a presumption of justifiability based on the properties that acts of discrimination are grounded in: should a court deem there to be a sufficiently strong claim of wrongful discrimination on the part of an administrative body, the fact that the discrimination occurred on the basis of, for example, hair colour and not sex will be of no defence.[145] This standard of reasonableness demanded of public bodies does not extend to private individuals precisely because it is designed to hold the state to a higher standard. As such, while statute has complemented the common law anti-discrimination principle by prohibiting public bodies from discriminating on the basis of explicitly protected characteristics, this should be understood as merely supplementary to a prior common law principle of non-discrimination.

An equality-based account of wrongful discrimination provides a unifying grounding for not only prejudicial discrimination, but also for liberty- or autonomy-violating discrimination. Supposedly non-equality-based forms of wrongful discrimination may also be prohibited through the administrative law doctrine of reasonableness and this doctrine may itself be informed by a

[142] Holmes (n 46) 190–91.

[143] I leave open the question whether the mere fact of these consequences renders the discrimination wrongful – if it does, it is wrongful but not impermissible; *cf* Fredman, *Discrimination Law* (n 10) Ch 1.

[144] Although if we accept that discrimination is a form of negligence and thus subject to a private law standard of reasonableness, finite lists may not, in fact, be needed. See Moreau, 'Discrimination as Negligence' (n 16).

[145] *Associated Provincial Picture Houses Ltd v Wednesbury Corpn* [1948] 1 KB 223, 229 (Lord Green MR).

commitment to legal equality and fidelity to the rule of law. While some forms of wrongful discrimination are wrongful for reasons unrelated to equality (at least on the surface), they may still violate a principle of equal subjection to law should they amount to unreasonable misuse of discretionary power.

We could say that all wrongful discrimination should be classed as demeaning discrimination by virtue of the disrespect for moral equality which it engenders. However, this would elide an important distinction between those forms of discrimination which can never be justified and those which are only determined to be violative of moral equality once a justification test has occurred. Thus, while demeaning discrimination is automatically unjustified because disrespect for moral equality is the primary grounding of the wrong, other forms of discrimination must be subject to greater analysis of the justification offered before such determinations can be made. The reason for this is that no overriding justification can allow the state to treat a citizen as an inferior, but one may be offered for failing to treat someone as an individual. To the extent that we conclude that this failure to respect individuality is unjustified, there is an indirect equality claim which necessarily obtains as a result of the discriminatory nature of the conduct in question. Should a compelling justification be found, the discrimination may be legally or morally permissible and the equality claim does not arise.

5

Discrimination and Judicial Review

DISCRIMINATION IS SOMETHING that governments do as an essential aspect of administration. Resources must be allocated fairly; burdens and benefits must be placed upon people unequally so as to further the public good. To do so, some must be treated less favourably than others and often this is done on the basis of personal characteristics. What matters for our purposes are those instances where discrimination is unjustified. It is often assumed that wrongful discrimination is not prohibited by the common law. Indeed, in 2003, Lord Hope in *Relaxion Group v Rhys-Harper plc* stated that:

> [A]lthough discrimination on whatever grounds is widely regarded as morally unacceptable, the common law was unable to provide a sound basis for removing it … Experience has taught us that this is a matter which can only be dealt with by legislation, and that it requires careful regulation by Parliament.[1]

As an assessment of the common law position with regard to wrongful discrimination in the private sphere, this is broadly correct. There have been some successful cases where the implied duty of an innkeeper to provide accommodation to guests on a reasonable basis has precluded hotels from refusing to provide a room on the grounds of the race of the prospective customer.[2] However, this has been of limited applicability. Attempts to invoke the common law of tort or contract to challenge wrongful discrimination were usually unsuccessful. Indeed, the Court of Appeal has acknowledged that there is no general prohibition in law on private actors refusing admittance to 'coloured people'.[3] A public law conception of reasonableness seems to have been the decisive factor in distinguishing these two kinds of cases. Innkeepers, while operating private businesses, were seen to perform a public function and so were subject to a public law requirement that their refusal to admit persons be grounded on a reasonable basis. However, in the private context, the reasonable man was not expected to be free from racial bias.[4] Reasonableness, when construed in its public law context, is informed by constitutional principle, including the

[1] *Relaxion Group v Rhys-Harper plc* [2003] UKHL 33, [78].

[2] See eg *Constantine v Imperial Hotels Ltd* [1944] KB 693.

[3] *Scala Ballroom (Wolverhampton) Ltd v Ratcliffe* [1958] 3 All ER 220.

[4] Although, recent case law suggests that the distinction between public law reasonableness and private law reasonableness may be collapsing, at least in the contract context. See *Braganza v BP Shipping Ltd.* [2015] UKSC 17, [30].

principle of equality before the law. Thus, while the common law has generally offered little protection against wrongful discrimination in the private context, the same cannot be said of the public law, even if a coherent articulation of the common law principle of legal equality has been absent.[5]

It has long been established that public authorities act unlawfully if they treat people in an unequal manner with no reasonable justification for doing so. The coherence of this doctrine is revealed only when our conception of administrative lawfulness extends beyond the consistent application of discrete rules to encompass underlying commitments to constitutional principle, including a commitment to respecting the rule of law and, by extension, the equal dignity of legal subjects.[6] A court, in applying a principle of legal equality, must necessarily extend its gaze beyond the text of a statute; 'unjust and illegal discriminations between persons' in the application of neutral legal rules are also forbidden. It is thus unconstitutional 'if it is applied and administered by a public authority with an evil eye and an unequal hand'.[7] As Lord Nicholls notes in *Ghaidan v Godin-Mendoza*, '[d]iscriminatory law undermines the rule of law because it is the antithesis of fairness. It brings the law into disrepute. It breeds resentment. It fosters an inequality of outlook which is demeaning alike to those unfairly benefited and those unfairly prejudiced.'[8] This connection between the rule of law, non-discrimination, and fairness or non-arbitrariness is vital to the proper understanding of the role of non-discrimination within the principles of judicial review.

However, while there is this history of drawing a connection between unreasonableness and wrongful or unjustified discrimination, the common law has often failed to properly articulate a coherent conception of legal equality that could manifest within existing constitutional principles. Indeed, even within its traditional home of reasonableness review, the principle of non-discrimination has been criticised for deficiencies in both coherence and consistency.[9] This has resulted in commentators advocating for equality or non-discrimination to

[5] See C O'Cinneide, 'Equality: A Core Common Law Principle, or 'Mere' Rationality?' in M Elliott and K Hughes (eds), *Common Law Constitutional Rights* (Hart Publishing, 2020).

[6] On the relationship between judicial review and constitutional principle, see P Craig, 'Ultra Vires and the Foundations of Judicial Review' (1998) 57 *Cambridge Law Journal* 63; TRS Allan, 'The Constitutional Foundations of Judicial Review: Conceptual Conundrum or Interpretative Inquiry' (2002) 61(1) *Cambridge Law Journal* 87; *cf* M Elliott, 'The Ultra Vires Doctrine in a Constitutional Setting: Still the Central Principle of Administrative Law' (1999) 58 *Cambridge Law Journal* 129. On the connection between the rule of law and equal dignity, see Ch 3.

[7] *Yick Wo v Hopkins*, 118 US 356 (1886). See also PG Polyviou, *The Equal Protection of the Laws* (Duckworth, 1980); TRS Allan, *Law, Liberty, and Justice: The Legal Foundations of British Constitutionalism* (Clarendon Press, 1993) 164.

[8] *Ghaidan v Godin-Mendoza* [2004] UKHL 30, para 9. Note that, although this case was decided after the coming into force of the Human Rights Act 1998, this statement clearly concerned the rule of law and is therefore not particular to any statutory or international law regime.

[9] See A Lester and G Bindman, *Race and Law* (Penguin, 1972); B Hepple, *Race, Jobs and the Law in Britain* (Penguin, 1970); A McColgan, *Discrimination, Equality and the Law* (Hart Publishing, 2014).

form an independent ground of review. This chapter will argue that wrongful discrimination on the part of the state is unreasonable and should be – indeed *is* – covered under existing standards of review. To fully account for this, however, one must properly understand the constitutional nature of judicial review and the importance of both moral and legal standards in prohibiting the unreasonable misuse of public power.

There are two main reasons why the common law is sometimes critiqued for failing to advance a clear principle of non-discrimination. The first is an undue focus on ground-sensitivity rather than a more capacious analysis of unjustifiably treating an individual or group less favourably than others. The focus on grounds coalesces around finite lists of personal characteristics, leaving commenters to look for where the common law has dealt with racial or sexual discrimination (and so on) explicitly. But the principle of non-discrimination is far more foundational than its application to these forms of discrimination. Under the common law of judicial review, we must instead look to the more general principles of reasonableness and fairness if we are to fully articulate a principle of non-discrimination. Otherwise we would be doing the equivalent of attempting to fully articulate a the rule against bias by looking exclusively at cases where family members of decision-makers are involved. That might be an example of the rule against bias but it cannot provide a coherent or comprehensive account of the rule without being abstracted to a more general level.

The second reason why the common law is often critiqued for failing to manifest a clear principle of non-discrimination is the direct mirror of the first: an undue focus on abstract, speculative principle, unmoored from context. The common law, particularly administrative law principles of natural justice and reasonableness, are extremely context dependent. This does not mean that there are not principles or standards at play, it simply means that the application of those principles involves extremely contextualised reasoning. To someone looking for a principle of non-discrimination, protecting a school teacher from being fired for her hair colour or prohibiting bribes in planning permission decisions might not seem like obvious examples. But there is absolutely a principle of non-discrimination at work there.

Part of this may be informed by the focus on a finite list of protected characteristics at the legislative level and a presumption that common law, if it were to protect against wrongful discrimination, would look very similar to the Equality Act 2010. But this fails to adequately distinguish between legislation and common law. Where the Equality Act articulates clear rules which address discrimination across a wide range of contexts, the common law, in the context of judicial review, is focused more narrowly on the misuse of executive discretion and more widely on general standards of fairness which need not be confined to a finite list of protected characteristics in the same way.

There is no need for a separate ground of review for wrongful discrimination. If we recall the distinctions set out in the previous chapter, we can conclude that most forms of unlawful conduct on the part of a public authority can be classed as wrongfully discriminatory if they amount to treating one person or group less favourably than another on the basis of some property in an unjustified manner. In many instances the justifiability of the conduct will be determined by reference to our well-established common law standards of procedural fairness and reasonableness. Nevertheless, there may be good reason to pay particular attention to the kinds of demeaning discrimination which directly disrespect the moral equality of persons. These forms of discrimination directly engage the commitment to equality embedded within our legal order and are usually what commentators have in mind when they call for wrongful discrimination to be classed as a separate ground of review.

I. REASONABLENESS AND RELEVANCY

A constitutional principle of non-arbitrariness concerns actions or decisions made by legislative or administrative bodies on the basis of irrelevant considerations or where relevant considerations have not been taken into account in the legislative or administrative process. The presumption against arbitrariness is a longstanding and central pillar of constitutional and administrative law. Closely related to the common law principles of natural justice and the rule against bias, a principle of non-arbitrariness finds its home among the collection of duties associated with a fair hearing, the maxim of *audi alteram partem*, and the right to a reasoned decision taking proper account of pertinent evidence and arguments.[10] In its most basic form, arbitrariness is a lack of reason. As Endicott notes, '[a]rbitrary government is a distinctive form of government; it is a departure from the rule of law, in favor of rule by the mere will of the rulers'.[11] The rule of law is often described as protecting each citizen from arbitrary expressions of power, shielding the individual from abuses of legality, and guaranteeing some degree of liberty and freedom from the will of others.[12] When reduced to one short sentence, the rule of law is said to be contrasted with arbitrary power.

We cannot draw a sharp distinction between the various grounds of review, particularly those of rationality, reasonableness, or proportionality.[13] This is

[10] See generally P Cane, *Administrative Law*, 5th edn (Oxford University Press, 2011) 69–76.

[11] T Endicott, 'Arbitrariness' (2014) 27 *Canadian Journal of Law and Jurisprudence* 49, 49.

[12] See AV Dicey, *An Introduction to the Study of the Law of the Constitution* (JWF Allison ed, Oxford University Press, 2013) 119. See also Aristotle, 'Politics' in J Barnes (ed), *The Complete Works of Aristotle* (Princeton University Press, 1984) bk III, 16; TRS Allan, *Law, Liberty, and Justice: The Legal Foundations of British Constitutionalism* (Clarendon Press, 1993) 22–28; F von Hayek, *The Constitution of Liberty* (Routledge & Kegan Paul, 1960) 113; N Simmonds, *Law as a Moral Idea* (Oxford University Press, 2008).

[13] See TRS Allan, *The Sovereignty of Law: Freedom, Constitution, and Common Law* (Oxford University Press, 2013) Ch 7.

partly because the rule of law itself cannot be reduced to one singular principle or requirement; it is 'an amalgam of standards, expectations, and aspirations'.[14] It is also because the precise boundaries of judicial review and of the grounds of review cannot be reduced to simple rules. They are general principles, not susceptible to exhaustive definition in some speculative fashion: '[t]hey take shape from the context in which they are applied'.[15] What exactly will count as an arbitrary decision is debatable. Legal arbitrariness is strongly contextual, heavily dependent upon differences in standards and meanings, and the different purposes and interests which are at stake within particular cases.[16] Indeed, it would itself be arbitrary to draw too sharp a distinction between reasonableness, relevance, and fairness, given the connections that exist between rational behaviour, the practice of taking into account relevant considerations (and refusing to take into account irrelevant considerations), and adhering to proper procedures of adjudication. Due process demands not just procedural fairness but also a reasonable and fair-minded decision which is in conformity with constitutional principle.[17]

This is particularly evident in review for wrongful discrimination. It is now well established that wrongful or unjustifiably discriminatory decisions are unlawfully arbitrary. In *Slattery v Naylor*,[18] Lord Hobhouse noted that the court may set aside some bye-laws as unreasonable 'such, for instance, as a bye-law providing that the Roman Catholic cemetery should be closed to the Roman Catholic community, but remain available for others', or if it were 'capricious or oppressive'.[19] Similarly, in *Kruse v Johnson*,[20] Lord Russell suggested that bye-laws would be unlawful '[i]f, for instance, they were found to be partial and unequal in their operation as between different classes'.[21] Subsequent judicial dicta have indicated that wrongfully discriminatory policies are prohibited by the common law doctrine of rationality. For example, Lord Hoffmann, in *Matadeen v Pointu*, notes that 'treating like cases alike and unlike cases differently is a general axiom of rational behaviour. It is, for example, frequently invoked by the courts in proceedings for judicial review as a ground for holding some administrative act to have been irrational.'[22] As Lord Sumption notes in *R (Rotherham Metropolitan Borough Council) v Secretary of State for Business, Innovation and Skills*, a commitment to treating like cases alike absent objective justification for doing otherwise is 'fundamental to any rational system of law'.[23]

[14] Allan, *Law, Liberty, and Justice: The Legal Foundations of British Constitutionalism* (n 7) 21.

[15] M Elliot and R Thomas, *Public Law*, 3rd edn (Oxford University Press, 2017) 497.

[16] R Wright, 'Arbitrariness: Why the Most Important Idea in Administrative Law Can't Be Defined, and What This Means for the Law in General' (2010) 44 *University of Richmond Law Review* 839.

[17] Allan, *The Sovereignty of Law* (n 13) 252–53.

[18] *Slattery v Naylor* (1888) 13 AC 446.

[19] ibid 453.

[20] *Kruse v Johnson* [1898] 2 QB 91.

[21] ibid 99.

[22] *Matadeen v Pointu* [1999] 1 AC 98, [8].

[23] *R (Rotherham Metropolitan Borough Council) v Secretary of State for Business, Innovation and Skills* [2015] UKSC 6, [26].

In addition, McCombe J concluded in *Gurung v Ministry of Defence* that unjustifiable racial or ethnic distinctions were 'irrational and inconsistent with the principle of equality that is the cornerstone of our law'.[24] Further still, Lady Hale evidently endorsed a strong connection between requirements of non-discrimination and broader constitutional principle in the Belmarsh case,[25] echoing her previous statement that 'democracy is founded on the principle that each individual has equal value'.[26] Similarly, Lord Bingham has suggested that laws which discriminate on status grounds such as race and sex cannot be based on 'objective differences', and as such violate the rule of law.[27] Unjustifiably treating one person or group less favourably than another lacks a rational foundation. Often such conduct is described as motivated by prejudice, bias and other kinds of 'bad faith' reasoning.[28] However, while animus or bad motive is sometimes present in such cases, it is not necessary for a decision to be wrongfully discriminatory. To establish discrimination, it is sufficient for there to be a disparity in treatment. Then, a question of justification will arise that might lead to a conclusion of unreasonableness and therefore wrongfulness. As Daly argues, this would amount to an 'indicium' of irrationality which would generate a presumption of unreasonableness and demand some objective justification.[29]

While judicial scrutiny of wrongful discrimination is usually covered under the auspices of reasonableness review, it can also violate the procedural requirement to take relevant considerations into account and to avoid taking irrelevant considerations into account. This should come as no surprise; often the most blatant examples of wrongful discrimination concern the incorporation of specific characteristics such as race or sex into one's decision-making where there is no justifiable reason to do so. However, many other decisions falling foul of the relevancy requirement are instances of wrongful discrimination, albeit not what we might commonly associate with discrimination, given the general focus that commentators have on the list of protected characteristics contained in legislation.

Since the common law is not confined by any finite list of protected characteristics, our determination of wrongful discrimination must rest on an assessment of the justifiability of treating some person or group less favourably than another on the basis of some property. When an irrelevant consideration is taken into account or a relevant one is not taken into account, an administrative decision will be unlawful.[30] In circumstances where the consideration in question

[24] *Gurung v Ministry of Defence* [2002] EWHC 2463 (Admin), [55]. See also M Foran, 'The Cornerstone of Our Law: Equality, Consistency, and Judicial Review' (2022) 81 *Cambridge Law Journal* 249.

[25] *A v Secretary of State for the Home Dept* [2004] UKHL 56, [237]–[238].

[26] *Ghaidan v Godin-Mendoza* [2004] UKHL 30, para 132. See also *R v Immigration Appeal Tribunal, ex p Manshoora Begum* [1986] Imm AR 385.

[27] T Bingham, *The Rule of Law* (Allen Lane, 2010) Ch 5.

[28] B Hale, 'The Quest for Equal Treatment' [2005] *Public Law* 571.

[29] P Daly, 'Wednesbury's Reason and Structure' [2011] *Public Law* 237.

[30] *Hanks v Minister of Housing and Local Government* [1963] 1 QB 999; *Padfield v Minister of Agriculture, Fisheries and Food* [1968] AC 997.

relates to some property of the claimant, say their height or their hair colour or the fact that they are not a relative of the decision-maker, the court, in concluding that the decision in question is unlawful, has also concluded that it amounts to wrongful discrimination. Indeed, the classic example of *Wednesbury* unreasonableness is a decision of exactly this kind: 'the red-haired teacher, dismissed because she had red hair'.[31]

Thus, it is clear that multiple grounds of review may obtain in circumstances where a wrongfully discriminatory decision has been made. Indeed, Lord Greene, in *Wednesbury*, was quite right to stress that these grounds are often hard to clearly distinguish, noting that dismissing the red-haired teacher 'is unreasonable in one sense. In another sense it is taking into consideration extraneous matters. It is so unreasonable that it might almost be described as being done in bad faith; and, in fact, all these things run into one another'.[32] Acting for improper purposes, acting in bad faith, and engaging in *Wednesbury* unreasonableness all amount to instances of acting on irrelevant considerations and, should these instances treat some less favourably than others on the basis of some property they have, will also amount to unlawful discrimination.

In articulating the grounds for review, Lord Greene can be seen to express the familiar juxtaposition between the rule of law and arbitrariness: an unlawful decision, as determined through the established processes of judicial review, is necessarily unreasonable. A failure to follow proper procedure or to comply with requirements of relevancy is something no reasonable *public authority* can lawfully do. Even if those in the position of a public official may have good reason to disregard their legal obligations, to do so is to no longer act in a public role. The distinction between public and private reasonableness is illuminating in this context: an individual may have good reasons for embezzling public funds for their private gain. As immoral as such conduct is, it cannot be described as irrational in the sense that it is devoid of logic.[33] It is nevertheless unlawful because there is no *public* reason, compatible with the rule of law, to justify it.[34] Reasonableness is, in this context, a common law construct, informed by legal principle and the rule of law, and a general descriptor of the grounds of review as a whole; it 'expresses the *conclusion* of legal analysis, which encompasses all the relevant rule-of-law criteria as they apply to the facts or circumstances in view'.[35] The requirements of rationality are not simply requirements that public officials act in a logical manner; they must also be justified in that they act to further the common good, eschewing private gain in favour of public service.

[31] *Associated Provincial Picture House Ltd v Wednesbury Corpn* [1948] 1 KB 223, 229. See also Warrington LJ in *Short v Poole Corpn* [1926] Ch 66, 90, 91.

[32] ibid.

[33] Except insofar as one sees any immoral action as irrational by virtue of its unjustifiability.

[34] In the statutory context, discretion must be exercised only 'to promote the policy and objects of the Act' in question: *Padfield v Minister of Agriculture* [1968] AC 997, 1030.

[35] Allan, *The Sovereignty of Law* (n 13) 113.

II. AN OVERLY RESTRICTIVE STANDARD?

Notwithstanding the above, there remains the concern that reasonableness review is not an appropriate avenue for dealing with wrongful forms of discrimination, primarily because rationality seemingly cannot fully encapsulate the deeper concerns animating the principle of equal dignity from which non-discrimination derives. In addition to this, there is the concern that the nature of rationality review leads too quickly to the perception that discriminatory practices, particularly those based on prevailing biases and stereotypes, are perfectly rational, given the prevalence of bias and embedded assumptions in the broader social sphere within which the court operates.[36] This, coupled with a perceived reluctance of the court to invalidate a decision unless it is on the extreme end of unreasonableness, leads to the conclusion that some innovation is warranted if the common law is to live up to this ideal. This critique is intelligible only if we draw a sharp distinction between reasonableness (substantive) review and procedural review, a distinction which Lord Greene seemed to reject and which it would be wise to question.[37]

It is a mistake to presume that the court has exclusively confined itself to asking whether a decision is 'so unreasonable that no reasonable authority could ever have come to it',[38] or whether it is one 'which is so outrageous in its defiance of logic or of accepted moral standards that no sensible person who had applied his mind to the question to be decided could have arrived at it'.[39] This standard, *Wednesbury* unreasonableness, is but one instantiation of the principles of judicial review, all of which amount to a form of unreasonableness, once reasonableness is properly understood within its constitutional context.[40]

There seems to be a disconnect between this narrow conception of unreasonableness and the underlying commitment to legal equality which explains why decisions found to be 'partial and unequal in their operation as between different classes', or 'capricious and oppressive' are unlawful.[41] Nowhere is this more evident than in *R v Ministry of Defence, ex p Smith*.[42] This case concerned the lawfulness of dismissing members of the British Armed Forces solely on the grounds of their sexual orientation. The government's policy was that homosexuality was incompatible with service in the Armed Forces. Service personnel who were known to be homosexual or who were known to have engaged in homosexual activity were administratively discharged. While this case predated the Human Rights Act 1998, Lord Bingham in the Court of Appeal placed

[36] See McColgan (n 9) 12.
[37] See Allan, *The Sovereignty of Law* (n 13) Ch 7.
[38] *Associated Provincial Picture Houses Ltd v Wednesbury Corpn* [1948] 1 KB 223, 230.
[39] *Council of Civil Service Unions v Minister for the Civil Service* [1985] AC 374, 410.
[40] Mark Elliott makes a similar argument with regards to the *Ultra Vires* doctrine: Elliott, 'The Ultra Vires Doctrine in a Constitutional Setting' (n 6).
[41] *Kruse v Johnson* [1898] 2 QB 91, 99; *Slattery v Naylor* (1888) 13 App Cas 446, 453.
[42] *R v Ministry of Defence, ex p Smith* [1996] QB 517.

weight on the fact that the claimants' 'rights as human beings' were 'very much in issue', at the very least gesturing towards the common law commitment to equal dignity.[43] This indicated the need for a more searching form of review than appeared to be the standard in *Wednesbury*: 'The more substantial the interference with human rights, the more the court will require by way of justification before it is satisfied that the decision is reasonable.'[44] One way of explaining the reason behind this is that there is a presumption that reasonable people do not infringe upon human rights without good reason.[45] However, this would reveal a common misunderstanding concerning rationality review: the belief that the assessment of the lawfulness of administrative action is determined by reference to standards applicable to private actors. It makes little difference whether reasonable *people* would infringe upon fundamental rights; what matters is whether a reasonable *public authority* would do so. It must not be forgotten that reasonableness, in this context, is a legal standard, determined by reference to constitutional principle, not every-day meaning.[46] Craig is thus mistaken to assume that a decision is even capable of being reasonable if it is based on a legally irrelevant consideration or pursued outside of its statutory remit.[47]

Indeed, this elision between constitutional and other standards of reasonableness lies at the heart of the *Smith* judgment. The court accepted that the government's justification for the ban – that military effectiveness and morale would be undermined by the presence of homosexual personnel – was unconvincing, reflecting a 'wrong view … that rests too firmly upon the supposition of prejudice in others and which insufficiently recognises the damage to human rights inflicted'.[48] However, it nevertheless concluded that the policy was not unlawful because it was supported by both Houses of Parliament and 'reflected the overwhelming consensus of service and official opinion'.[49]

It seems the court simultaneously confined itself to assessing only for extreme defiance of logic or moral standards while also empowered and, indeed, obligated to review for breach of constitutional principle, given the presumption that Parliament intends administrative agencies to adhere to the rule of law. The lawfulness of administrative action cannot depend on whether members of government support their own policies. Reasonableness review, as the court itself

[43] ibid 556.

[44] ibid 554. See also *R (Gurung) v Secretary of State for the Defence* [2008] EWHC 1496 (Admin), [54], [60].

[45] Elliott and Thomas (n 15) 541.

[46] M Foran, 'The Constitutional Foundations of Reasonableness Review: Artificial Reason and Wrongful Discrimination' (2022) 26 *Edinburgh Law Review* 295.

[47] P Craig, 'The Nature of Reasonableness Review' (2013) 66 *Current Legal Problems* 131, 136. The sharp demarcation between relevancy and reasonableness review must be rejected as inaccurate. While Craig is correct to stress that considerations of weight are relevant for reasonableness review, it is not the case that considerations of relevancy are sharply removed to some antecedent deliberation prior to reasonableness review.

[48] *R v Ministry of Defence, ex p Smith* [1996] QB 517, 540.

[49] ibid 553.

accepted, concerns whether the decision is beyond the range of responses open to a reasonable decision-maker.[50] That range cannot depend on what responses the government, or even both Houses of (but not the King in) Parliament, thinks a reasonable decision-maker would make. As Allan stresses, 'The court's own appraisal should be independent and impartial, bowing to official opinion only when it falls within a legitimate range of balanced judgement, focused on the rights in question.'[51]

If the court is going to accept that the justification offered for the ban was unconvincing, too firmly reliant upon the prejudice of others, and insufficiently attuned to the legal rights at issue, then it cannot decide that, as a matter of public policy, it has parliamentary support and for that reason it is lawful. To do so would be to collapse review for lawfulness into an assessment of the political merits of the policy in question. Even on the most extreme reading of the ultra vires school of judicial review, it is the Crown in Parliament that is Sovereign, and it is only through legislation, interpreted by the courts, that the sovereign will is known. Executive policy is not, as a matter of constitutional principle, immune from constraints of reasonableness, even if supported by both Houses. In the court's interpretation, the general requirement that discretionary powers should be exercised in accordance with the rule of law is presumed to be the sovereign intention of the Crown in Parliament, even if the detailed grounds of review are supplied by the common law.[52]

Lord Bingham is correct to distinguish the court's role from that of the 'primary decision-maker' who can rely on purely consequentialist reasoning and many other kinds of considerations it would be improper for the court to engage in. It was 'not the constitutional role of the court to regulate the conditions of service in the armed forces of the Crown'; but the court is nevertheless bound by 'the constitutional role and duty of ensuring that the rights of citizens are not abused by the unlawful exercise of executive power'.[53] In focusing on parliamentary support for a policy as a metric of assessing its lawfulness, the court in *Smith* erred, ignoring its stated assessment that the justification offered was not sufficient, and confused a legal standard of reasonableness with official (but not sovereign) opinion.

The issue with *Smith* was not a failure of reasonableness review. It was a failure to adequately account for both context and constitutional principle: 'we should not confuse the propriety of the test with the bungled application of it'.[54] Nor should we fall into the orthodox trap of presuming that proportionality review would or does dictate a wholly different standard of review from

[50] ibid 554 (endorsing counsel's formulation of the correct approach).

[51] Allan, *The Sovereignty of Law* (n 13) 245.

[52] M Elliott, *The Constitutional Foundations of Judicial Review* (Hart Publishing, 2001) Ch 4; Allan, *The Sovereignty of Law* (n 13) 225.

[53] *R v Ministry of Defence, ex p Smith* [1996] QB 517, 556.

[54] Allan, *The Sovereignty of Law* (n 13) 248.

reasonableness review. The recognition in *Smith* of the important weight that fundamental rights must have in reasonableness review blurs any neat distinction between it and proportionality review and renders it, at most, a distinction of degree and not kind.[55]

Separating the grounds of judicial review into distinct categories is misguided and leads to the presumption that reasonableness review is confined to only the most extreme of cases. It suggests that the judiciary may only interfere with a public authority that has lost its mind and defied all logic. Indeed, it has resulted in judges suggesting that the law has changed or needs to change to strengthen its assessment of discretionary powers.[56]

The courts have never been so restricted in their assessment of the legality of administrative action. Reasonableness is a common law construct, reflective of legal principle and necessarily attuned to context. There is a significant difference between reviewing the regulation of cinemas by a local authority and reviewing the detention of a person without trial. *Habeas corpus* is not confined to those detentions which are made by someone who has completely defied all logic or moral standards. Indeed, if we recall *Kruse v Johnson*, decisions may be quashed not simply because they 'could find no justification in the minds of reasonable men', but because they were 'partial and unequal in their operation as between different classes, if they were manifestly unjust, if they disclosed bad faith, if they involved such oppressive or gratuitous interference with the rights of those subject to them' *such that* there could be no reasonable justification for them.[57] It is the failure of an administrative body to adhere to the rule of law and to respect fundamental common law rights that gives rise to the conclusion that no reasonable public authority would make such a decision. Where fundamental rights are not threatened, the court's assessment of reasonableness may be different, and it may be more inclined to look only to whether there is an appropriate connection between means and ends or whether the decision was consistent with statute.[58]

Similarly, in *R v Home Secretary, ex p Khawaja*, the House of Lords reviewed the decision of an immigration officer as to whether a person could be classed as an illegal immigrant.[59] In so doing, it did not ask whether the decision was one which no reasonable person could have made. Indeed, it explicitly rejected the application of such a stringent standard: 'Such exclusion of the power and duty of the courts runs counter to the development of the

[55] ibid 246; M Elliott, 'The Human Rights Act 1998 and the Standard of Substantive Review' (2001) 60(2) *Cambridge Law Journal* 301, 311–15.

[56] See *Kennedy v Charity Commission* [2014] UKSC 20, [54]; *R (Sandiford) v Secretary of State for Foreign and Commonwealth Affairs* [2014] UKSC 44, [66]; *Pham v Home Secretary* [2015] UKSC 19, [113]; *Keyu v Foreign Secretary* [2015] UKSC 69, [132], [303]–[304]; *Youssef v Foreign Secretary* [2016] UKSC 3 [51]–[61].

[57] *Kruse v Johnson* [1898] 2 QB 91, 99–100.

[58] See Daly (n 29).

[59] *R v Home Secretary, ex p Khawaja* [1984] AC 74.

safeguards which our law provides for the liberty of the subject.'[60] Discussing *Wednesbury* unreasonableness, Lord Scarman noted that it 'is undoubtedly correct in cases where it is appropriate'.[61] Where fundamental rights to liberty or legal equality are threatened, the court is obliged to ensure that a public body is not simply *sane*, but *justified* in its actions. Such standards are essential to the common law and do not arise solely as a result of the European Convention on Human Rights, as is evidenced by Blake J in *Limbu*: 'the common law and Convention principle essentially walk hand in hand together, although the common law principle [of equality] has to be applied through the public law doctrine of rationality'.[62]

This does not mean that the court may substitute its own judgement for the judgement of the primary decision-maker. Review must be done to ensure that administrative authority is exercised in accordance with legal principle, but the court may not step in simply because it disagrees. It must point to a justified standard of lawfulness; a *kind* of unreasonableness that is recognised at law. But this is exactly what the court did in *Smith*, while nevertheless refusing to quash the discriminatory policy. If, as the court stated in *Wednesbury*, unreasonableness includes the failure to adequately account for relevant considerations, it makes no sense for the court in *Smith* to conclude both that the rights of the claimants were not adequately accounted for and that the policy was nevertheless reasonable.

III. REASONABLENESS AND RATIONALITY

One way of explaining the difficulty presented here is to draw a distinction between 'unreasonableness' as a breach of common law principle which provides normative grounding for certain aspects of judicial review and 'irrationality' as a particular form of unreasonableness that fits somewhere on the extreme end of the spectrum between legally justified decisions and those with no reasonable justification whatsoever. Indeed, this maps onto the tendency of the court to refer to *Wednesbury* unreasonableness as irrationality.[63]

Again, irrationality must be understood as a common law construct, even in this context. According to its ordinary meaning, an irrational decision is one that is inexplicable, devoid of any intelligible purpose. However, to the English public lawyer, an irrational decision is defined, in part, by reference to constitutional

[60] ibid 109–10.

[61] ibid 109.

[62] *R (on the application of Limbu) v Secretary of State for the Home Department* [2008] EWHC 2261 (Admin), [50].

[63] See eg *Council of Civil Service Unions v Minister for the Civil Service* [1985] AC 374, 410; *R v Minister of Defence, ex p Walker* [2000] 1 WLR 806, 812, 816; *Tesco Stores v Environment Secretary* [1995] 1 WLR 759, 780; *R (McDonald) v Kensington and Chelsea Royal LBC* [2011] UKSC 33, [28].

principles which preclude certain considerations or purposes from the realm of legitimate considerations or purposes that a public authority my adopt. Many of these considerations or purposes may be perfectly intelligible.

Imagine if the government has decided not to employ members of a racial or cultural minority in the police force because it is aware of the prejudicial attitudes of the majority of the populace and fears that police officers from non-majority backgrounds would be less effective, at heightened risk of assault, and liable to lead to a widespread breakdown of trust between the state and the general populace. Let us assume that these fears are likely to come to pass should members of minority groups be admitted into the police force. In this case, a decision to preclude certain applicants because of their race or skin colour would manifestly be discriminatory.[64] But is it arbitrary? It seems that, far from being based on irrational or irrelevant considerations such as prejudicial or stereotypical beliefs concerning these minority groups, the government is acting on what might be seen as perfectly relevant considerations relating to efficiency, safety, and public order. Thus, it would be odd to conclude that this is an example of arbitrary decision-making, even where there is a general presumption that racial distinctions are arbitrary. Yet, such a decision would most definitely be quashed as unreasonable and unlawful.[65] We can make sense of this only if we recognise that rationality and reasonableness are not understood by the court in abstraction from constitutional principle. What matters is whether the decision in question took into account all relevant legal considerations and ignored legally irrelevant ones. But an important legal consideration is the moral equality of persons, the cornerstone of our law.[66]

Another example may be useful, this time from a recent case. In *R (on the application of Adath Yisrole Burial Society) v HM Senior Coroner for Inner North London*, the High Court held that a religiously discriminatory policy was, by that virtue, incapable of rational justification.[67] The claimants, a charitable organisation responsible for managing and facilitating the burials of a large proportion of the orthodox Jewish community in Inner North London, and an elderly Jewish woman resident in the area, challenged the lawfulness of a policy adopted by the defendant which stated that:

> No death will be prioritised in any way over any other because of the religion of the deceased or family, either by the coroner's officers or coroners.[68]

[64] This is so despite no evidence of discriminatory intent. See Hepple (n 9) 17–31, 175–76.

[65] It might be noted that the facts in this hypothetical example bear some similarities to the *Smith* case, further supporting the argument that the court erred in relying on institutional homophobia as a legitimate defence to the policy in question. It is quite unlikely, given the decision in *Gurung*, that a prevalence of racism would be enough to justify a similar policy.

[66] Foran (n 24).

[67] *R (on the application of Adath Yisrole Burial Society) v HM Senior Coroner for Inner North London* [2018] EWHC 969 (Admin).

[68] ibid [2].

The policy in question was described as a 'cab rank rule' and 'an equality protocol'.[69] The purpose of the policy (for there evidently was a purpose) was to 'ensure that the bereaved whose loved ones fall within the remit of HM Coroner for Inner North London are treated fairly, and the best use is made of overall of ... inadequate resources'.[70] The reasoning here (for there evidently was cogent reasoning) was that it would be unfair and unjust to 'prioritise one sector of the community above others' and that previous policies allowing Jewish families to engage in 'queue jumping places those who are pushed back further in the queue at a material disadvantage'.[71]

So, we have a policy which seems to be rationally connected to a legitimate purpose that a coroner might have – ensuring that the bereaved are treated fairly given a lack of resources. The policy is defended on the basis of cogent reasoning grounded in considerations of fairness. Against this, we have the claimant's argument that 'for certain faith groups, in particular the Jewish faith and the Muslim faith, it is very important that a funeral should take place as soon as possible, ideally on the day of death itself'.[72] They claimed that a failure to adopt a more nuanced and flexible policy was wrongfully discriminatory and unreasonable. What is a court to make of this? If we adopt an uncontextualised reading of the *Wednesbury* unreasonableness doctrine, then it is very difficult to see how this policy is 'so unreasonable that no reasonable authority could ever have come to it'.[73] Nevertheless, attuned to context as the Court must inevitably be, it concluded that the policy:

> precludes taking into account representations which have a religious basis and it thereby singles out religious beliefs for exclusion from consideration. There is no good reason for this exclusion. It is discriminatory and incapable of rational justification.[74]

It is interesting that the court began by noting that the pertinent question in this instance is whether the policy is 'capable of rational justification' but then concludes that it is the fact that the policy is not grounded in *good* reason that renders it incapable of rational justification. Clearly there are some reasons that could be offered to justify the policy. Indeed, some of those reasons are grounded in an equality framework and the value of equal treatment. However, the court is not assessing whether there are *any* reasons that might justify the policy; it is concerned with reasons which are themselves compatible with constitutional principle. It is lawfulness, not persuasiveness, that the court is reviewing for.

[69] ibid.
[70] ibid [45].
[71] ibid [50].
[72] ibid [58].
[73] *Associated Provincial Picture Houses Ltd v Wednesbury Corpn* [1948] 1 KB 223, 230.
[74] *R (on the application of Adath Yisrole Burial Society) v HM Senior Coroner for Inner North London* [2018] EWHC 969 (Admin), [91].

A blanket ban on considerations arising from religious belief may treat people equally, but it does not treat them as equals. It does not take irrationality in the lay sense before the courts will declare a decision or policy to be unlawful by virtue of its unreasonableness. Rationality review, or *Wednesbury* unreasonableness, occurs when a decision 'is *so* unreasonable that even though the administrative authority has a wide discretionary power … it is no breach of comity for judges to interfere with its exercise'.[75] It would therefore be incomplete to describe a decision as 'irrational' if the reasoning 'reveals no true flaw of logic but rather an inadmissible or collateral purpose'.[76]

This willingness to probe beyond review for absurdity is not a recent development of the common law. As far back as *Rooke v Withers*, the courts have limited administrative discretion with 'the rule of reason and Law'.[77] This case concerned a statutory scheme authorising an administrative agency to survey banks and ditches and other flood defences in need of repair, to build or repair according to their discretion and to charge landowners the cost of doing so as seemed most convenient. The agency repaired a bank along the Thames estuary and charged Mr Rooke the cost. He owned seven acres of meadow along the riverside where the repairs were made. However, Rooke was not the only landowner who benefited from these repairs: some 800 acres of land were at risk of flooding and many landowners put at risk if the bank was not repaired. Was it reasonable for the agency to place this financial burden on Rooke and Rooke alone? Sir Edward Coke concluded that it was not. Part of his reasoning for finding as such was that it was radically unfair to charge someone for the full cost of repairs when they occupy less than 1% of the land that benefited from the works.

A significant factor in this decision was undoubtedly the fact that the decision in question was to take Rooke's property. Such a threat to common law rights warrants more searching judicial review than a test for mere rationality understood in the lay sense. Given this, the decision was unreasonable in the *Wednesbury* sense: no reasonable authority would require the occupier of less than one per cent of the land to cover the costs of saving 807 acres. But this does not mean that the decision was irrational in the lay sense of that term. Rooke had been maintaining the bank before the task was brought under the purview of the government. It makes perfect sense to maintain the status quo, particularly when it would be easier to collect the cost of maintenance in one lump sum from one person. So, there were intelligible reasons behind the decision; there was both purpose and logic to it. And still, the radical unfairness rendered it unlawful.

[75] T Endicott, *Administrative Law*, 4th edn (Oxford University Press, 2018) 246.

[76] *R (Bancoult) v Foreign Secretary (No 2)* [2007] EWCA Civ 498 [59], per Sedley LJ. See also Craig (n 47) 136.

[77] *Rooke v Withers* (1597) 5 Co Rep 99, 100a.

IV. DEMEANING DISCRIMINATION AS DISTINCT FROM INCONSISTENCY

Sir Jeffrey Jowell, in 1994, argued that the moral equality of persons has become an established value within the British constitution and that the courts should be more explicit in their reliance on it to develop the common law.[78] In particular, he argued that the common law should give effect to the 'equality principle' in its supervision of public authorities, precluding them from acting in a way that fails to adequately respect the equal status of legal subjects.[79] But what is more, Jowell also argued that this principle of legal equality should manifest as a free-standing ground of judicial review, rather than operating as a 'well-disguised rabbit to be hauled occasionally out of the *Wednesbury* hat'.[80] This approach has gained some traction among public law scholars working on this topic. As will be clear from the previous sections in this chapter, the central thrust of this critique is grounded in the mistaken conception of common law reasonableness as a test for manifest absurdity. Instances, such as *Smith*, where the court has confined its analysis to an overly restrictive assessment of mere logic or whether the policy in question has ministerial support manifest a failure to live up to internal legal standards committed to respecting equal dignity.

Once analysis includes common law principle, it becomes clear that reasonableness review, even *Wednesbury* unreasonableness, must be attuned to moral as well as factual standards of reasonableness.[81] Common law values are central to our understanding of both fairness and relevancy. These values evidently include a commitment to respecting the dignity and autonomy of persons. It is only then that we can make sense of the common law position that decisions will be unlawful by virtue of unreasonableness if they are 'capricious or oppressive',[82] if they are 'found to be partial and unequal in their operation as between different classes',[83] or if they are 'inconsistent with the principle of equality that is the cornerstone of our law'.[84]

Within this analysis, it is important to be clear about the different kinds of wrongful discrimination and how they may render an administrative action unlawful. It has been established that wrongful discrimination can generally be covered under existing principles of judicial review because, very often, it is a failure to conform to the principles of due process, relevancy, and reasonableness that renders a discriminatory decision wrongful in the first place. In this sense, we can conclude that wrongful discrimination breaches the rule of law, given that the rule of law ultimately grounds and justifies judicial review

[78] J Jowell, 'Is Equality a Constitutional Principle?' (1994) 7 *Current Legal Problems* 1.

[79] ibid 18.

[80] ibid 14.

[81] On whether discrimination can be morally arbitrary even when it is not factually arbitrary, see P Singer, 'Is Racial Discrimination Arbitrary?' (1978) 8 *Moral Matters* 185.

[82] *Slattery v Naylor* (1888) 13 App Cas 446, 453.

[83] *Kruse v Johnson* [1898] 2 QB 91, 99.

[84] *Gurung v Ministry of Defence* [2002] EWHC 2463 (Admin), para 55.

of administrative wrongdoing.[85] There remains the separate issue of whether a commitment to legal equality could itself be operative in a determination that an administrative action is unlawful by virtue of its unreasonableness. It would be here where the concept of demeaning discrimination mentioned in the previous chapter would become salient. The case law discussed above seems to suggest that demeaning discrimination on the part of a public body would be unlawful precisely because it is capricious or oppressive. If we conceive of reasonableness as an umbrella term for the various grounds of review, it may be the case that demeaning discrimination, to the extent that it cannot be covered under existing grounds of review, is nevertheless unlawful. On this view, unreasonableness and disproportionality, when they occur against the backdrop of lawful conduct, amount to breaches of the equal dignity of those affected. As Allan argues:

> A disproportionate interference with constitutional rights, having regard to the relative urgency of countervailing public interests, is a denial of the equal status of those affected: it is *unreasonable* (or irrational) in its primary legal sense of failing to accord equal respect to all those persons subject to the jurisdiction of the relevant public authority.[86]

Whether demeaning discrimination needs to be covered under a separate ground of review depends on how we conceptualise common law unreasonableness. If we follow Allan and see this as the culmination of our constitutional deliberation rather than the starting point,[87] then perhaps we already have grounds for review that include concerns for legal equality, albeit demonstrative of a hitherto underemphasised connection between unlawfulness and inequality. On that reading, the unreasonableness of firing a schoolteacher for having red hair is derived from a broader constitutional commitment to moral equality.

It may be desirable, for clarity's sake, to explicitly set out demeaning discrimination as a ground for review. However, this would not require anything drastic in the realm of common law evolution. Rather, all that would be required is the acknowledgement that reasonableness review includes constitutional standards and that legal equality is one of them.

As such, we can say that discriminating in such a way that it demeans or treats persons as inferiors in some way can be prohibited as unreasonable whether or not it is recognised as a separate ground of review. Nevertheless, there remains an additional distinction that has caused some confusion among scholars attempting to make sense of the role of discrimination within judicial review. One could point to the courts' repeated insistence that *equal treatment* is

[85] See TRS Allan, 'Constitutional Dialogue and the Justification of Judicial Review' (2003) 23 *Oxford Journal of Legal Studies* 563; Allan, 'The Constitutional Foundations of Judicial Review: Conceptual Conundrum or Interpretative Inquiry' (n 6); Elliott, *The Constitutional Foundations of Judicial Review* (n 52); Craig (n 6).

[86] TRS Allan, 'The Moral Unity of Public Law' (2017) 67 *University of Toronto Law Journal* 1, 2; see also Allan, *The Sovereignty of Law* (n 13) Ch 3.

[87] Allan, *The Sovereignty of Law* (n 13) 113.

not a separate ground of review and infer from this that executive action cannot be reviewed on equality-based grounds.[88] However, as has been explained in Chapter 2 above, while legal equality is an important constitutional standard, this does not mean that there is a general ground of review for inconsistency or a right to equal treatment.

Legal equality, through the presumption that persons are moral equals, demands appropriate justification for departures from equal treatment. So long as this is compatible with the value of equal dignity, it is generally not, for that reason alone, subject to judicial review. Equally, however, the fact that inconsistency is not a separate ground of review does not mean that the demands of equal dignity cannot manifest within the principles of judicial review. It must always be remembered that equal treatment is ultimately derived from the deeper commitment to treating persons *as equals*. The court in *Gallaher* was thus entirely correct to reject consistency as an independent ground of review. But this has very little to say about the place of demeaning discrimination in assessing the lawfulness of an administrative action. Treating a person or group as an inferior, through capriciousness or oppression is evidently unreasonable, even if it might be rational in the lay sense that it is not manifestly absurd.

Lord Hoffmann offers an alternative account in *R (Carson) v Work and Pensions Secretary*.[89] Here he notes that determinations as to whether cases are relevantly similar are partly a matter of values and partly a matter of rationality.[90] As such, a principle that like cases should be treated alike involves both a commitment to notions of 'the respect due to the individual' and a commitment to drawing distinctions on rational and relevant grounds. This being the case, however, he argues that it may be rational to prefer to employ men over women because more women than men choose to leave employment to take up childcare responsibilities.[91] Importantly, Lord Hoffmann stresses that, while the courts, 'as guardians of the right of the individual to equal respect', will carefully examine the reasons offered to justify distinctions which violate the respect due to individuals, the determination of what counts as an irrelevant consideration is ultimately to be left to the elected representatives of the people.[92] Lord Hoffmann, in this analysis, has made the crucial error of presuming that rationality and reasonableness can be determined in abstraction from constitutional principle. He is right that the principle that like cases should be treated alike does not automatically give rise to a principle of equal dignity. However, he is wrong to draw such a sharp distinction between the constitutional requirement of equal respect and the notion of legal rationality. He is also mistaken to

[88] See *R (on the application of Gallaher Group Ltd and others) v The Competition and Markets Authority* [2018] UKSC 25, [24]; *Matadeen v Pointu* [1999] 1 AC 98, [9]; *R (O'Brien) v Independent Assessor* [2007] 2 AC 312, [30].

[89] *R (Carson) v Work and Pensions Secretary* [2005] UKHL 37.

[90] ibid [15].

[91] ibid [16].

[92] ibid [16]–[17].

presume that all of these concerns are grounded in the principle that like cases should be treated alike, given that this principle is itself derived from the more foundational commitment to legal equality.

It is important to note that the standard in *Slattery v Naylor* is one which renders decisions unlawful if they are capricious *or* oppressive. Motive is not of primary concern here; what matters is whether, through malice or negligence, someone is treated in a manner which fails to adequately respect their equal dignity. Thus, while capricious motive is sufficient to establish unlawfulness, it is not necessary. Oppression in this context must be read consistently with common law principles and rights such that their breach will amount to oppressive and unreasonable conduct. The principle of equality that is the cornerstone of our law is not one which demands equal treatment in all contexts. Rather, it demands appropriate respect for the equal dignity of persons in the justification of departures from consistent treatment. Judicial review generally captures this standard through reasonableness review, should reasonableness be understood within its appropriate constitutional context. There is, however, another way in which concern for wrongful discrimination manifests within judicial review.

V. THE RULE AGAINST BIAS AND THE IMPORTANCE OF EXPRESSION

To act in conformity with the rule of law, decision-makers must respect the principles of natural justice and due process. While this requirement may be defended on purely instrumental grounds relating to the likelihood that this will produce better decisions overall,[93] the rule of law provides a foundational defence which focuses on the demands of human dignity. To properly be respected as an autonomous moral agent, as legality requires, one must be treated fairly and impartially, without fear of bias or undue favour.[94] Under the common law, bias amounts to an improper attitude which predisposes an authority to decide against a party's interests, regardless of the merits of the case itself. A biased decision-maker 'unfairly regard(s) … with favour, or disfavour, the case of a party to the issue under consideration by him'.[95]

We can recall from the previous chapter that discrimination may be wrongful depending on the attitude that one holds or expresses while discriminating. In general, bias in this context amounts to the unfair prejudgement of a case.[96] Prejudgement arises from the connection between a biased attitude – one which, among other things, may manifest a failure to respect moral equality – and

[93] See DJ Galligan, *Due Process and Fair Procedures: A Study of Administrative Procedures* (Oxford University Press, 1996). See also *Secretary of State for the Home Department v AF (No 3)* [2009] UKHL 28, [60], per Lord Philips; *Raji v General Medical Council* [2003] UKPC 24, [13].

[94] See TRS Allan, 'Procedural Fairness and the Duty of Respect' (1998) 18 *Oxford Journal of Legal Studies* 497.

[95] *R v Gough* [1993] AC 646, 670 (Lord Goff).

[96] *R v Cowle* (1759) 2 Burr 834, 862–63 (Lord Mansfield).

the decision-making processes which are subject to judicial review. The rule of law and the principles of natural justice prohibit sham hearings where a decision-maker will rule a particular way, regardless of what they hear by way of argument.

It should be evident that all instances of bias, especially when operative within an institutional setting such as a legal system, disrespect the equal dignity of persons by failing to treat them as individual moral agents with equal rights under law. This can occur in circumstances where the decision-maker is prejudiced or biased *against* one party by virtue of a property of theirs, or where the decision-maker is unduly *preferencing* their own or another's interests above the rights of one party. For example, a decision-maker having an improper interest in the outcome of a decision will result in the decision being quashed for lack of due process.[97] This is automatic in cases where a judge has a substantial financial interest in the case.[98] Similarly, a decision may fall foul of the rule against bias on account of the relation that the decision-maker has to one party to the dispute in question.[99] Again, this is automatic if the decision-maker is a party themselves, reflecting the 'fundamental principle … that a man may not be a judge in his own cause'.[100]

Of central concern to the rule against bias is the appearance of impartiality. As Lord Hewart famously said, 'it is not merely of some importance but is of fundamental importance that justice should not only be done, but should manifestly and undoubtedly be seen to be done'.[101] The emphasis placed upon the appearance of impartiality means that, often, decisions will be declared unlawful even if there is no actual prejudgement of a case. Thus, while a decision will be quashed if a decision-maker is actually biased, it will also be quashed if it can be shown that there is *apparent* bias. It is one thing to show that a decision-maker will personally stand to gain, financially or otherwise, from her decision; it is another thing to show that she was actually influenced by this fact.

One way of interpreting this principle is simply to focus on the difficulty of proving actual bias. However, something is missing if our concern with ensuring that justice is seen to be done arises from nothing more than evidentiary burden. Of foundational concern is the importance of both expression and perception. It is not, as Lord Goff mistakenly presumed, for the court to ask itself how *it* perceives things in determining if there is apparent bias.[102] Rather, what matters

[97] *R v Bow Street Metropolitan Stipendiary Magistrate, ex p Pinochet Ugarte (No 2)* [2000] 1 AC 119.

[98] *Locabail v Bayfield* [2000] QB 451, [50]; *Dimes v The Proprietors of the Grand Junction Canal* (1852) 3 HLC 759, 793.

[99] See eg *Re Medicaments (No 2)* [2001] EWCA Civ 1217; *Lawal v Northern Spirit* [2003] UKHL 35.

[100] *R v Bow Street Metropolitan Stipendiary Magistrate, ex p Pinochet Ugarte (No 2)* [2000] 1 AC 119, 132.

[101] *R v Sussex Justices, ex p McCarthy* [1924] 1 KB 256, 259.

[102] *R v Gough* [1993] AC 646, 670.

is 'whether the circumstances would lead a fair-minded and informed observer to conclude that there was a real possibility of bias'.[103]

Expressions and perceptions matter, and they matter legally. Knowing that a decision-maker appears to be biased against a claimant and choosing not to quash the decision is intrinsically disrespectful, even if the consequences of not quashing are minimal such that the decision itself is not actually biased. In this sense, the common law *definition* of bias is narrowly tailored to prohibit the favouring or disfavouring of one party to a particular case, and so does not include expressive wrongdoing. However, the *rule against* bias, as a common law principle, is more expansive than that and does indeed account for expressions of bias, even where there is no prejudice. Returning to the distinctions set out in the previous chapter, it is the illocutionary meaning of the decision in question (as determined by the fair-minded and informed observer) and not the perlocutionary consequences that render it unlawful according to the rule against bias.

Demeaning discrimination, therefore, can be prohibited by the rule against bias both when the decision-maker is actually prejudiced against a party and where they act in a manner which is conventionally understood to manifest bias. The state is under a positive obligation to ensure not only that it treats legal subjects with appropriate respect, but also that it is seen to treat them with respect. Legal officials, including both judges and administrative decision-makers,[104] acting in accordance with the principle of natural justice and legal equality, must therefore make appropriate efforts to consider and appreciate the social meaning that their actions may carry and to avoid acting in ways that express prejudice or denigration. It is for this reason that a decision will be quashed as biased if a judge jokes about whether an Arab sheikh would disappear on his flying carpet.[105] While it is possible for a decision-maker to make such jokes and remain free from bias or prejudice, the law will not allow such conduct to stand regardless. Similarly, taking someone's race or sex into account during the decision-making process, where there is no reasonable justification, will not only fall foul of the relevancy requirement or the principle of reasonableness, it will very likely give rise to the appearance of a real possibility of bias and breach principles of natural justice and due process.

It should be stressed, however, that, although there is a concern with the integrity and reputation of the institutions of state, the rule against bias can plausibly be interpreted to also, perhaps primarily, be concerned with demanding respect for the equal dignity of legal subjects. An expression of inferiority, as occurs where there has been demeaning discrimination, does not simply give rise

[103] *Porter v Magill* [2001] UKHL 67, [102]–[103], adapting the test in *Re Medicaments and Related Classes of Goods (No 2)* [2001] 1 WLR 700.

[104] *R v Secretary of State for the Environment, ex p Kirkstall Valley Campaign Ltd* [1996] 3 All ER 304.

[105] *El-Farargy v El Farargy* [2007] EWCA Civ 1149.

to the appearance of a real possibility of bias – although that would be sufficient to render the decision unlawful – it also wrongs those affected in a manner that cannot be explained solely by focusing on the reputation of the public body itself. A wrong has been done to the victim of prejudice which grounds a claim that can underpin the unlawfulness of a decision or action beyond simply the instrumental justification that expressing bias is bad for business.

Once one accounts for the interconnected nature of the grounds of judicial review as informed by constitutional principle, it becomes clear that wrongfully discriminatory decisions have long been prohibited by the common law. There are a number of errors that many make in their analysis of equality-based concerns as they manifest within judicial review. The first is the presumption that the court's refusal to recognise consistency as a ground of judicial review means that they will not declare an administrative decision to be unlawful if it violates the equal dignity of persons. We can see from this chapter that this is manifestly false. However, the persistence of this presumption rests on another, more prevalent presumption: that the court will only review for unreasonableness when an administrative agency has taken complete leave of its senses. It is simply not true that reasonableness review cannot or, indeed, does not cover wrongfully discriminatory and demeaning administrative decisions.

A cause of these errors may well be the tendency of scholars to focus more on distinctions and demarcations between the grounds of review than they do on the important connections which exist between them. It is in the threads that tie these grounds together under the auspices of reasonableness that we can begin to identify the principles of equal dignity. It is sometimes forgotten that constitutional principle and the rule of law inform the particularities of judicial review and not a concern with efficient administration.[106]

There is, however, another line of reasoning that leads some to conclude that existing grounds of review are inadequate in addressing equality concerns. On this view, equal dignity requires something transformative in nature. This argument will be addressed in the next chapter where the distinction between formal and substantive equality will be analysed. As valuable as these equality goals are, the limits of public law mean that such goals can only be legitimately pursued through the legislative and executive processes.[107] The role of the court in judicial review, absent statutory obligation, is to ensure the lawfulness of administrative action by reference to common law duties to refrain from unreasonable conduct. Assessing the merits of decisions by reference to state policy goals can only be done by a court where there is express legislative authorisation and obligation. However, this does not mean that the existing grounds of review are incapable of addressing the problem of wrongful discrimination.

[106] This is so, even if the justification of judicial review lies in the ultra vires doctrine. It is the common law which provides the grounds of review, even if parliament is presumed to legislate in conformity with the rule of law. See Elliott, 'The Ultra Vires Doctrine in a Constitutional Setting' (n 6).

[107] See Ch 2 above.

Once we account for the important distinction between wrongful discrimination as a breach of constitutional duty, and the pursuit of substantive equality as tied to consequentialist policy goals, it becomes clear that the common law approach to judicial review of wrongful discrimination is perfectly capable of addressing the concerns that the separation of powers permits it to address. Anything transformative beyond that must necessarily arise at the legislative and executive level and cannot be plausibly required of the principles of judicial review. To fail to respect this distinction is to collapse the important distinction between appeal and review.

6

Indirect Discrimination and Substantive Equality

When we prohibit acts of wrongful discrimination, what precisely are we trying to do? Are we seeking to protect individuals from wrongful forms of treatment? Are we attempting to promote the interests of certain social groups and transform society to reduce or eliminate advantage gaps that exist between those groups? Some argue that we are pursuing both of these aims and that such legislative provisions are informed by multiple normative foundations.[1]

This raises an important challenge to the account of wrongful discrimination set out in the previous two chapters, which focuses on whether a policy or administrative decision breaches fundamental constitutional principle, including a deontic requirement to treat legal subjects with appropriate respect. On this rival account, anti-discrimination rights are portrayed as concerned with both the treatment of individuals and the 'relative treatment of groups', mandating the prohibition of both harm to individuals and harm to groups.[2] In particular, principles prohibiting indirect discrimination, by requiring 'disparate impact on the group', are said to incorporate consideration of the relative status of social groups into anti-discrimination duties, even if they mediate these group-based concerns through individual rights.[3]

The claim here is not that principles of non-discrimination give rise to both individual rights and group rights. Rather, it is that certain forms of discrimination harm both individuals and social groups but that legal mechanisms mediate these harms through the lens of individual rights.[4] In addition to this, because

[1] See T Khaitan, *A Theory of Discrimination Law* (Oxford University Press, 2015); H Collins and T Khaitan, 'Indirect Discrimination Law: Controversies and Critical Questions' in H Collins and T Khaitan (eds), *Foundations of Indirect Discrimination Law* (Hart Publishing, 2018) 29; C O'Cinneide, 'The Uncertain Foundations of Contemporary Anti-Discrimination Law' (2011) 11(1–2) *International Journal of Discrimination and the Law* 7, 11–12.

[2] D Hellman, 'Equality and Unconstitutional Discrimination' in D Hellman and S Moreau (eds), *Philosophical Foundations of Discrimination Law* (Oxford University Press, 2013) 55. See also K Karst, *Belonging to America: Equal Citizenship and the Constitution* (Yale University Press, 1989); O Fiss, 'Groups and the Equal Protection Clause' (1976) 5 *Philosophy & Public Affairs* 107, 124.

[3] S Fredman, 'Direct and Indirect Discrimination: Is There Still a Divide' in Collins and Khaitan (eds) (n 1) 47; Khaitan (n 1) 86–87.

[4] See Fiss (n 2) 124–27, 145–46; Khaitan (n 1) 137–38.

it focuses on the group harm, the statutory prohibition of unjustified indirect-discrimination is said to further the aim of reducing or eliminating advantage gaps which exist between particular social groups in a way that the prohibition of direct-discrimination does not.[5] In this way, a connection is drawn between anti-discrimination rights and substantive equality, understood as a transformative principle designed to reduce or eliminate advantage gaps which exist between various social groups.

This chapter, drawing on the framework established throughout the book, will argue that prohibitions on wrongful discrimination, operating within a deontological framework of individual rights, do not necessarily prohibit group-based harm; nor do they directly further the aim of reducing or eliminating advantage gaps between social groups. This is the same for both common law prohibitions and statutory prohibitions on wrongful discrimination. Ultimately, acts of wrongful discrimination, even acts of demeaning discrimination, do not necessarily harm social groups, even if they may (and often do) contingently harm them. This is not to say that there can be no legal measures to directly further consequentialist equality goals. However, these measures cannot be contained within or entailed by rights to non-discrimination.[6] Rather, they are best seen as associated with group *interests*, affirmative action, and the public sector equality duty.[7]

I suggest that statutory principles of non-discrimination, including those prohibiting indirect discrimination, follow a similar deontic structure to common law duties and are thus conceptually distinct from principles of affirmative action. While these provisions often operate harmoniously to foster respect for the moral equality of persons, they each have a general affinity with distinct ethical traditions: deontology and consequentialism respectively. Given public law's focus on constraining government action only for breach of deontic constitutional principle, affirmative action policies and the furtherance of substantive equality may be pursued only through the legislative and executive branches

[5] See Khaitan (n 1); T Khaitan and S Steel, 'Wrongs, Group Disadvantage and the Legitimacy of Indirect Discrimination Law' in Collins and Khaitan (eds) (n 1); Fredman, 'Direct and Indirect Discrimination: Is There Still a Divide' (n 3).

[6] Khaitan draws a distinction between duties which are rights-generating (direct and indirect discrimination duties) and duties which are non-remedial: Khaitan (n 1) 143–45. This maps quite easily onto Holmes' distinction between action-regarding principles and non-action-regarding principles: E Holmes, 'Anti-Discrimination Rights without Equality' (2005) 68 *Modern Law Review* 175, 184. Note, however, that Khaitan conceives of all discrimination law as pursuing consequentialist equality goals such as the reduction or elimination of advantage gaps and, as such, would not accept the claim that non-discrimination rights are individual rights, unconcerned with group harm or the reduction of advantage gaps between different groups. This is so even though he grounds his conception within a liberty-based account and not an equality-based one: Khaitan (n 1) 113–15, 130–34.

[7] Equality Act 2010, s 149. Similarly, Owen Fiss, in his analysis of the Equal Protection Clause of the US Constitution, argues that an anti-discrimination principle must be supplemented with a group-disadvantage principle in the interpretation of the clause specifically because an anti-discrimination principle fails to account for group interests: Fiss (n 2) 147–56.

of state and cannot be reasonably contained within common law principles of non-discrimination.

This does not necessarily mean that the status of social groups has no place within philosophical accounts of discrimination. It is entirely possible that group-based disadvantage becomes salient within discrimination theory when one is identifying which personal characteristics of an individual are protected as grounds for discrimination.[8] This is one important difference between statutory and common law frameworks: the common law is not confined to a set list of protected characteristics and so a focus on why statutory frameworks protect race but not hair colour would provide little insight to the common lawyer interested in constitutional equality concerns arising from a commitment to the rule of law.[9]

Nevertheless, it is important to distinguish between the group disadvantage that might be necessary to identify a ground for discrimination and the claim that individual acts of discrimination necessarily harm social groups *qua* social groups.[10] Furthermore, it is important to distinguish between the identification of a ground of discrimination and the claim that prohibiting indirect discrimination advances group interests in reducing advantage gaps in a way that is meaningfully different from the prohibition of direct discrimination. Indeed, I have argued above that, at common law, there is no need for a distinction between direct and indirect discrimination given that wrongful discrimination is determined by reference to the principles of judicial review which do not confine their analysis to a finite list of protected characteristics.

Still, one may wish to introduce or maintain the concept of indirect discrimination at common law precisely because it is believed that the prohibition of indirect discrimination advances consequentialist equality goals. This chapter will argue that indirect discrimination in statute serves to identify a sufficient connection between a given policy and a protected characteristic but does not advance consequentialist equality goals. For this reason, common law frameworks need not adopt a rigid distinction between direct and indirect

[8] See for example; Khaitan (n 1) 31–38.

[9] On protected characteristics, see M Foran, 'Grounding Unlawful Discrimination' (2022) 28 *Legal Theory* 3.

[10] Incidentally, I take the position that this group disadvantage is a contingent but not necessary feature of a ground of discrimination. Following Lippert-Rasmussen, I argue that grounds of discrimination can be identified on the basis of the social salience of particular personal characteristics. See K Lippert-Rasmussen, *Born Free and Equal: A Philosophical Inquiry into the Nature of Discrimination* (Oxford University Press, 2013) 30–36; K Lippert-Rasmussen, 'The Badness of Discrimination' (2006) 9 *Ethical Theory and Moral Practice* 167, 169; H Baber, 'Gender Conscious' (2001) 18 *Journal of Applied Philosophy* 53. This salience often arises as a result of historic or ongoing disadvantage faced by particular social groups, but it does not necessarily do so. We can imagine a situation where there is significant tension between two religious groups, manifesting bias, negative stereotypes and inequality-laden attitudes while nevertheless both groups being comparably situated in terms of social and material advantage. In such a society, religion may still be a protected ground within discrimination law even if there are no advantage gaps between religious groups.

discrimination, nor is there a need to introduce a list of protected characteristics, notwithstanding the Equality Act 2010. It is one thing to say that people should not be treated less favourably because of their membership within a particular socially salient group; it is another thing entirely to say that treating an individual less favourably on this basis also treats the group that they are a part of less favourably or that the prohibition of this less favourably treatment necessarily advances substantive, consequentialist equality goals. This is so even where the actor in question is the state or a government minister. While the state certainly has the capacity to significantly affect entire social groups, not all administrative decisions will do so.

Thus, public bodies may be subject to two distinct anti-discrimination duties: the common law duty set out in the previous chapters and the statutory duty set out in the Equality Act 2010. This being the case, it could be argued that, while judicial review must be grounded within a deontic framework of rights and duties, the statutory framework need not. This is true, and some aspects of the Equality Act – most notably the public sector equality duty – evidently derive from a consequentialist or teleological foundation. Nevertheless, it will be argued that anti-discrimination duties, be they common law or statutory, are necessarily grounded in a deontic framework of individual rights. To that end, this chapter will begin by analysing the claim that wrongful discrimination, even on the basis of protected characteristics, necessarily harms social groups *qua* groups. It will be shown that, while discrimination may express denigration and therefore *wrong* individuals and, arguably, also groups, it does not necessarily *harm* groups in the sense that those groups have been particularly disadvantaged by individual instances of indirect discrimination. The test for indirect discrimination does not require that a provision, criterion, or practice put a social group at a particular disadvantage, just that it puts some persons who share a protected characteristic at a particular disadvantage. Of course, repeated, sustained, and widespread instances of discrimination may cumulatively harm social groups. However, discrimination can obtain where a social group has not been put at a particular disadvantage. Group harm is therefore not a necessary feature of wrongful discrimination, even if it may occur contingently.

From here, the connection between rights to non-discrimination and group interests in the reduction of advantage gaps will be explored. It will be shown that rights to be free from wrongfully discriminatory treatment, because they are entailed by action-regarding, deontic principles, do not directly advance the kinds of consequentialist equality goals that give rise to duties to reduce or eliminate advantage gaps, even in the statutory context. These goals are advanced by the positive duties associated with the public sector equality duty rather than by rights to non-discrimination. Affirmative action policies and positive duties to advance equality of opportunities are informed by group interests *qua* group interests. They are thus aimed at furthering the goal of reducing disparities between the social groups that they pertain to in a way that rights to non-discrimination, including rights to be free from indirect discrimination, are not.

Often, when discussing principles of non-discrimination and positive duties, a conceptual distinction between formal and substantive equality is invoked.[11] While none of the above principles are strictly egalitarian, this distinction is useful so long as the philosophical commitments latent within each concept are clearly identified. Nevertheless, it will be shown that prohibitions on indirect discrimination, while commonly considered to be examples of substantive equality, in fact find their home within a framework of formal equality due to their emphasis on removing formal barriers and prohibiting wrongful forms of treatment. In contrast, principles of substantive equality are non-action-regarding, consequentialist principles which focus on achieving a broadly redistributive goal that emphasises some degree of parity in opportunities or outcomes as between certain socially salient groups.

While principles of non-discrimination and affirmative action are both informed by a commitment to treat persons with equal concern and respect, the way that they do so is quite different, informed by different conceptions of equality.[12] Conceptions of formal equality operate within a broadly deontological framework, emphasising the rights of individuals to be free from certain forms of wrongful treatment, the removal of formal barriers, and the general pursuit of corrective justice. In contrast, I suggest that what distinguishes substantive equality from formal equality is an emphasis on broadly consequentialist frameworks, promoting the interests of social groups in the reduction or elimination of advantage gaps, and the general pursuit of distributive justice.

To the extent that equality of opportunities means the removal of formal barriers, this is not commonly associated with substantive equality, as evidenced by the fact that the prohibition of direct discrimination is not classed as furthering equality of opportunities even though it is clear that the removal of formal barriers does assist in increasing opportunities for those who were previously excluded by those barriers. Within the purview of a substantive equality framework, equality of opportunities demands more than simply the removal of barriers: using the metaphor of a race, the aim is to at the very least ensure that members of different groups have equal starting points, if not to ensure that there is parity in outcome. These goals simply do not fit well within a deontic framework of rights to be free from wrongfully discriminatory treatment and are best conceived as contained only within the provisions which entail positive duties to advance equality of opportunities as between groups.

[11] See S Fredman, *Discrimination Law*, 2nd edn (Oxford University Press, 2011) Ch 1; S Fredman, 'Substantive Equality Revisited' (2016) 14 *International Journal of Constitutional Law* 712; C Barnard and B Hepple, 'Substantive Equality' (2000) 59 *Cambridge Law Journal* 562; S Bedi, 'The Scope of Formal Equality of Opportunity' (2014) 42 *Political Theory* 716; C Daum and E Ishiwata, 'From the Myth of Formal Equality to the Politics of Social Justice: Race and the Legal Attack on Native Entitlements' (2010) 44 *Law & Society Review* 843.

[12] See Ch 2 above.

Rights to non-discrimination, as individual rights, do not necessarily pertain to group harm or the promotion of group interests. While the widespread vindication of non-discrimination rights can indirectly and contingently lead to the reduction of advantage gaps between certain social groups, the rights themselves do not take into account notions of group harm or group interest that underpin theories of substantive equality. If this is true, it may challenge attempts to provide unitary accounts of equality law frameworks, including not just anti-discrimination rights but also anti-harassment rights, anti-victimisation rights, reasonable accommodation duties, and affirmative action duties. In particular, it may challenge accounts which identify an overarching purpose in the reduction or elimination of relative group disadvantage.[13] Should anti-discrimination rights be conceptually distinct from consequentialist equality goals such as affirmative action, we must conclude that they necessarily pursue different legal ends using different legal means. Within the British statutory framework, anti-discrimination provisions do not pursue the reduction of relative group disadvantage, but rather the prevention of wrongful treatment suffered by individuals.[14] This is in line with the common law constitutional approach to non-discrimination. As such, equality law broadly construed pursues at least two distinct ends: the prohibition of discriminatory treatment; and the promotion of substantive equality. The upshot of this is that anti-discrimination rights may sometimes conflict with substantive equality goals, raising difficult questions concerning how one should resolve such a conflict. This is particularly important within public law because, if this argument is correct, it will mean that the promotion of consequentialist equality goals can only be done through legislative and administrative measures and must, consequently, be in conformity with constitutional principle if it is to remain lawful.

I. INDIRECT DISCRIMINATION AND HARM TO SOCIAL GROUPS

Indirect discrimination provisions, by focusing on the effects that facially neutral policies or practices have on social groups, are said to manifest a distinct shift towards group-based conceptions of harm. The nature of the wrong of indirect discrimination is such that it is felt by individuals but calculated by reference to

[13] See for example Khaitan (n 1); *cf* P Shin, 'Is There a Unitary Concept of Discrimination?' in Hellman and Moreau (eds) (n 2); *cf* Fredman, *Discrimination Law* (n 11) 130–39.

[14] It should be stressed that this analysis focuses on anti-discrimination rights as conceptually distinct from anti-harassment rights, anti-victimisation rights, rights to reasonable accommodation, or duties to engage in affirmative action. While these concepts are regularly addressed by a singular piece of legislation and all share a connection to the moral equality of persons, they pursue distinct legal ends and use distinct legal means. This paper argues that positive duties require consideration of group interests in the reduction of advantage gaps but that prohibitions on discriminatory treatment concern only wrongful treatment accorded to individuals, sometimes collections of individuals, but not necessarily social groups *qua* social groups.

the impact that discriminatory treatment has or would have on some members of particular social groups.[15] If a form of treatment puts or would put some members of one group at a particular disadvantage relative to some members of other groups distinguished by a protected characteristic, this establishes prima facie indirect discrimination, subject to a justification inquiry.[16] Thus, if there was a requirement that applicants be under the age of 28 to be eligible for employment as an executive officer in the Civil Service, this would place female applicants at a particular disadvantage compared to male applicants.[17] Women are far more likely to take time off during their twenties to have children and thus to enter (or re-enter) the labour market when they are over the age of 28. In these circumstances, an unjustified age requirement would amount to indirect discrimination on the basis of sex.[18] Similarly, unjustifiably refusing to hire employees under a certain height may amount to indirect sex discrimination by virtue of the connection between height and sex such that disproportionately fewer women would be able to comply with such a policy relative to their male counterparts.[19]

On a common law assessment of this policy, unlawfulness need not turn on the relationship that height has with sex. All that would matter would be whether the policy in question was unjustified according to the general heads of review, including reasonableness and proportionality (to the extent that we are drawing a sharp distinction between these two grounds). This policy could, therefore, be seen as unjustified height discrimination, even if an aspect of the unjustifiability derives from the impact that such a policy has upon women.

[15] Equality Act 2010, s 19. See also *Griggs v Duke Power Co*, 401 US 424 (1971); s 703 of Title VII of the US Civil Rights Act, 1991.

[16] Note that the severity of the disadvantage in question will be relevant to determining if there is justifiability but, nevertheless, these are distinct inquiries: Khaitan (n 1) 180–92. It could be argued that the relative disadvantage or advantage of the group that the victim of discrimination is a part of may impact upon the justification analysis. However, the justification test is primarily a test of proportionality, looking to whether the policy in question can be rationally defended as a proportionate means of achieving a legitimate aim. Such an inquiry is likely to be unaffected by who the victim of discrimination is. It would be almost arbitrary to conclude that a specific policy is a proportionate means of achieving a legitimate aim when those put at a particular disadvantage are Christian, but it is not a proportionate means when they are women.

[17] *Price v Civil Service Commission* [1977] IRLR 291 (EAT). See also *Edwards v London Underground (No 2)* [1998] IRLR 364. Developments in EU and UK law have resulted in the adoption of a 'rule of thumb' approach to identify particular disadvantage rather than a strict requirement to prove statistical disproportionality. See Equality Act 2010, s 19(2)(b); Framework Directive 2000/78/EC, Art 2(2)(b); *Homer v Chief Constable of West Yorkshire Police* [2012] UKSC 15; *Wards Cove Packing Co v Atonio*, 490 US 642 (1989); C-237/94 *O'Flynn v Adjudication Officer* [1996] 2 CMLR 103.

[18] Holmes argues that, in these circumstances, age should be seen as a proxy for sex. On this conception, tests for indirect discrimination are designed to broaden the range of characteristics protected by rights to non-discrimination rights: see Holmes (n 6) 184. As Lady Hale notes, indirect discrimination provisions scrutinise 'requirements which look neutral on their face but in reality work to the comparative disadvantage of people with a particular protected characteristic': *Homer v Chief Constable of West Yorkshire Police* [2012] UKSC 15, [17].

[19] C-409/16 *Ypourgos Esoterikon v Kalliri* [2018] IRLR 77.

While a group may be put at a particular disadvantage, that is not ultimately the deciding factor when assessing justifiability. The statutory context demands a specific relationship between the ground for a decision and a protected characteristic to even begin the justification inquiry; judicial review need not establish this relationship in order to assess for lawfulness. It is for this reason that a decision to fire a schoolteacher for the colour of her hair can be unreasonable and unlawful, despite there being no connection between red hair colour and any characteristic protected by statute. While social group disadvantage may be relevant to these kinds of inquiry, a policy need not place members of specific group at a particular disadvantage before it can be assessed for lawfulness.

References to 'groups' and 'disadvantage' here can be somewhat misleading. Gardner suggests that indirect discrimination looks to relative social disadvantage, assessed in relation to the disparities between two social groups, and reveals 'institutional disadvantage'.[20] This focus on social disadvantage is often seen as grounding indirect discrimination liability within a distributive justice framework.[21] However, the kind of disadvantage that is relevant for determining whether wrongful discrimination has occurred does not pertain to whether groups are *generally* disadvantaged (socially, economically, culturally, etc) but to the impact that a particular provision, criterion or practice may have on some members of some groups. So, for example, if a county council sets a hiring criterion which required applicants to commit to working on Sunday mornings, this may put Christian employees at a particular disadvantage, even if Christians as a group are not disadvantaged relative to other religious groups within that society. As such, indirect discrimination is always concerned with disadvantageous treatment that is felt by some persons who share a protected characteristic as compared to others who do not share that characteristic, but it is not always concerned with relative group disadvantage generally.[22]

As mentioned above, it is, of course, possible that the identification of statutorily protected characteristics is dependent on the relative disadvantage faced by particular social groups.[23] This is one of a number of competing explanations for why it is that certain characteristics are protected.[24] However, group

[20] J Gardner, 'Liberals and Unlawful Discrimination' (1989) 9 *Oxford Journal of Legal Studies* 1, 4–5. See also C McCrudden, 'Institutional Discrimination' (1982) 2 *Oxford Journal of Legal Studies* 303.

[21] See C McCrudden, 'Changing Notions of Discrimination' in S Guest and A Milne (eds), *Equality and Discrimination: Essays in Freedom and Justice* (ARSP Beiheft 21, 1985); RH Fallon and PC Weiler, 'Firefighters v Scotts: Conflicting Models of Racial Justice' [1984] *The Supreme Court Review* 1; B Eidelson, *Discrimination and Disrespect* (Oxford University Press, 2015) 6, 67–68.

[22] Khaitan would contest this point, arguing that discrimination against Christians is not a 'paradigmatic' case of discrimination: Khaitan (n 1) 31–38. This may be true. However, the point stands that, paradigmatic case or not, the test for indirect discrimination does not require proof of relative group disadvantage: it requires proof of disadvantageous treatment.

[23] Indeed, this forms the core of Khaitan's theory of discrimination law: ibid.

[24] Another prominent explanation is the immutability of protected characteristics. See K Balog, 'Equal Protection for Homosexuals: Why the Immutability Argument Is Necessary and How It Is Met

disadvantage in that context is distinct from the kind of harm that statutorily prohibited discrimination entails. Furthermore, even if anti-discrimination rights arise by virtue of group disadvantage, the rights themselves would be individual rights to be free from wrongful treatment and would not necessitate any analysis of how particular social groups have been treated. The test for disadvantage within an indirect-discrimination framework does not require a claimant to prove harm to groups as a whole: disadvantage is calculated based on whether it puts or would put *some members* of a group at a particular disadvantage. Using the above example, one must determine whether Christian *employees* would be put at a particular disadvantage relative to other employees, not whether Christians *as a group* would be disadvantaged. There is no requirement to prove that the provision, criterion, or practice actually affects the entirety of the group itself, nor that it affects groups *qua* groups. This can be seen when one examines the duty contained in the Equality Act 2010:

> a provision, criterion or practice is discriminatory in relation to a relevant protected characteristic of B's if … it puts, or would put, persons with whom B shares the characteristic at a particular disadvantage when compared with persons with whom B does not share it.[25]

There is no reference to harm to social groups as a whole here. All that is required is that some individuals who share a protected characteristic are put at, or would be put at, a particular disadvantage. This test is designed to identify circumstances where individuals are treated worse than others because of a protected characteristic, despite the treatment being facially neutral with regard to such characteristics. Thus, if an employer indirectly discriminated against their female employees, all that must be shown is that the employer's action would put female *employees* at a particular disadvantage relative to male *employees*; not that this action put women as a social group at a particular disadvantage relative to men as a social group.

References to adverse impact hypothesise how a particular provision, criterion, or practice might affect persons distinguished by a protected characteristic: if some persons who share a protected characteristic are disproportionately negatively affected, then there may be discrimination.[26] In these circumstances,

Note' (2005) 53 *Cleveland State Law Review* 545; S Marcosson, 'Constructive Immutability' (2001) 3 *University of Pennsylvania Journal of Constitutional Law* 646; S Hoffman, 'The Importance of Immutability in Employment Discrimination Law' (2011) 52 *William and Mary Law Review* 1483. *cf* J Clarke, 'Against Immutability' (2015) 125 *Yale Law Journal* 2. Note that Clarke, while rejecting immutability, argues in favour of an account which emphasises the irrationality and bias of discrimination rather than group disadvantage. Social salience could also explain why certain grounds are protected without necessarily requiring relative group disadvantage. See Lippert-Rasmussen, 'The Badness of Discrimination' (n 10) 169; Lippert-Rasmussen, *Born Free and Equal: A Philosophical Inquiry into the Nature of Discrimination* (n 10) 30–36.

[25] Equality Act 2010, s 19(2).

[26] It is for this reason that those put at a particular disadvantage may be hypothetical, even if the victim must be an identified claimant. Importantly, the hypothetical victims of discrimination

we can say that a ground which would otherwise not be prohibited (say height) becomes prohibited because of the relationship it bears to a protected characteristic (say sex) such that, should it not be justified, disadvantageous treatment on the basis of the non-prohibited ground is treated as if it *were* on the basis of the protected characteristic.[27] As Holmes notes, the disparate impact test is not qualifying or altering a non-discrimination principle but determining its application.[28]

There is never a requirement to show that social groups *qua* social groups are actually affected by discriminatory practices. While it is certainly true that discriminatory acts and relative group disadvantage often coincide with each other, it is not the case that one is conceptually dependent upon the other.

That being said, such an interpretation is not likely to be accepted by some theorists in this area who ground their conception of indirect discrimination in group harm and relative group disadvantage. For example, Collins and Khaitan argue that 'indirect discrimination is always about groups: the question is whether a protected group is disproportionately disadvantaged by an action'.[29] Khaitan and Steel define indirect discrimination as '[a]n act, policy or practice that – while facially neutral- nonetheless has a disproportionate impact on a group protected by discrimination law (such as Blacks or women)'[30] and argue that 'the comparison required is between two groups'.[31] McCrea notes that 'the

must be individuals in a sufficiently similar situation to the claimant. For example, the hypothetical employees must be employees of the employer in question. Reliance on hypothetical employees to establish particular disadvantage does not necessitate analysis of how the social group that the claimant is a part of has been treated or of how the social group is comparatively situated relative to other social groups. It is only a sub-set of the group that must be put at a particular disadvantage.

[27] Holmes (n 6) 184. Note that disability and age discrimination appear to be outliers within this context as there are a number of features of disability and age discrimination which set them apart from other forms of discrimination. In particular, while justification requirements generally only occur within indirect discrimination provisions, a directly discriminatory policy on the grounds of disability or age may be justified. For example, a refusal to hire the blind as pilots or truck drivers is not disability discrimination whereas a refusal to hire Jews would be. Indeed, it may be the case that impermissible cases of disability-based disadvantageous treatment occur only when they are arbitrary, whereas most other cases of discrimination can be wrongful even when they are not arbitrary. See L Alexander, 'What Makes Wrongful Discrimination Wrong? Biases, Preferences, Stereotypes, and Proxies' (1992) 141 *University of Pennsylvania Law Review* 149, 151; D Wasserman, 'Is Disability Discrimination Different?' in Hellman and Moreau (eds) (n 2); D Wasserman, 'Distributive Justice' in A Silvers et al (eds), *Disability, Difference, Discrimination: Perspectives on Justice in Bioethics and Public Policy* (Rowman & Littlefield, 1998); M Kelman, 'Defining the Antidiscrimination Norm to Defend It' (2006) 43 *San Diego Law Review* 735; P Singer, 'Is Racial Discrimination Arbitrary?' (1978) 8 *Moral Matters* 185. *cf* M Crossley, 'Reasonably Accommodation as Part and Parcel of the Antidiscrimination Project' (2004) 35 *Ruthers Law Journal* 861; P Karlan and G Rutherglen, 'Disabilities, Discrimination, and Reasonable Accommodation' (1996) 46 *Duke Law Journal* 1.

[28] Holmes (n 6) 184.

[29] Collins and Khaitan (n 1) 19. See also ibid 15.

[30] Khaitan and Steel (n 5) 197–98.

[31] ibid 199.

key issue in relation to indirect discrimination is group disadvantage'.[32] Fredman stresses that indirect discrimination focuses on both 'individual detriment as well as group impact'.[33] Hepple argues that indirect discrimination is concerned with 'the adverse impact or effects on the group (eg women or an ethnic minority) to which B belongs'.[34] Blum argues that discrimination is wrong 'in ways that wrong individuals *and also* in ways that wrong or harm groups'.[35] In some cases, theorists appear to recognise that indirect discrimination does not, in fact, harm social groups *qua* groups and that it usually harms only a sub-set of a group. This is particularly evident when analysis focuses on the difficulty of identifying the appropriate 'pool' of comparison.[36] However, it would be wrong to conclude from this that the issue is simply imprecise language; some theorists do endorse a group-harm (*qua* group-harm) account of indirect discrimination and others rely on group impact to ground indirect discrimination provisions within a substantive equality framework, repeatedly emphasising the transformative nature of those provisions and distinguishing them from direct discrimination provisions, which are seen as examples of formal equality.

Khaitan and Steel have recently engaged in some depth with the group harm condition set out above.[37] They argue that, in circumstances where it can be shown that a provision, criterion, or practice might put some persons at a particular disadvantage relative to other persons defined by a protected characteristic, one should conclude that the defendant's act caused a particular disadvantage to a social group *qua* group and that the claimant suffered because they are a member of that group.[38] To explain this point, they invite us to consider two hypothetical scenarios arising from the imposition of a facially neutral test, passing which is a prerequisite for securing employment. In the first scenario, no particular racial group disproportionately failed the test. In the second, Black candidates were only 25 per cent as likely as their white counterparts to pass the test. In these examples, Ifelmelu, a Black woman, failed both times. They argue that in the first scenario, no claim for indirect discrimination could arise as Ifelmelu's failure is best explained by chance or luck. However, in the second

[32] R McCrea, 'Squaring the Circle: Can an Egalitarian and Individualistic Conception of Freedom of Religion or Belief Co-Exist with the Notion of Indirect Discrimination?' in Collins and Khaitan (eds) (n 1) 156.

[33] Fredman, 'Direct and Indirect Discrimination: Is There Still a Divide' (n 3) 32.

[34] B Hepple, *Equality: The Legal Framework*, 2nd edn (Hart Publishing, 2014) 81. See also McCrudden, 'Changing Notions of Discrimination' (n 21); McCrudden, 'Institutional Discrimination' (n 20).

[35] L Blum, 'Racial and Other Asymmetries: A Problem for the Protected Categories Framework for Anti-Discrimination Thought' in Hellman and Moreau (eds) (n 2) 195–96.

[36] See Khaitan (n 1) 75, 156–59; Collins and Khaitan (n 1) 14; T Khaitan, 'Indirect Discrimination' in K Lippert-Rasmussen (ed), *The Routledge Handbook of the Ethics of Discrimination* (Routledge, 2017); Fredman, *Discrimination Law* (n 11) 185–86. See also *Jones v Chief Adjudication Officer* [1990] IRLR 533 [36].

[37] Khaitan and Steel (n 5).

[38] ibid 203–204.

scenario, they argue that, once chance has been ruled out, the most plausible conclusion to draw is that: (i) the defendant's act caused a particular disadvantage to Blacks as a group and, consequently; (ii) Ifelmelu suffered some adversity because she is a member of that group.[39] Khaitan and Steel recognise that UK law does not require such group harm to be proven.[40] However, they suggest that, nevertheless, the best interpretation of anti-discrimination provisions is one which views them as taking these two presumptions as given in circumstances similar to the second scenario.

There is a disconnect here between the use of a theoretical framework which stresses disadvantageous treatment of social groups and a statutory framework which is concerned only with wrongs to some members of some groups. It seems that the clearest way for us to resolve this difficulty is to note that, while individuals are wronged, the determination of this requires analysis of how particular policies, criteria, or practices might disadvantage members of different groups should those individuals be affected by the policy, criterion, or practice in question. Crucially, the victims of indirect discrimination are not entire groups. They are some members of those groups: the employees, applicants, customers, and so on, who are demonstrably impacted by the policies and actions in question. In light of this, the most plausible conclusion to be drawn from the second scenario is not that the test puts Blacks as a group at a particular disadvantage. Rather, it is that this test puts Black *applicants* at a particular disadvantage relative to white applicants.[41]

Indeed, this interpretation not only conforms with the tests set out in statute, it is also necessary for Khaitan and Steel's later argument that the harm to groups accrues as a result of the knock-on effects of the harm to individuals.[42] They claim that there is 'a direct correspondence between adverse effects on a sub-set of a group and on the group as a whole' and stress that the extent of this harm may be trivial or significant.[43] For example, an employer with a small

[39] ibid. Khaitan and Steel are quite explicit in stating that they view the second causal claim as entailed by the first and that the first claim pertains to what they refer to as the general duty not to harm a group which is protected by discrimination law (say, Blacks) *as a group*: ibid 206.

[40] Indeed, Khaitan, in his previous work, stresses that the group comparison is limited by a choice of 'pool'. In this analysis, Khaitan notes that, while the comparison is between two groups, we will often come to different conclusions relating to whether a given policy disproportionately harms women dependent on what we choose as our relevant pool (the entire population of the jurisdiction, only the persons qualified for the job in question, or simply the workforce of the employer): Khaitan (n 1) 75, 156–59. This analysis appears to be consistent with my own arguments in as much as we agree that test for discrimination does not look to the impact upon women as a group and instead looks to the effect on some women. However, Khaitan goes further, stressing that, even if the legal tests do not require proof of harm to social groups *qua* groups, we should *presume* that this is exactly what discrimination does.

[41] Of course, this disadvantage may be compounded by the fact that Blacks as a group are already comparatively disadvantaged and may itself compound that disadvantage. See D Hellman, 'Indirect Discrimination and the Duty to Avoid Compounding Injustice' in Collins and Khaitan (eds) (n 1); M Selmi, 'Was Disparate Impact Theory a Mistake?' (2001) 53 *UCLA Law Review* 701, 704–706.

[42] Khaitan and Steel (n 5) 206.

[43] ibid.

workforce who indirectly discriminates against his female employees is, according to Khaitan and Steel, likely to only marginally harm women as a group. In contrast discriminatory laws are likely to have a significantly greater impact on a group. The argument can be summarised as follows: individual acts of indirect discrimination directly harm particular individuals (the employers, applicants, customers, and so on) and also produce knock-on effects which harm the group that those individuals are a part of *qua* social group. The more individuals who are directly harmed by an act of indirect discrimination, the greater the knock-on harm to the group. However, this argument contradicts Khaitan and Steel's previous argument that an act of indirect discrimination causes 'a particular disadvantage to Blacks as a group' and that, consequently, the claimant suffered because of her membership within that group.[44]

Khaitan and Steel repeatedly stress that the particular harm done to individuals is causally entailed by the general harm done to the group and also that the harm done to the group is the result of knock-on effects from the harm done to individuals. So, which is it? They 'take the assumption that there is some knock-on effect on the group as a whole to hold in most, if not all, cases'.[45] They then argue that the 'causal presumption in the particular duty, it should be obvious, hangs on the prior breach of the general duty'.[46] So, the particular harm to individuals is dependent on general harm to the group which is in turn dependent on knock-on effects produced by particularised harm to individuals. These claims are mutually incompatible. Using the example above, either the employment test harms Blacks as a group and thus harms Ifelmelu because she is a part of that group, or the test harms Black applicants such as Ifelmelu and also produces knock-on harms that affect Blacks as a group. The group harm accrues either top-down or bottom-up; it cannot do both simultaneously.

It has been shown that the claim that indirect discrimination directly harms groups *qua* groups is incorrect. This leaves us with the second claim: that indirect discrimination harms individuals but produces knock-on effects which harm groups as a whole. This is entirely plausible in some circumstances, for example where discrimination comes in the form of a sufficiently broad legislative enactment which targets the group *qua* group. However, it is not clear at all how an act of discrimination against only a small number of individuals harms the group that they are a part of *qua* group. So, when a county council discriminates against Christian applicants via its hiring practices, it is unclear precisely how this will harm all Christians, either in that county or in the country as a whole. Khaitan and Steel rest their argument on the empirical claim that an employer's discrimination against two employees who are female has an effect on all women and thus contributes to making women as a group less free.[47] This

[44] ibid 203–204.
[45] ibid 206.
[46] ibid 207.
[47] This approach grounds Khaitan and Steel within a liberty-based conception of discrimination. See S Moreau, 'In Defense of a Liberty-Based Account of Discrimination' in Hellman and Moreau

seems extremely unlikely. Indeed, most forms of indirect discrimination, even by public authorities, plausibly harm only a small number of individuals either directly or through knock-on effects. It is unlikely that individual acts of indirect discrimination will have any effect, direct or otherwise, on people in another city on the other side of the country.

In contrast, Khaitan and Steel describe the harm of indirect discrimination with reference to the harm done to a group's opportunities.[48] Specifically, they argue that a victim is harmed because, where race becomes a factor in determining if they will get a job, their opportunities become rationally less attractive and so less valuable.[49] On this view, harm accrues not because Ifelmelu did not get the job, but because her chances of doing so have been reduced.[50] As such, Khaitan and Steel argue that Ifelmelu is harmed even if she was successful in obtaining employment, noting that '[s]ince autonomy requires the possession of a wide set of valuable options, the diminishment in the value of an option has an impact on an agent's autonomy'.[51] Again, Khaitan and Steel premise these conclusions on strong empirical claims arguing that '[e]ven if this loss to particular individuals may be small in some cases, the systemic effect on the group, many of whose members do not even apply, is often significant'.[52]

The problem is that Khaitan and Steel present us with no evidence to support the claim that this individual loss of opportunities felt by three female applicants necessarily, or even often, results in women as a group losing opportunities, or in the diminishment of the value of their opportunities. The fact that such harm does not need to be proven by a claimant reinforces the point that this is not a necessary feature of wrongful discrimination, even if it may occur contingently. We can easily imagine circumstances where this knock-on effect has not occurred and where nevertheless there has been wrongful discrimination. As such, even if it were the case that many instances of indirect discrimination produce knock-on effects which diminish the value of opportunities at a group level, this group harm is not conceptually necessary for the existence of wrongful discrimination. Group harm is a contingent feature of discrimination, where it occurs at all.[53]

However, by definition, wrongful discrimination does *wrong* individuals and may also wrong groups, even if it does not necessarily harm them.

(eds) (n 2); D Hellman, 'Two Concepts of Discrimination' (2016) 102 *Virginia Law Review* 895; Khaitan (n 1).

[48] Khaitan and Steel (n 5) 208–10. See also S Moreau, 'What Is Discrimination?' (2010) 38 *Philosophy & Public Affairs* 143.

[49] Khaitan and Steel (n 5) 209–10.

[50] ibid 209.

[51] ibid 210.

[52] ibid.

[53] Although some would argue that the denial of opportunities does not, in-and-of itself, amount to sufficient harm to ground a justification for legal intervention in the private sphere, even if it may be sufficient at public law should it correspond with a breach of constitutional principle. See Gardner (n 20) 6. Of course, if the denial of opportunities does not ground justification, it is clear that the diminishment of the value of certain opportunities does not either.

Lippert-Rasmussen has argued that we can distinguish disadvantageous treatment from treatment that causes harm.[54] For example, he argues that refusing to hire an applicant who is better qualified treats them disadvantageously even if, as a result of this rejection, she is successful in landing herself a better job.[55] Another example would be the discriminatory refusal to allow a person to board an aeroplane which then crashed. In these cases, the victim of discrimination has been wronged even though they have ultimately benefited from this wrongful treatment and so cannot be reasonably seen to have been harmed. Conversely, you can treat someone advantageously while harming them overall if, by hiring them, despite a more qualified candidate applying, they unknowingly lose out on getting a much better job as a result.[56] Thus, Lippert-Rasmussen argues that one can experience disadvantageous treatment and be wrongfully discriminated against even if, overall, one has not been harmed or may even benefit from the treatment itself.[57] So when we speak of less favourable treatment being a necessary feature of discrimination, it is the treatment itself that is pertinent, independent of the consequences which might arise from such treatment. As Hellman notes, the wrongness of discrimination is not reducible to the harm that one may inflict in discriminating, even though discrimination often does considerable harm.[58]

Thus, for example, we can see that indirect discrimination might put Christian employees at a particular disadvantage and thus wrong them should this be unjustified (even if it does not ultimately harm them) but that it does not necessarily put Christians as a social group at a particular disadvantage relative to other religious groups. Furthermore, if we take an expressivist account of discrimination, grounded in the contention that discrimination is wrongful when it demeans or expresses attitudes of unequal moral worth, it is entirely possible for indirect discrimination to wrong social groups by expressing the attitude that the group *qua* group is inferior.[59] However, it should be stressed that whether this individual wrongful expression has an impact on social groups as a whole is contingent upon a number of variable factors, including the scope of the discrimination, the institutional or social position of the discriminator, and the publicity of the expression.

Nevertheless, Khaitan and Steel evidently do not endorse an expressivist account of discrimination. Their account is grounded within a liberty-based conception of discrimination and not equality- or dignity-based conceptions

[54] Lippert-Rasmussen, *Born Free and Equal: A Philosophical Inquiry into the Nature of Discrimination* (n 10) 18.

[55] ibid.

[56] ibid.

[57] ibid. See also J Gardner, 'Discrimination as Injustice' (1996) 16 *Oxford Journal of Legal Studies* 353.

[58] Hellman, *When Is Discrimination Wrong?* (Harvard University Press, 2011) 26–27.

[59] See Hellman, *When Is Discrimination Wrong?* (n 58); Hellman, 'Indirect Discrimination and the Duty to Avoid Compounding Injustice' (n 41). See also Ch 5 above.

which can identify the wrong of discrimination in the action itself and not its consequences.[60] As such, if they wish to claim that single instances of indirect discrimination put social groups at a particular disadvantage, they must establish some material harm that is done to the group's (and not merely some members) liberty interests. This focus on effects and particular disadvantage precludes any reading of their claim which would see it as grounded in expressive wrongdoing. Even if it did account for expressive wrongdoing, this is distinct from the claim that indirect discrimination necessarily puts social groups at a particular disadvantage.

II. INDIRECT DISCRIMINATION AND FORMAL EQUALITY

Discrimination, where it is unjustified, is a form of treatment that wrongs and often harms individuals. This wrong is comparative in nature, primarily grounded within frameworks of corrective justice.[61] As such, statutory provisions, just like common law principles, prohibiting wrongful discrimination are action-regarding, deontic principles which identify wrongful forms of conduct rather than non-action-regarding, consequentialist principles which mandate the distribution of some resource or the achievement of a particular state of affairs.[62]

Wrongful discrimination is sometimes characterised as a failure to distribute fairly.[63] While this is often true, it would be wrong to say that a right to be free from discriminatory treatment entails a right to have particular goods or resources distributed to you. A principle of non-discrimination precludes certain kinds of distribution to be sure, and in that sense can be said to be premised on avoiding distributive injustice. Nevertheless, a lack of fair distribution on its own is not sufficient to prove wrongful discrimination at common law or according to the Equality Act 2010.[64] It is on this basis that Morris draws a distinction between corrective and distributive schemes, noting that 'corrective schemes generally require some element beyond mere disturbance of a distributive scheme before corrective rights and duties are implicated'.[65]

[60] Khaitan and Steel (n 5).

[61] See Aristotle, 'Nicomachean Ethics' in J Barnes (ed), *The Complete Works of Aristotle* (Princeton University Press, 1984) ll 1130a30-1131b25. For more on the comparative nature of discrimination, see Hellman, 'Equality and Unconstitutional Discrimination' (n 2); Hellman, 'Two Concepts of Discrimination' (n 47); Lippert-Rasmussen, 'The Badness of Discrimination' (n 10) 168–69, 173.

[62] Holmes (n 6). See also A Morris, 'On the Normative Foundations of Indirect Discrimination Law: Understanding the Competing Models of Discrimination Law as Aristotelian Forms of Justice' (1995) 15 *Oxford Journal of Legal Studies* 199.

[63] See for example; Gardner (n 57).

[64] Morris (n 62) 205.

[65] ibid.

Thus, in *R v Drybones*, the Canadian Supreme Court struck down a law which made it an offence for an aboriginal Canadian to be intoxicated when off a reserve.[66] The court held that a law creating an offence applying only to members of a particular race violated the guarantee of equality before the law contained within the Bill of Rights 1960.[67] While it is possible to see this as a form of distributive injustice in the sense that certain legal burdens were distributed unfairly, it would be odd to conclude that the prohibition of such discriminatory laws sought to promote a distributive aim of reallocating resources or advantages to aboriginal Canadians. If non-discrimination has a distributive element to it, it is not the kind of consequentialist distributive goal that we regularly identify with principles of affirmative action or positive duties which seek to alter the composition of various social structures to be more diverse in terms of particular identity groups. Such a goal is exclusively distributive in nature, focusing explicitly on directing the allocation of a shared set of advantages and burdens across a given community.[68] A principle of non-discrimination may indirectly result in some degree of redistribution of this kind, but it is not the explicit aim of such principles, nor are such principles capable of independently ensuring this redistribution. Indeed, it may be the case that principles of non-discrimination actually preclude redistribution on the basis of protected characteristics.[69]

As we have seen above, statutory frameworks prohibiting wrongful discrimination regularly rely on a conceptual distinction between direct and indirect discrimination, where both forms of discrimination are said to pursue different aims and to be founded on different conceptions of equality. Direct and indirect discrimination are mutually exclusive and conceptually distinct, even if it is sometimes difficult identify where the boundaries lie.[70] Often, this distinction is supplemented by reliance on another distinction between 'formal' equality and 'substantive' equality.[71] This dichotomy is usually invoked to explain the

[66] *R v Drybones* (1969) DLR (3rd) 473.

[67] Specifically, s 1(b) which protects the right of the individual to equality before the law and the protection of the law 'without discrimination by reason of race, national origin, colour, religion or sex'.

[68] Aristotle (n 61) ll 1131a1, 22–28; R Nozick, *Anarchy, State, and Utopia* (Basic Books, 1974) 153–55. See also Gardner (n 20) 9. Here, Gardner argues that distributive justice as a justification for state intervention focuses exclusively on patterns of advantage and disadvantage, not on further factors which go beyond the injustice of particular states of affairs and look to 'how, and by whose agency, they arose'.

[69] See B Havelkova, 'Judicial Scepticism of Discrimination at the ECtHR' in Collins and Khaitan (eds) (n 1); W Reynolds, 'Individualism vs Group Rights: The Legacy of Brown' (1984) 93 *Yale Law Journal* 995; O'Cinneide (n 1); C O'Cinneide, 'Justifying Discrimination Law' (2016) 36 *Oxford Journal of Legal Studies* 909.

[70] See Lady Hale in *R (E) v Governing Body of JFS* [2010] 2 AC 72, [57]; Mummary LJ in *R (Elias) v Secretary of State for Defence* [2006] EWCA Civ 1293, [117]–[118]: 'The conditions of liability, the available defences to liability and the available defences to remedies differ'. *cf* Fredman, 'Direct and Indirect Discrimination: Is There Still a Divide' (n 3).

[71] See Fredman, *Discrimination Law* (n 11) Ch 1; N Bamforth, 'Conceptions of Anti-Discrimination Law' (2004) 24 *Oxford Journal of Legal Studies* 693; Barnard and Hepple (n 11); C Albertyn,

inadequacies of prohibitions on direct discrimination (seen as examples of formal equality) and the necessity of prohibitions on indirect discrimination (seen as examples of substantive equality).[72] However, it is sometimes unclear precisely what theorists have in mind when they distinguish between formal and substantive conceptions of equality. In particular, there is a certain degree of ambiguity when it comes to substantive equality which has seemingly come to represent anything that might be described as 'true' equality or 'real' equality.[73] In this sense, substantive equality could be described by reference to what it is not (formal equality) rather than what it is. Such an approach is unsatisfying, however. There is clearly something which distinguishes formal from substantive equality, beyond simply the idea that substantive equality is more normatively or politically desirable than formal equality, even if one must build upon the other to be truly valuable.

I suggest that formal equality is characterised by a focus on treatment and the attainment of corrective justice through the protection of individual rights correlatively entitled by directed duties. In contrast, substantive equality is focused on addressing group-based disadvantage and achieving parity of outcomes or opportunities as between social groups through the transformation of social structures, the broadening of social inclusion, and the attainment of redistributive justice.[74] Formal equality, by focusing on the elimination of discriminatory treatment, is often critiqued for failing to account for disparities in group status. As a result, it is argued that the achievement of formal equality does little to advance 'the eradication of social disadvantage', a goal which is necessary for the achievement of substantive equality.[75]

Substantive equality has gained political and legal prominence largely as a response to the perceived inadequacies of formal equality, and the inability of direct discrimination provisions to achieve the redistributive goal that is the aim of substantive equality. To encapsulate the thrust of this critique in a sentence: formal equality within an unequal society does little to close advantage gaps that exist between various social groups. To rectify this, substantive equality is focused, in one way or another, on bringing about social change such that inequalities between groups is lessened or removed.

'Substantive Equality' (2007) 23 *South African Journal on Human Rights* 209; Fredman, 'Substantive Equality Revisited' (n 11).

[72] Barnard and Hepple (n 11) 564; Hepple (n 34) 12–13, 24–29, 81; Fredman, *Discrimination Law* (n 11) 10.

[73] C Bourn and J Whitmore, *Anti-Discrimination Law in Britain*, 3rd edn (Sweet & Maxwell, 1996) 4–5. This is in contrast with formal equality which is often defined by reference to the principle that likes should be treated alike. See Fredman, *Discrimination Law* (n 11) 8–14. However, I suggest that the operative principle here is not one which equalises treatment but one which prohibits wrongfully discriminatory treatment. See Holmes (n 6). Note however that, while Holmes is correct that principles of non-discrimination are not strictly egalitarian in this way, they are nevertheless grounded within an equality-based framework and consequently can be described as principles of 'formal' equality should this distinction be in play.

[74] Fredman, *Discrimination Law* (n 11) 11–12.

[75] Bourn and Whitmore (n 73) 4–5.

It is this desire to bring about social change which is often associated with prohibitions on indirect discrimination. Indeed, many commentators have concluded that the introduction of such prohibitions into statutory frameworks was done with the express aim of effecting distributive justice as between various social groups, manifesting a distinct shift in focus away from the corrective concerns of direct discrimination, and the formal conception of equality which informed them.[76] Thus, Hepple notes that 'indirect discrimination aims to achieve substantive equality' and associates it with 'a procedural notion of equality of opportunity'.[77] Similarly, Fredman argues that the concept of indirect discrimination attempts to address the 'redistributive and restructuring goals of equality'[78] by bringing to mind 'the graphic metaphor of competitors in a race' and 'asserts that true equality cannot be achieved if individuals begin the race from different starting points'.[79] As such, Hepple stresses that '[t]he aim is to equalise the starting points',[80] resulting in indirect discrimination provisions focusing on the 'redistribution of wealth and opportunities'.[81]

Recently, Fredman has argued that substantive equality should not be collapsed into a single formula.[82] Rather, it should remain responsive to those who are disadvantaged by adopting a multi-dimensional approach with the aim to: 'redress disadvantage; address stigma, stereotyping, prejudice, and violence; enhance voice and participation; and accommodate difference and achieve structural change'.[83] This approach indicates that perhaps substantive equality is simply a collection of disparate normative positions and commitments. Nevertheless, it seems to me that there is a central thread which runs through all conceptions of substantive equality: a notable shift towards accounting for and advancing group interests *qua* group interests. These substantive equality goals manifest a distinct conception of how one is to properly respect the moral equality of persons that moves away from deontological concerns that focus on treatment which wrongs persons towards a teleological approach which identifies certain interests that must be promoted and a state of affairs which must be

[76] See for example: Collins and Khaitan (n 1) 19, 29–30; Hepple (n 34) 12–13, 81; Moreau, 'What Is Discrimination?' (n 48) 144–45; Eidelson (n 21) 6, 67–68; H Collins, 'Discrimination, Equality and Social Inclusion' (2003) 66 *Modern Law Review* 16, 20; Barnard and Hepple (n 11) 564. Note that Collins argues that social inclusion is aimed at combating persistent or absolute disadvantage that particular groups face, as opposed to combating relative group disadvantage. Nevertheless, the goal is still broadly redistributive. See also Fiss (n 2) 143; Gardner (n 20) 3–5, 8–11; C McCrudden et al, *Racial Justice at Work: Enforcement of the Race Relations Act 1976 in Employment* (Policy Studies Institute, 1991); Morris (n 62) 207–208; R Arneson, 'Discrimination, Disparate Impact, and Theories of Justice' in Hellman and Moreau (eds) (n 2) 108–109.

[77] Hepple (n 34) 81, 25.

[78] S Fredman, *Discrimination and Human Rights: The Case of Racism* (Oxford University Press, 2001) 23.

[79] S Fredman, *A Critical Review of the Concept of Equality in UK Anti-Discrimination Law* (Cambridge University Press, 1999) paras 3.10–3.16.

[80] Hepple (n 34) 26.

[81] R Townshend-Smith, *Discrimination Law: Texts, Cases and Materials* (Cavendish, 1998) 262.

[82] Fredman, 'Substantive Equality Revisited' (n 11) 712.

[83] ibid 713–14.

striven towards. Within a substantive equality framework, the duty is to bring about the realisation of particular ends such as structural and cultural change, rather than a duty to refrain from treating persons wrongfully.

Bearing this in mind, the duty not to indirectly discriminate is best characterised, if we are using the metric of formal/substantive equality, as an example of formal equality, focused primarily on corrective rather than distributive justice, and the protection of individual rights rather than the promotion of group interests.[84] Within the context of indirect discrimination, the classification of a provision, criterion, or practice as prima facie discriminatory will be determined based on the effects of that treatment. However, while indirect discrimination looks to the effects of particular policies or procedures, this does not mean that focus has shifted from treatment to outcomes or opportunities in the sense that substantive equality envisages. Fundamentally, there has been no shift from corrective to distributive justice as might occur with the introduction of laws which entail positive duties or affirmative action policies.[85]

The emphasis on the effects of conduct on members of particular groups results in increased forms of conduct being classed as discriminatory. It does not directly manifest anything in the way of redistribution, nor does it do much to increase the opportunities of particular social groups *qua* groups. It could, of course, *indirectly* contribute to redistribution or the increase of opportunities through the prohibition of wrongful conduct. However, this is a by-product of the removal of formal barriers, not a necessary feature. As such, a lack of redistribution does not invalidate the remedy offered for breach of the duty not to indirectly discriminate.[86]

Indeed, this has caused some theorists to critique indirect discrimination for failing to achieve the transformative goals of substantive equality.[87] For example, Khaitan notes that '[t]he antidiscrimination duty, on its own, cannot close pervasive, abiding, and substantial advantage gaps between groups'.[88] Fredman, while stressing that the aim of laws prohibiting indirect discrimination is to equalise starting points, notes that, while opportunities are opened up, there is no guarantee that more women, or members of ethnic minorities will actually be in

[84] Morris (n 62). Here, Morris argues that indirect discrimination law is coherent only when conceived through the lens of corrective justice. Specifically, '[t]o the extent that an interpretation strays from the corrective thesis, the law's features lose conceptual coherence and the law loses apparent efficacy towards any point.' ibid 208.

[85] This is of crucial importance. While it may be argued that there is a distributive element within the concept of discrimination law (Khaitan and Steel (n 5) 38–41), affirmative action is necessary to achieve a broader distributive goal of closing advantage gaps: Morris (n 62) 216, 222–24.

[86] Indeed, very often the remedy offered is simply the removal of the barrier in question. Some might see this as evidence of the institutional focus of indirect discrimination. However, this does not mean that these provisions should be classed as advancing a substantive equality framework any more than the prohibition of direct discrimination does seeing as direct discrimination provisions also remove barriers.

[87] See for example; Fredman, *Discrimination Law* (n 11) 180–83; Fredman, 'Direct and Indirect Discrimination: Is There Still a Divide' (n 3) 49–50.

[88] Khaitan (n 1) 215.

a position to take advantage of those opportunities.[89] Hepple similarly argues that, even though indirect discrimination laws advance equality of opportunities, this alone is not sufficient to achieve 'true' equality and affirmative action is therefore necessary to sidestep many of the limitations of indirect discrimination provisions.[90] However, there is a central flaw in the above analysis: the assumption that the prohibition of indirect discrimination actually seeks to equalise starting points or opportunities. Principles prohibiting indirect discrimination do what all anti-discrimination principles do: they mandate the removal of formal barriers and the prohibition of wrongful forms of treatment. Prohibiting indirect discrimination removes more barriers than prohibiting direct discrimination alone does because there is a shift in focus from overt barriers to hidden barriers. This does not mean that prohibitions on indirect discrimination do anything other than remove barriers and prohibit wrongful forms of treatment. Sticking with our race analogy, principles of non-discrimination remove hurdles or handicaps during the race, but they do not equalise starting positions.

Laws prohibiting indirect discrimination do not do anything all that different from laws prohibiting direct discrimination; they certainly do not do anything so different that we could conclude that the prohibition of direct discrimination was a manifestation of formal equality while the prohibition of indirect discrimination was a manifestation of substantive equality. Indirect discrimination relies on disparate impact coupled with a justification test to determine the application of direct discrimination standards to conduct which would not ordinarily be classed as discriminatory. Any transformation of society that occurs as a result of indirect discrimination laws is that which would naturally occur in a system free of formal barriers. This is exactly the same kind of transformation which occurs as a result of the prohibition of direct discrimination.

Thus, we must conclude that the prohibition of wrongful discrimination, be it direct or indirect, is an individual right, which does not necessarily promote the interests of social groups. Nevertheless, the public sector equality duty and the provision for voluntary affirmative action policies by private actors do recognise and advance the interests of particular social groups *qua* groups. However, where an individual right comes into conflict with a group interest, UK law vindicates the rights of the individual to be free from wrongfully discriminatory treatment.

III. GROUP INTERESTS AND AFFIRMATIVE ACTION

The introduction of public sector positive duties and permissible voluntary affirmative action policies within the private sector mark a distinct shift in focus

[89] Fredman, 'A Critical Review of the Concept of Equality in UK Anti-Discrimination Law' (n 79) 3.12–3.16.

[90] Hepple (n 34) 25–27.

away from the prohibition of wrongful forms of treatment contained within anti-discrimination duties towards a theoretical and political framework which takes into account the interests of particular social groups *qua* groups. The focus is not on ensuring that individuals are free from wrongful forms of treatment; rather, the goal is to transform society such that advantage gaps between certain groups is lessened or eliminated or that those groups are not wronged or harmed by the policies or decisions of public bodies.[91] Within UK law, there are two ways that this is attempted. The first is the public sector equality duty, which requires public authorities to have due regard to the need to advance 'equality of opportunity'. The second is the explicit setting out of permissible conduct that can be voluntarily engaged in should private bodies wish to assist in the reduction of advantage gaps between social groups. The Equality Act 2010 frames the public sector equality duty as follows:

> A public body must, in the exercise of its functions, have due regard to the need to –
>
> (a) eliminate discrimination, harassment, victimisation and any other conduct that is prohibited by or under this Act;
>
> (b) advance equality of opportunity between persons who share a relevant protected characteristic and persons who do not share it ...[92]

The Act replaced earlier provisions for race, sex and disability, and also extends the duty to include age, gender reassignment, pregnancy and maternity, religion or belief, and sexual orientation.[93] In addition, there is a separate requirement on certain authorities to 'have due regard to the desirability' of exercising their functions 'in a way that is designed to reduce the inequalities of outcome which result from socio-economic disadvantage'.[94] This duty is quite onerous. The Act applies to any function of a public authority and imposes:

> a heavy burden upon public authorities in discharging the public sector equality duty and in ensuring that there is evidence available, if necessary, to demonstrate that discharge. It seems to have been the intention of Parliament that these considerations of equality of opportunity (where they arise) are now to be placed at the centre of formulation of policy by all public authorities, side by side with all other pressing circumstances of whatever magnitude.[95]

However, while these duties are wide-ranging, they do not require public bodies to engage in ineffective or unfruitful actions where the needs identified in the

[91] See ibid 22; S Fredman, *Human Rights Transformed: Positive Rights and Positive Duties* (Oxford University Press, 2008); S Albertyn, 'Substantive Equality and Transformation in South Africa' (2007) 23 *South African Journal of Human Rights* 253; Khaitan (n 1) Ch 8; Khaitan and Steel (n 5).

[92] Equality Act 2010, s 149(1).

[93] ibid s 149(7).

[94] ibid s 1(1).

[95] *R (Bracking) v Secretary of State for Work and Pensions* [2013] EWCA Civ 1345, [59].

Equality Act clearly do not arise.[96] Nevertheless, an authority should consider whether an impact assessment, along with other means of obtaining information, is required.[97] Positive duties have opened up new avenues for policy decisions to be challenged on the ground that they have failed to take into consideration the interests of particular social groups *qua* social groups. Thus, in the *Southhall Black Sisters* case, a decision to remove funding from an organisation which provided services to Afro-Caribbean and Asian women who are victims of domestic violence, due to a change in policy which would instead fund a borough-wide service provider catering to all individuals irrespective of gender or ethnicity, was held to be unlawful.[98] The reason for this was that the Council had failed to carry out a racial equality impact assessment when formulating this new funding criterion. If it cannot be shown that a decision-maker has paid proper attention to each of the statutory considerations, a public authority may be in breach of the duty, even when 'there has on any view been very substantial compliance with these equality duties'.[99]

Importantly, the statutory duty to have due regard to the need to advance equality of opportunities is not 'a duty to promote equality of opportunities between the appellants and persons who were members of different racial groups' and as such might not even be an example of substantive equality in the sense that it appears to pursue the goal of preventing harm done to social groups as a result of disadvantageous policies or practices rather than pursuing the goal of actually reducing or eliminating advantage gaps between those groups.[100] In this context, 'due regard' is 'the regard that is appropriate in all the circumstances', including the way that a disadvantaged group is affected, but also including 'such countervailing factors as are relevant to the function which the decision-maker is performing'.[101] As such, the duty is a procedural one to prepare and use equality impact assessments when making decisions or taking actions which might impact upon particular social groups.

The public sector equality duty is, as Endicott notes, 'a particularly intense, statutory form of the doctrine of relevant considerations'.[102] Because of this, if public bodies consider the group impact that their decisions or conduct has in circumstances where the duty to have due regard arises, their evaluation of the impact 'will only be treated as unlawful where it is "unreasonable or perverse"'.[103] In this sense, we can conclude that the statutory framework acts

[96] *R (Elias) v Defence Secretary* [2005] EWHC 1435 (Admin), [96]; *R (Aspinall) v Secretary of State for Work and Pensions* [2014] EWHC 4134 (Admin), [123].

[97] *R (Brown) v Secretary of State for Work and Pensions* [2008] EWHC 3158 (Admin), [89].

[98] *R (Kaur) v London Borough of Ealing* [2008] EWHC 2062 (Admin).

[99] *R (Hurley) v Secretary of State for Business Innovation and Skills* [2012] EWHC 201 (Admin), [95].

[100] *R (Baker) v Secretary of State for Communities and Local Government* [2008] EWCA Civ 141, [31].

[101] ibid.

[102] T Endicott, *Administrative Law*, 4th edn (Oxford University Press, 2018) 294.

[103] *R (S) v Justice Secretary* [2002] EWHC 1819, [99].

as a supplement to existing common law principles of judicial review. Indeed, nowhere is this clearer than with regard to indirect discrimination itself. It is not the disparate impact that results in a finding of unlawfulness; rather, disparate impact simply gives rise to a question of justification which, at least in the administrative context, is likely to be resolved by reference to the existing principles of judicial review. It is thus unclear precisely what the Equality Act is adding to assessment of the justifiability of indirect discrimination in the administrative context, except perhaps the identification of suspect characteristics which, should discrimination be on those grounds, demand a heightened degree of scrutiny than other characteristics such as hair colour or height.

This is not to say that the Equality Act does not add anything else to administrative law. It also has identified certain forms of discrimination which the court is now precluded from deeming justified. Direct discrimination on the basis of these protected characteristics can simply no longer be justified without breaching statute. Furthermore, the public sector equality duty has fundamentally restructured policy-making by mandating that public authorities consider group interests where they are implicated. However, because this duty requires consideration of how policies affect groups, it arguably is really just an indirect discrimination test which has a particularly large 'pool' for comparison and may ultimately be unable to guarantee the reduction or elimination of advantage gaps, even if it ensures that public authorities must pay attention to the impact that their policies and actions have on particular groups. Nevertheless, it is evident that this duty necessarily requires consideration of the treatment of social groups and the interests of those groups *qua* groups whereas most duty-bearers must only account for the impact that their policies will have on a sub-set of the group. Public authorities are expected to take into account the impact that their policies will have on social groups *qua* groups because, as public bodies, they are subject to higher standards of conduct and are far more likely to affect entire groups.

In addition to the public sector equality duty, sections 158 and 159 of the Equality Act set out what is permissible should a private body or individual seek to assist in the reduction or elimination of advantage gaps between groups. These provisions are permissive, not mandatory, and apply to all protected characteristics. Section 158 clarifies that the Equality Act 2010 does not prohibit a person from taking any action which is a proportionate means of achieving any of the follow three aims:

(a) enabling or encouraging persons who share a protected characteristic to overcome or minimise a disadvantage connected to that characteristic;
(b) meeting those needs of persons who share a protected characteristic that are different from the needs of persons who do not share it; or
(c) enabling or encouraging participation in an activity where participation by persons who share that characteristic is disproportionately low.[104]

[104] Equality Act 2010, s 158(2). See also Hepple (n 34) 129–30.

For example, these measures could include targeting members of particular disadvantaged groups for the provision of additional training to enable them to gain employment.[105] Within the employment context, 'tie-breaks' in recruitment and promotion are permitted under the Equality Act to the extent that they are genuine tie-breaks and do not amount to automatic policies. Section 159 permits an employer to take a protected characteristic into account when deciding who to recruit or promote, where persons who have that characteristic generally suffer a disadvantage or are underrepresented as a group. The provision can only be used in genuine tie-break situations where the candidates in question are 'as qualified as' each other.[106] However, determination of what counts as equally qualified need not be confined to formal qualifications. The intention of the Act is that if an employer reasonably thinks that candidates are of a comparable standard, the protected characteristic can be invoked as a tie-break.[107] This approach is in line with the jurisprudence of the European Court of Justice, which allows for preference to be given where candidate have 'substantially equivalent merits'.[108]

While the above provisions may not be sufficient to fully close advantage gaps between social groups, they are clearly grounded within a substantive equality framework in a way that deontic principles of non-discrimination are not. They constitute what McCrudden describes as 'an important, indeed radical, shift of regulatory philosophy in the area of equality legislation compared with what has gone before'.[109] So, what exactly has shifted? The introduction of a positive duty on public bodies to have due regard to the need to advance equality of opportunity is striking.[110] However, while is it unclear what precisely is required to achieve equality of opportunity, positive duties evidently manifest a movement away from treatment-based, deontic principles of non-discrimination towards the achievement of *some* form of consequentialist equality between particular social groups. It is the desire to reduce or eliminate advantage gaps which exist between these groups, however that is done, that motivates these duties. The radical shift that occurred was the introduction of group interests *qua* group interests into legal frameworks that had previously only dealt with individual rights to be free from discriminatory treatment.

Note that public authorities fulfilling their positive duties, and others who wish to take positive action on a voluntary basis, are limited by the principle of

[105] Explanatory Notes to the Equality Act 2010, para 511.

[106] Equality Act 2010, s 159(4)(a).

[107] Explanatory Notes to the Equality Act 2010, para 518.

[108] C-407/98 *Abrahamsson v Fogelqvist* [2000] ECR I-5539.

[109] C McCrudden, 'Equality Legislation and Reflexive Regulation: A Response to the Discrimination Law Review's Consultative Paper' (2007) 36 *Industrial Law Journal* 255, 266.

[110] Particularly as the correct definition of 'equality of opportunity' has been a topic of great contention within political and legal philosophy in recent decades See R Dworkin, *Sovereign Virtue: The Theory and Practice of Equality* (Harvard University Press, 2000); J Rawls, *A Theory of Justice*, rvsd edn (Harvard University Press, 1971); A Sen, *Inequality Re-Examined* (Clarendon Press, 1992); G Cohen, *If You're an Egalitarian, How Come You're So Rich* (Harvard University Press, 2000); Bedi (n 11); W Sadurski, *Equality and Legitimacy* (Oxford University Press, 2008).

non-discrimination. As such, the use of a protected characteristic as a criterion for treating some more favourably than others is prohibited as discriminatory by statute. Therefore, quotas which exist on the basis of protected characteristics are unlawful and employers engaged in 'tie-breaks' must not have a policy of automatically treating persons with one characteristic more favourably than others.[111] It is here that we can see the greatest need for conceptual clarity. We can only identify the conflict between principles of non-discrimination and principles of affirmative action or positive duties if we recognise that non-discrimination is an individual right which does not include conceptions of group harm or group interest and that positive duties are grounded primarily in consequentialist equality principles and group-based interests.[112]

Positive duties to advance equality were introduced into the UK legislative context as a result of criticisms which were levied against anti-discrimination laws for their failure to advance substantive or consequentialist equality goals. As has been shown above, those same criticisms can be levied against principles prohibiting indirect discrimination because, even though there is a shift to focus on the effects of wrongful treatment, these principles are nevertheless still action-regarding, deontic principles which seek to remove formal barriers through the protection of individual rights, but do not manifest anything that resembles the conception of group-based social transformation envisioned by substantive equality.

It seems that principles of substantive equality, as they are described by scholars and advocates, are not, strictly speaking, egalitarian principles because they do not wish to equalise anything.[113] Rather, they are principles which seek to take into account the interests of groups *qua* groups and consequently focus on reducing or eliminating gaps which exist between certain social groups by advancing the relative position of disadvantaged groups such that they are brought into parity with advantaged groups. In this sense they are far more associated with prioritarianism than egalitarianism and so descriptions of substantive or formal equality are primarily rhetorical in nature.[114] We do not actually want equalisation when we speak of substantive equality; we use the language of equality because it carries political weight. Equality, when used in this context, is a proxy for other, more nuanced, philosophical commitments.

We might conclude from this, as Holmes does, that principles of non-discrimination (as well as principles of substantive equality) are not actually connected to equality in any meaningful sense.[115] However, this would be a mistake. While these principles are not egalitarian in nature, where egalitarianism is defined by

[111] Equality Act 2010, s 159(4)(b).
[112] *cf* Ch 5.
[113] See Ch 2 above.
[114] Holmes (n 6) 191–92. See also P Westen, 'The Empty Idea of Equality' (1982) 95 *Harvard Law Review* 537.
[115] Holmes (n 6) 187–94.

the desire to equalise some 'thing', it is clear that these principles are nevertheless grounded within the value of equality.[116] Specifically, both the individual right to be free from wrongful discrimination and the group interest to reduce relative group disadvantage are informed by a commitment to respecting the moral equality of all persons, even if they are distinct methods of doing so. The desire to reduce advantage gaps between particular groups is only intelligible once we recognise that membership within either of these groups has no impact upon the moral status of those members. It is for this reason that we can account for the desirability to reduce advantage gaps between Blacks and whites or men and women as well as for the undesirability of attempts to equalise any gaps which may exist between murderers and non-murderers.

Ultimately, these principles relate to what treatment or conditions we are entitled to as moral equals operating within a legal system. While the use of labels such as 'formal equality' or 'substantive equality' may be primarily rhetorical in practice, a conceptual distinction still exists between principles of non-discrimination and principles of affirmative action. At its core, this distinction is between individual rights and group interests: formal equality pertains to individual rights to be free from both direct and indirect discrimination, and substantive equality pertains to group interests to reduce or eliminate advantage gaps between particular social groups.

IV. CONCLUSION

Modern anti-discrimination principles are often characterised as hybrid concepts, built upon multiple normative foundations and seeking to pursue divergent aims and goals. The reason for this has been a continued insistence that certain aspects of indirect discrimination previsions rely on group harm and seek to achieve some redistributive goal such as the reduction or elimination of advantage gaps between particular social groups. This group-based conception of harm leads scholars to conclude that indirect discrimination provisions are examples of substantive equality, manifesting a movement away from the formal equality which is associated with the prohibition of direct discrimination. These

[116] And not necessarily liberty. See Hellman, *When Is Discrimination Wrong?* (n 58); Hellman, 'Equality and Unconstitutional Discrimination' (n 2); Hellman, 'Two Concepts of Discrimination' (n 47). *cf* Moreau, 'In Defense of a Liberty-Based Account of Discrimination' (n 47); Moreau, 'What Is Discrimination?' (n 48); Khaitan (n 1); Khaitan and Steel (n 5). See also Fredman, *Discrimination Law* (n 11) 33–34. This analysis may ostensibly be favouring an equality-based account of discrimination and affirmative action over a liberty-based account. However, as Moreau correctly notes, these accounts can be analysed at two levels: one which explains *what* we are entitled to; the other which explains *why* they are entitled to it: Moreau, 'In Defense of a Liberty-Based Account of Discrimination' (n 47) 74–75. While one could account for the wrong of discrimination and the wrong of group-based inequality by reference to liberty claims, at a foundational level, these liberty claims are claims to *equal* liberty and are informed by a commitment to respecting the moral equality of those who differ with respect to certain characteristics.

assumptions are false. Principles of non-discrimination are examples of formal equality and formal equality only.

A right to non-discrimination is an individual right to be free from wrongful forms of treatment. Respect for group-based interests in redistribution is contained within the public sector equality duty and the voluntary affirmative action provisions within the Equality Act 2010. In this sense we can say that UK equality law can broadly be divided into two strands: one concerned with individual rights;[117] the other with group-based consequentialist equality interests. For the most part, these two strands work harmoniously, complementing each other by ensuring that those who consistently face discrimination are not only free from such harmful treatment, but that their group-based interests in advancing equality of opportunities is taken into account by public bodies in their administrative decision-making. However, these two strands may sometimes conflict.[118] Public or private bodies are prohibited from wrongfully discriminating, even where the goal is to advance group interests in substantive equality. As such, quota systems or automatic policies in tie-break situations are not permitted under UK law. Where individual rights conflict with group interests, the rights of the individual are preferred.[119]

It could be argued that all positive actions are wrongfully discriminatory in that they indirectly discriminate even where there is no quota or automatic policy. However, as indirect discrimination includes a justification test, it is only legally problematic where affirmative action amounts to direct discrimination which is automatically prohibited by statute. There is a fine line, but a line nonetheless, between incorporating the need to advance group interests into decision-making processes and basing a decision on a protected characteristic. Determining precisely when that line has been crossed is difficult but possible. Ultimately, such determinations will seek to identify where a provision, criterion or practice can be reasonably said to be 'based on' or 'grounded in' a protected characteristic and when we can reasonably conclude that someone has been treated less favourably 'because of' or 'on the basis of' a protected characteristic.

[117] Including rights to not only non-discrimination but also non-harassment, non-victimisation, and reasonable accommodation.

[118] When such conflicts arise, they cannot be resolved by appeals to moral equality, as we have here a clash of interpretations regarding how best to treat people with equal concern and respect, similar to when utilitarians and deontologists disagree over how best to respect the equality of persons. Rather, to resolve these conflicts, one must look to other philosophical commitments latent within these principles. As Fredman notes, this is a clash of values not logic: Fredman, *Discrimination Law* (n 11) 2.

[119] Notwithstanding the requirement of non-discrimination, there is significant room for UK law to expand on the current substantive equality provisions without infringing upon individual rights. The public sector equality duty currently only requires public bodies to have *due regard* to the need to advance equality of opportunities. There is no explicit duty to actually advance group interests. Similarly, many of the affirmative action policies which are permitted at law could be made mandatory without infringing upon rights to non-discrimination so long as those measures do not result in a protected characteristic becoming the determinative factor in decision-making.

These questions turn first on whether affirmative action policies are always discriminatory policies, and second on whether the advancement of group interests is sufficient to justify a breach of individual rights to non-discrimination.

On the first point, there is precedent to suggest that, where a policy uses a protected characteristic as one of several factors in decision-making, such policies are not 'based on' protected characteristics and will consequently not amount to a breach of anti-discrimination rights.[120] On the second point, a determination that affirmative action policies are discriminatory may not be sufficient to negate or override the desire to advance substantive equality. Equality law frameworks which attempt to incorporate both anti-discrimination rights and affirmative action policies will always have to strike a balance between the rights of the individual and the interests of the group. The Equality Act 2010 has indicated that affirmative action policies which incorporate protected characteristics, but which do not base decisions solely on those characteristics, are not directly discriminatory, even if they may be examples of justified indirect discrimination. As such, UK law holds that some, but not all, affirmative action policies are unlawful and that, where a policy is directly discriminatory, the rights of the individual to be free from discrimination takes primacy over group interests in the reduction or elimination of advantage gaps. Whether this is the best way to strike that balance is clearly a topic of contentious debate. Before such debates can be resolved, however, we need to be clear about the precise location of this conflict.

Conceptual analysis of discrimination provisions has consistently identified group interests within non-discrimination rights, implying that these rights advance both formal and substantive equality. In light of the arguments set out above, we can conclude that rights to non-discrimination, including the right to be free from indirect discrimination, are individual rights, grounded within formal equality, and which do not require proof of group harm or seek to advance group interests in the way that substantive equality envisages. The conflict within the UK statutory context is between rights to be free from direct discrimination and a few specific affirmative action policies, not between differing requirements of non-discrimination principles, or between anti-discrimination rights and affirmative action policies in general. An effective theory of discrimination is one which accurately accounts for the deontological, individual rights-based nature of anti-discrimination provisions and the ways in which these rights may complement – but also sometimes conflict with – the consequentialist equality goals associated with substantive equality.

[120] See *Regents of the University of California v Bakke*, 438 US 265 (1978); *Grutter v Bollinger*, 539 US 306 (2003).

7

Political Discretion and the Common Good

THIS BOOK BEGAN with a discussion of the role that value plays within constitutional theory. Given the nature of the substantive claims advanced since then, it is only fitting that it should end with a discussion of the role that politics does – or should – play within constitutional theory. While focused on the concept of legal equality, this book has operated at the intersection between general constitutional theory and British public law. This approach may present a difficulty for scholars who place emphasis on the uniqueness of the political aspects of British constitutional practice. Yet, when one ponders on the attempt to draw a sharp distinction between law and politics in this context, it becomes unclear precisely what characterises the legitimate boundaries between judicial, legislative, and executive power. An internal perspective which focuses on the principles of the common law must draw upon both theory and doctrine in its interpretation of existing and proposed practice. The question then becomes, insofar as the judiciary develops common law standards, informed by institutional history and constitutional theory, to what extent can the legal limit or affect the political?

Put another way, the focus of this book so far has been on the equality-based duties that constitutional government appropriately respectful of the rule of law necessarily entails. But both the rule of law and the ideal of legal equality speak to more than minimum duty. There is an element of supererogation at play here, what Lon Fuller would have described a 'morality of aspiration' as distinct from a morality of duty.[1] By this he sought to describe aspects of the rule of law which move beyond 'the basic rules without which an ordered society is impossible or without which an ordered society directed towards certain specific goals must fail of its mark'.[2] While these basic rules and duties are essential, they are a floor not a ceiling. The morality of aspiration then focuses on what can be done in pursuit of an ideal in addition to this. It is about the good not the right: '[i]t is the morality of the Good Life, of excellence, of the fullest realization of human powers'.[3] Within the context of legal equality, this represents the ways in which

[1] L Fuller, *The Morality of Law*, rvsd edn (Yale University Press, 1969) Ch 1.
[2] ibid 5–6.
[3] ibid 5.

public power can be directed towards the achievement of equality-based goals. It captures principles of equality which cannot be described entirely by reference to individual rights but which instead manifest within a diverse range of policies from wealth redistribution to affirmative action, to the establishment of a universal healthcare system.

A recurring theme within this book has been the need to carefully delineate the distinctly legal aspects of legal equality such that the ideal does not collapse into what one might describe as 'pure politics'. But that should not be taken to mean that legal equality and the rule of law are exclusively concerned with minimum duty. Once it is accepted that legal equality demands more than this, however, it raises a question of how constitutional law should deal with these aspirational aspects of equality. In this chapter, I defend the contention that these concerns are properly within the realm of legitimate political discretion. This is not to say that they can be entirely abandoned by a political authority if it chooses. It would undermine of both the rule of law and the principle of legal equality to fail to do anything in this regard. But the choice of what to do is a feature of legitimate political determination, so long as it is within a range of reasonable options that respect the rights of all. Equally, there may be actions which are so inimical to any plausible conception of the public good that they cannot be lawful.

Requirements of fundamental legal equality, manifesting a commitment to the equal dignity of persons, ground the rule of law as a defensible scheme of public justice. But this commitment also demands that law be ordered towards a politics which views the flourishing of each and every member of our community as an essential feature of its own success. Put simply, the normative commitments latent within the ideal of legality are not and cannot be neutral as to the ends of just government. There is an internal moral standard within the rule of law which manifests principled constraints on what officials can do in pursuit of the common good.[4] But there must be more than that if the rule of law is to live up to its fullest potential. There must also be limits on what constitutes the public interest which extend beyond rights-based constraint to include conceptions of what law can enable and facilitate. This aspect of legality – what law must be directed towards if it is to meet its internal commitment to just governance – must be included within any account of legal equality which pays appropriate attention to both law and equality.

[4] See TRS Allan, 'Constitutional Rights and Common Law' (1991) 11 *Oxford Journal of Legal Studies* 453; TRS Allan, 'Political Obligation and Public Law' in L Crawford et al (eds), *Law Under a Democratic Constitution: Essays in Honour of Jeffrey Goldsworthy* (Hart Publishing, 2019); TRS Allan, 'Why the Law Is What It Ought to Be' (2020) 11 *Jurisprudence* 574, 575–77; TRS Allan, 'Law as a Branch of Morality: The Unity of Practice and Principle' (2020) 65 *American Journal of Jurisprudence* 1, 7–8; TRS Allan, *The Sovereignty of Law: Freedom, Constitution, and Common Law* (Oxford University Press, 2013) 293.

I. EQUALITY AND THE PUBLIC INTEREST

When thinking about the rule of law, it is tempting to see it only as a check on abuses of state power. It is often described as having only a negative virtue, useful to prevent harms done through law but providing very little, if anything, in the way of positive benefit.[5] The reason for this is the way in which political authority is envisaged, often tacitly, to manifest only as an expression of will. In contemporary democracies this translates into the view that the public interest is identified as a kind of majoritarian aggregation of views or, in a more refined sense, as the will of a representative political body such as a legislature or government.[6] Viewed as such, politics loses much of its intrinsic virtue as it collapses into an instrumental vector for the consolidation and implementation of a public will which is itself only contingently valuable so long as the public adopt broadly correct political views. In that context, the rule of law becomes a shield to protect the individual from abuse of power, a counter-majoritarian check to mediate between the public interest and the private citizen.

This conception of the public interest is impoverished. It captures an important aspect of modern democratic theory but fails to ground that within an account of the purposes of both law and politics, properly understood. In this framework, the individual and the community stand in conceptual tension with each other. This has two worrying implications. The first is that this way of framing the relationship between the individual and the community makes it difficult to conceive of a politics which is directed towards the common interests of all, where each person is valued equally. Instead, we see a concern for protecting the vulnerable translate into a distrust for political authority which focuses heavily on constraining state power.[7] While it is important to prevent the abuse of power, an exclusive focus on constraint can result in a failure to take seriously the good that can be done by the well-ordered use of legal authority, directed towards the achievement of ends that advance the collective interests of the community as a whole.

The second worrying implication of this kind of framework is an impoverishment of our theoretical language such that it becomes difficult to conceive of important constitutional concepts except as checks on the abuse of power. When the public interest is collapsed into majoritarianism and the public therefore set up in conceptual tension with the individual, rights become the last great

[5] See J Raz, 'The Rule of Law and Its Virtue' in *The Authority of Law: Essays on Law and Morality*, 2nd edn (Oxford University Press, 2009).

[6] G Webber and P Yowell, 'Securing Human Rights through Legislation' in G Webber et al (eds), *Legislated Rights: Securing Human Rights through Legislation* (Cambridge University Press, 2018) 4–5.

[7] This can sometimes be described as a 'red light' approach to the rule of law. See C Harlow and R Rawlings, *Law and Administration*, 4th edn (Cambridge University Press, 2022).

defence of the individual against an encroaching state demanding their sacrifice for the benefit of the rest of society.[8]

A commitment to legal equality must recognise the equal rights of all legal subjects. But it is bolstered when informed by a conception of the public interest which is grounded in the moral equality of persons, one which views the point and purpose of politics and law as the flourishing of each and every member of the community. This has echoes in the classical legal tradition. On this view, the public interest or the public good is not in tension with the rights and interests of legal subjects. Rather they are co-constitutive of each other. What is good for an individual cannot be separated from what is good for the community as a whole. This is partially because one's life is better when their friends' lives are better,[9] and partially because it is good for people to live within a society that values them and their fellow citizens as equals. Being valued equally is a necessary aspect of this but it is not sufficient. Membership within a civic community grounds the bonds of civic friendship that connect all members of a polity.[10] But a flourishing society is one which utilises collective political agency to establish and maintain social institutions which benefit all of its members.

It is in this vein that we can begin to conceptualise a vision of the public interest that embraces legal equality without being exhausted by individual rights. An important aspect of the classical natural law tradition, stretching back to the Greeks and Romans, is the view that the purpose of political institutions is to ensure that members of the political community can flourish and lead good lives.[11] Law therefore plays a vital role in helping to establish and sustain social institutions directed towards this goal.[12] It serves a social function by providing a framework of rules and principles which protect the vulnerable from the predations of bad actors and allow people to plan their lives, secure in the confidence that the contracts they enter will generally be upheld and the wrongs they suffer will be adequately rectified.[13] But this must be supplemented by a political arena actively seeking to advance the best interests of the governed, bolstered by other social institutions such as the local community and the family which reduce the need for coercive law.[14]

[8] Even certain communitarian thinkers set things up like this, proposing that the needs of society should justify breach of individual rights in some cases. See for example A Etzioni, 'The Common Good and Rights: A Neo-Communitarian Approach' (2009) 10 *Georgetown Journal of International Affairs* 113, 115–17.

[9] J Finnis, *Natural Law and Natural Rights* (Oxford University Press, 1980) 4, 6.

[10] See J Maritian, *The Person and the Common Good* (University of Notre Dame Press, 1966) Ch 4.

[11] See H Rommen, *The Natural Law: A Study in Legal and Social History and Philosophy* (Thomas Hanley tr, Liberty Fund, 1998) Ch 1.

[12] NE Simmonds, 'Constitutional Rights, Civility and Artifice' (2019) 78 *Cambridge Law Journal* 175.

[13] On the social function of law, see L Fuller, *The Principles of Social Order: Selected Essays of Lon L Fuller*, rvsd edn (K Winston ed, Hart Publishing, 2001).

[14] A Etzioni, 'The Common Good and Rights: A Neo-Communitarian Approach' (2009) 10 *Georgetown Journal of International Affairs* 113, 115.

Law is a form of social order which helps to guide human conduct, but which also helps to constitute and maintain relationships of respect among a community of equals. As such, it can never be neutral with regard to ends, be they political or human. The rule of law cannot be separated from a robust theory of law and law can never be neatly separated from the proper ends of politics: the common good. It is thus both deontic and teleological, concerned as much with ensuring respect for the natural rights of legal subjects as it is with maintaining the conditions necessary for human flourishing. This idea that law could be defined by reference to the social function that it serves is central to Fuller's project of eunomics: the principles of good social order.[15] Thus, to Fuller, the principles of legality 'though they concern a relationship to persons generally, demand more than forebearances … to meet these demands human energies must be directed towards specific kinds of achievement and not merely warned away from harmful acts'.[16] As such, the rule of law appeals to 'a sense of trusteeship and the pride of the craftsman' on the part of the lawgiver.[17]

A good custodian, embodying both Fuller's ideal of reciprocity and the related concept of civic friendship, must not violate the fundamental rights of subjects.[18] But it cannot neglect their flourishing either. If we conceive of law – and the rule of law – as tied to this more expansive tradition oriented towards the collective benefit of all, we can begin to make sense of the communal or collective claims which are internal to the rule of law. Rather than being conceived as entirely within the purview of external political morality, a commitment to peace, justice, and the collective flourishing of all members of a community becomes core to an ideal of custodianship necessary to give meaning and coherence to the disparate principles we call the rule of law. This is only possible if we abandon any pretence to neutrality as to either political morality or the good life. To be a good custodian is to take an interest in improving the lives of those under one's charge. To do that one must have some vision of how to achieve this; there must be some conception of what would constitute an improvement.

The core insight of the classical natural law tradition is that it is much better (for you) to live in a society of flourishing equals than to be extravagantly wealthy in a crumbling dystopia.[19] Law in its central sense is oriented towards facilitating the advancement of the best interests of all within a society.[20] Raz, perhaps unintentionally, reveals the important link between this traditional way

[15] See Fuller, *The Principles of Social Order: Selected Essays of Lon L. Fuller* (n 13).

[16] Fuller, *The Morality of Law* (n 1) 42.

[17] ibid 43.

[18] On reciprocity, see ibid 19–27, 39–40, 48, 61–62, 137–40. On civic friendship, see Finnis (n 9) 141–56.

[19] See A Vermeule, *Common Good Constitutionalism* (Polity Press, 2022); C Casey, 'Common-Good Constitutionalism and the New Battle over Constitutional Interpretation in the United States' [2021] *Public Law* 765; M Foran, 'Rights, Common Good, and The Separation of Powers' (2022) 86 *Modern Law Review* 599.

[20] On the central case of law, see Finnis (n 9) Ch 1.

of thinking about law and the modern concept we call the rule of law by tying legality to an ideal of custodianship.[21] He thus tacitly accepts that there is more to the rule of law than simply checks on state power or the protection of individual liberties. A failure on the part of legal officials to maintain a system of peace, justice, and prosperity is a threat to the rule of law itself, constituting a failure to maintain the conditions necessary for law to serve the social function that it should.

Raz demonstrates this by way of an example of the misuse of public funds.[22] A hereditary monarch using the public purse to purchase an expensive diamond ring for his lover breaches the rule of law by failing to distinguish the rights and powers of governments from the rights and powers of private owners: 'even though he controls the public purse, he does not own it'.[23] A core insight here is that breaches of the rule of law need not include failure to guide conduct but can instead manifest in what we might call the privatisation of a public good: the use of a public good for private ends. But if this is true – and it is – then we have two categories that we can use to describe the ends of government: public ends and private ends. The rule of law then directs government to pursue public ends and curtails the pursuit of private ends. But now we must determine what these categories entail.

Traditionally, the distinction between public and private ends was encapsulated within the idea of the common good, itself grounded within the value of equality: 'In the classical account, a genuinely *common* good is a good that is unitary ("one in number") and capable of being shared without being diminished. Thus it is inherently non-aggregative; it is not the summation of a number of private goods'.[24] As such, the common good presupposes the moral equality of persons and conceives of politics as properly ordered towards those goods which can genuinely be shared in common; peace, justice, and abundance, 'extrapolate[d] to modern conditions to include various forms of health, safety, and economic security' (emphasis omitted).[25] Each of these goods can be enjoyed by all members of a community without diminishing them. What is more, the full enjoyment of such goods can only be achieved when one shares in their enjoyment with a community of moral equals. Indeed, rather than the interests of the community being in some conceptual tension with the individual, 'the good of the community is itself the good for individuals'.[26] A commitment to the common good is therefore to be contrasted with tyranny and factionalism,

[21] J Raz, 'The Law's Own Virtue' (2019) 39 *Oxford Journal of Legal Studies* 1.
[22] ibid 6.
[23] ibid.
[24] Vermeule (n 19) 28.
[25] ibid 7.
[26] ibid 29. See also C de Koninck, 'The Primacy of the Common Good against the Personalists: The Principle of the New Order' in R McInerny (ed), *The Writings of Charles de Koninck*, vol 2 (Notre Dame Press, 2016).

where state power is either used for private benefit or so weak that it cannot or will not prevent the abuse of the vulnerable at the hands of powerful private actors.[27]

The rule of law is therefore undermined not just by the privatisation of public goods but also by their neglect. We can see this starkly when we look to the underfunding of the justice system. A failure to provide adequate resources to maintain a functioning justice system is a direct threat to the rule of law. That much is accepted by virtually all rule of law theorists. Usually, however, the fact that the rule of law requires positive action on the part of the state to set up and run vital social institutions is rarely extrapolated to inform wider thinking on the concept. But if we accept the idea that legality is tied to good custodianship in the best interests of the governed, then it becomes much easier to see how this requirement to positively invest in the community is a central rather than peripheral instantiation of the rule of law.

II. DISCRETION

The idea that legal and political authority should be directed towards the best interests of all should not be dismissed as trite or banal. The dominant strands of both jurisprudence and constitutional theory do not tend to focus on these communal concerns, preferring instead to emphasise individual rights and questions of institutional design. Part of the reason for this is a legitimate concern with constitutionalising what is better seen as a matter of pure politics. But this concern can sometimes result in these communal aspects of constitutional theory being under-theorised or abandoned altogether. A careful balance must be struck between appropriate deference and abdication of responsibility.

In public law, a court must recognise and afford appropriate respect to the fact that it is not the primary decision-maker and so cannot decide for itself what constitutes good policy. In our modern administrative law, this translates into the maxim that courts will review the outmost limits of discretion but will not act as appellate bodies tasked with retaking the decision themselves. In these cases, courts recognise an alternative, perhaps superior, voice speaking on behalf of the community – even if they must interpret that voice when adjudicating cases, drawing upon principles of justice in so doing. It is this authority which explains the courts' deference to the more political organs of state. It is for this reason that Laws suggests that 'deference marks the courts' recognition that as regards the merits of the use of discretionary power in any given instance, the public body to which the power has been delegated by Parliament is the primary decision-maker'.[28]

[27] Vermeule (n 19) 26–27.
[28] J Laws, *The Constitutional Balance* (Hart Publishing, 2021) 90.

The approach of the common law to questions of deference echoes the natural law concept of *determinatio*. In the classical legal tradition, the decisions of executive or legislative authorities were attempts to provide greater determination to the very general requirements of justice and the natural law. With that in mind, there exists a range of plausible concretisations of these requirements in any given context. As Aquinas notes, general ideas must be made particular, 'for example the craftsman needs to turn the general idea of a house into the shape of this or that house'.[29] This mirrors Fuller's argument that the rule of law appeals to 'a sense of trusteeship and the pride of the craftsman' mentioned above.[30]

Within the bounds of reason, such determinations as to these particulars must be contextualised to varying circumstances across time and place: 'The general principles of the natural law cannot be applied to all men in the same way because of the great variety of human circumstances; and hence arises the diversity of positive laws among various people.'[31] Here we see the classical roots of the principle of deference that is owed by courts to legitimate political authority, where it acts within the realm of its lawful authority. Determination will inevitably be in some way discretionary, so that, once within the bounds of reasonable disagreement, it may even be 'rationally arbitrary'.[32] In this sense, respect for political discretion helps to identify the proper scope of both political and legal authority. The basis of discretion is that 'deference is how law respects the discretionary space of the public authority to engage in determination'.[33]

In the context of equality, we have seen throughout this book that there is scope for quite considerable disagreement over the best way to respect the moral equality of persons. There is a delicate balance to be struck when theorising a constitutional conception of equality. On the one hand, one must not be too prescriptive, insinuating that there is only one, entirely speculative and acontextual way to respect and advance legal equality. On the other hand, there is a real danger that the theorist will instead be so concerned with respect for discretion that she says virtually nothing at all of substance. Yet, while purely speculative accounts of constitutional theory should generally be resisted, theory is not doctrine. It cannot provide the kind of detailed exposition of rules that manifest within a given legal history. What it can do, when it is successful, is situate doctrine within a framework of general principles that lend it coherence and weight.

Thus, while a strictly utilitarian economic structure might plausibly be defended from within an equality-based framework, it is not one which is

[29] T Aquinas, *Summa Theologica* pt I-II, q 95, Art 2 in Aquinas, *Political Writing* (RW Dyson ed, trans, Cambridge University Press, 2002) 130.

[30] Fuller, *The Morality of Law* (n 1) 43.

[31] Aquinas (n 29) 130.

[32] A Vermeule, 'Rationally Arbitrary Decisions in Administrative Law' (2015) 44 *The Journal of Legal Studies* S475.

[33] Vermeule (n 19) 46.

compatible with constitutional governance as it has been theorised and practised within the common law world. The individual is a locus of rights and responsibilities within this framework, not a vessel for utility that can be abandoned or sacrificed for the sake of the majority. There may be room for quite dramatic policy divergence, but fundamental rights and their entailed duties are in one form or another essential to rule of law compliance. There may be debate over the content of such rights, but the fact that legal subjects have rights, informed by foundational constitutional principle, is not itself negotiable.

Rights which are necessary for the rule of law are, in a constitutional democracy, not subject to legislative or executive override once their scope is properly determined. They are not up for reasoned debate or renegotiation in the way that ordinary statutory rights might be. However, it is important to understand that reasonableness, in this context, takes on the meaning attributed to it within public law: to be reasonable is to conform to constitutional principle. It is therefore incumbent upon any constitutional theorist to remain cognisant of the distinction between those rights which are essential for constitutional governance and those which are merely politically desirable.

Respect for the equal dignity of citizens entails acceptance of the legitimacy of moral disagreement and the need for a framework of constitutional principle which enshrines democratic processes to resolve these disagreements without undermining the commitment to moral equality that justifies those processes in the first place. The obligation to obey the law does not derive from official consensus or the assertion of governmental power. Rather, it is grounded in our political obligations to one another to respect the legitimate processes of resolving these disagreements in a manner which pays due attention to the moral and political equality of persons.[34] If we are to take this commitment seriously, we must accept that there may be legitimate executive or legislative intervention to better flesh out what is in the public interest, as well as to resolve sincere disagreement about the best ways to respect the dignity and moral rights of persons. However, we must also accept that the normative foundations of this obligation necessitate that political power is exercised in a manner which itself respects the moral equality of persons.

The connection between legality and constitutional legitimacy ensures that the obligation to obey the law flows from a relationship we have with the political community that we belong to, one which is premised upon a shared commitment to moral equality. When political institutions do not even strive for justice, when equality, 'the core of justice' is repudiated, then there can be no genuine legal obligation.[35] A judge, tasked with the interpretation of statute

[34] Allan, 'Political Obligation and Public Law' (n 4) 250, 253.

[35] ibid 253; see also G Radbruch, 'Statutory Lawlessness and Supra-Statutory Law' (2006) 26 *Oxford Journal of Legal Studies* 1; R Alexy, 'A Defence of Radbruch's Formula' in D Dyzenhaus (ed), *Recrafting the Rule of Law: The Limits of Legal Order* (Hart Publishing, 1999); TRS Allan, 'In Defence of Radbruch's Formula: Injustice, Interpretation, and Invalidity' in M Borowski et al (eds), *Rechtspjilosophie und Grundrechtstheorie* (Mohr Siebeck, 2017).

or the assessment of the legality of executive action, must guide her analysis by reference to this fundamental precept of constitutional legitimacy. She must operate on the assumption that the application of law is intended to respect constitutional rights such that the pursuit of the public interest does not disrespect the equal dignity of persons.[36]

This book has sought to explore this aspect of constitutional legitimacy, focusing primarily on the structure and history of the common law. In particular, it has shown that wrongful and unjustified discrimination is precluded by the general principles of judicial review as arbitrary and unreasonable, often resulting from a failure to adhere to principles of relevancy or the rule against bias. Central to this is a coherent understanding of the nature of discrimination as a comparative form of treatment which can be unjustified and wrongful for many reasons. Additionally, the principle of legal equality names a very particular form of discrimination which is wrongful precisely because it does not treat those affected as moral equals by failing to afford due and equal regard to their interests or proper respect for their dignity. To act in accordance with constitutional principle, administrative and judicial bodies must pay appropriate attention to the social meaning that is likely to attach to their actions and policies. It is a fundamental precept of the rule of law that 'justice should not only be done but should manifestly and undoubtedly be seen to be done'.[37] The rule of law manifests a relationship of reciprocity and respect between ruler and ruled. One cannot maintain such a relationship if there is the reasonable and justified perception that administrative agencies are biased against particular individuals or groups.

The core of legal equality and the rule of law is impartiality, with legal rules being constructed and applied without favouritism or prejudice: '[t]he distinctions drawn between persons must be justifiable not merely by reference to immediate political aims, but also in the light of fundamental duties of impartiality and fairness'.[38] These have been foundational principles of judicial review since its inception. The principles of fairness and proportionality captured in *Rooke's* case are informed by and informative of the common law commitment to constitutional justice.[39] They are essential to the very concept of rule by law, fundamentally in contrast with arbitrariness or caprice.[40] The application of these principles may change over time as context changes, but at their core they capture a commitment to natural justice.

[36] Allan, 'Political Obligation and Public Law' (n 4) 255.

[37] *R v Sussex Justices, ex p McCarthy* [1924] 1 KB 256, 259.

[38] Allan, 'Political Obligation and Public Law' (n 4) 257.

[39] *Rooke* (1597) 5 Co Rep 99. See also P Craig, 'Proportionality and Constitutional Review' (2020) 3 *University of Oxford Human Rights Hub Journal* 87.

[40] See Allan, *The Sovereignty of Law* (n 4); TRS Allan, *Law, Liberty, and Justice: The Legal Foundations of British Constitutionalism* (Clarendon Press, 1993); TRS Allan, *Constitutional Justice: A Liberal Theory of the Rule of Law* (Oxford University Press, 2001).

This is not to say that the rule of law demands judicial intervention in circumstances where there is legitimate disagreement regarding how best to balance conflicting constitutional values, themselves informed by a commitment to respecting human dignity. For example, in *Nicklinson* the court was faced with a sincere conflict between individual autonomy and the sanctity of life when tasked with determining whether a prohibition on assisted suicide was compatible with the European Convention on Human Rights.[41] Respect for dignity might inform much of our constitutional order, but that does not mean that dignity is itself independently justiciable absent some attachment to constitutional principles of reasonableness or proportionality. However, this does not preclude dignity from *informing* legal principle.

Whether the actions or policies of the executive are lawful will depend, in part, on whether they are reasonable and proportionate, and whether they are reasonable and proportionate will itself depend on whether they appropriately respect the equal dignity of legal subjects. Nevertheless, in circumstances where there is a genuine conflict, with each side resting on a plausible account of the public interest, and where the executive is acting in accordance with constitutional principle, the common law does not permit judicial intervention. Of course, legislation such as the Human Rights Act 1998 can provide sufficient grounding and justification of judicial assessment of the compatibility of executive action or even legislation with international human rights law. But this is evidently contingent upon legislative authorisation and not an essential feature of the rule of law. Even so, the rule of law demands that such questions relating to the meaning of particular rights be answered by reference to legal principle and the existing law and not by recourse to abstract moral reasoning unmoored from domestic or international law.

Fundamental rights are the floor below which no rule-of-law-compliant system can fall, but a society directed towards the flourishing of its members will obviously go beyond that. The court's role vis-à-vis Parliament and the executive, from Coke to Dicey, has been understood to police the outermost limits of reason so that statute and the related limits on executive action are interpreted in 'the spirit of legality'.[42] There is therefore a careful balance that must be struck to ensure that action can be taken within the legitimate realm of discretion afforded to the political branches of state without that discretion leading to abuse.

Within this context, it must be remembered that the public interest is distinct from that which is to be determined by the democratic processes. Here, the public interest that matters is the interest in ensuring that the government acts within its lawful bounds, pursuing the public good and refraining from committing

[41] *R (Nicklinson) v Ministry of Justice* [2014] UKSC 38.

[42] AV Dicey, *An Introduction to the Study of the Law of the Constitution* (JWF Allison ed, Oxford University Press, 2013) 273.

public wrongs: 'fundamentally the issue is not about individual rights but about public wrongs'.[43] This may be the basis of a distinction between political and constitutional principle, with one focusing on the duties that public authorities are subject to under the common law as opposed to legal rights broadly construed. But here careful consideration must be given to the precise nature of the public good and its connection to the legal limits on legislative, executive and judicial power.

III. LEGAL REASONING AND THE COMMON GOOD

When speaking of the contrast between policy and principle, it is best to construe this as a distinction between the use of law to pursue a particular goal and the appropriate use of judicial power to ensure that public bodies act within their constitutional limits. On this reading, the public interest is the combination of public policy (determined by the political processes) and constitutional principle (informed by the rule of law and enforced by the courts). The judiciary acts in the public interest when it enforces constitutional principle and refrains from pursuing its view of appropriate public policy. Likewise, the executive and legislature act in the public interest when they pursue the common good, suitably tailored to meet the needs of the moment via a process of determination. Allan is therefore entirely correct that 'the law must be regarded as a public asset, intended to serve the public good: it cannot be merely an instrument for promoting the interests of a ruling elite'.[44] As such, 'it is necessarily implicit that … a legislature, even if sovereign … must act for the public good'.[45]

In most areas, but particularly when dealing with equality-based theory, political morality will often conceive of the common good or the public interest in a manner which cuts across the principle/policy divide. The attainment of a perfectly just society will necessarily require the achievement of concrete ends in addition to a system of rights and duties. It might be tempting to conceive of this distinction as capturing two concepts which are wholly separate and suitably distinct. Conceived as such, the judiciary can be given its own sphere of authority – principle – which acts upon and checks the other organs of state who deal with policy. But this neat division must be challenged.

Liberal constitutionalists inspired by Ronald Dworkin sometimes rely on this distinction between principle and policy in their work.[46] But a sharp contrast

[43] B Hale, 'Who Guards the Guardians?' (2013) www.supremecourt.uk/docs/speech-131014.pdf; see also M Elliott, 'Standing, Judicial Review and the Rule of Law: Why We All Have a "Direct Interest" in Government According to Law' (*Public Law for Everyone*, 2013) www.publiclawforeveryone.com/2013/07/29/standing-judicial-review-and-the-rule-of-law-why-we-all-have-a-direct-interest-in-government-according-to-law/.

[44] Allan, 'Why the Law Is What It Ought to Be' (n 4) 575.

[45] Allan, *The Sovereignty of Law* (n 4) 293.

[46] See R Dworkin, *A Matter of Principle* (Clarendon Press, 1986) Ch 4; Allan, *Law, Liberty, and Justice: The Legal Foundations of British Constitutionalism* (n 40) 54–55.

between the principled protection of fundamental rights and the pursuit of the public good as mere policy misconstrues the basis of each. To Dworkin, constitutionalism must adopt a kind of liberal neutrality: the requirement 'that governments must be neutral on what might be called questions of the good life … that political decisions must be, so far as is possible, independent of any particular conception of the good life or of what gives value to life … liberalism takes [this] as its constitutive political morality'.[47] Dworkin argued that this neutrality is what distinguishes liberalism from rival left-wing and right-wing doctrines which all embrace non-neutral conceptions of the good life and attempt to mobilise state power to establish a flourishing society.[48] Yet this is difficult to reconcile with his account of policy, informed by arguments pertaining to how a given decision will work to promote the general welfare or the public interest.[49]

How can it be the case that government must remain neutral on the good life while policy decisions about the public interest remain the unique purview of government? This only makes sense if the public interest is not related to members of the public leading good lives. Indeed, this is exactly how Dworkin construes the public interest: either a utilitarian calculus or an aggregate of majoritarian preferences.[50] But this account of the public interest – the proper realm of policy determination on this view – is manifestly in conflict with a commitment to legal equality which takes the rights of subjects seriously. Indeed, that seems to be the point. If framed in this way, it is easy to see why one might argue for the primacy of the judiciary over the more political branches of state: the public good is conflated with an aggregative idea of the 'greater' good,[51] to be contrasted with rights under justice which can then act as 'trumps' against the collective will.[52] But this conception of both rights and the common good is mistaken. Properly understood, rights and the common good do not conflict.[53] This can only be fully understood once one breaks from the mistaken belief that the common good is some utilitarian aggregative concept.[54] Thus, while

[47] R Dworkin, 'Liberalism' in S Hampshire (ed), *Public and Private Morality* (Cambridge University Press, 1978).

[48] ibid 128.

[49] Dworkin, *A Matter of Principle* (n 46) 221 ff. See also Allan, *Law, Liberty, and Justice: The Legal Foundations of British Constitutionalism* (n 40) 54.

[50] See R Dworkin, 'Social Sciences and Constitutional Rights – the Consequences of Uncertainty' (1977) 6 *Journal of Law and Education* 1, 10; R Dworkin, *Taking Rights Seriously* (Harvard University Press, 1977) 22, 90.

[51] See JS Mill, 'Utilitarianism' in JM Robson (ed), *The Collected Works of John Stuart Mill, Vol X, Essays on Ethics, Religion and Society* (University of Toronto Press, 1969); P Singer, *Practical Ethics*, 2nd edn (Cambridge University Press, 1993); R Hare, *Moral Thinking: Its Levels, Method, and Point* (Clarendon Press, 1981); *cf* D Brink, 'The Separateness of Persons, Distributive Norms, and Moral Theory' in RG Frey and C Morris (eds), *Value, Welfare, and Morality* (Cambridge University Press, 1993).

[52] See Dworkin, *Taking Rights Seriously* (n 50).

[53] See Foran (n 19).

[54] See P Yowell, 'A Critical Examination of Dworkin's Theory of Rights' (2007) 52 *American Journal of Jurisprudence* 93.

Laws contends that '[p]oliticians, governments, are by necessity utilitarians',[55] this should be replaced with an understanding that legislatures and governments are engaged in reasoned deliberation in pursuit of the common good, which can include deliberation over rights, obligations, and goals.[56]

Properly understood, political authority in the form of legislative or administrative action is reasoned action, furthering the principles which underpin our existing practice, and not a mere act of aggregative will.[57] But if we accept that 'policy' cannot be sharply distinguished from principle, then neutrality on the good life or on the common good of the community is unsustainable. The commitment to a morally engaged legal practice is not compatible with attempts to remain neutral on the good life. Moral neutrality is impossible on matters of legal principle and the actions of legislatures and executives when they pursue the common good are far more a matter of legal principle than they are of aggregative will.

This does not mean that judges should necessarily create 'policy' or pursue some private version of the public good, however. The role of the common law judge is not to 'decide' within a realm of discretion how best to order society to the common good, but rather to interpret the decisions or actions of other actors such as political authorities in the form of legislatures or the executive, presuming that such decisions are reasonably directed towards the common good. There is a space for political authority to engage in reasoned action to pursue the common good within a realm of discretion here. But this should not be sharply removed from the reasoned elaboration of legal principle and the determination of legal rights and duties.[58] In all areas of legal reasoning, including legislative or administrative reasoning, will and reason must operate in harmony, reflecting the vital admixture of critical and positive morality such that no action of a legal authority can be described as a mere act of brute will.[59] This is so, even if courts must respect the acts of legitimate political authority to make choices in pursuit of the common good: that respect must be given, but it cannot amount to an abandonment of a court's duty to uphold the rule of law and the related commitment that government proceed in the interests of the governed.

The forced depopulation of Diego Garcia, the largest of the Chagos Islands, serves as a powerful illustration. The Commissioner, established as a legislature

[55] Laws (n 28) 41.

[56] See Webber and Yowell (n 6); Vermeule (n 19) 3.

[57] Allan, 'Why the Law Is What It Ought to Be' (n 4) 576; Allan, 'Law as a Branch of Morality: The Unity of Practice and Principle' (n 4) 14.

[58] Allan, *Law, Liberty, and Justice: The Legal Foundations of British Constitutionalism* (n 40) 55.

[59] Allan, *The Sovereignty of Law* (n 4) 64; *cf* L Fuller, 'Reason and Fiat in Case Law' (1946) 59 *Harvard Law Review* 376; M Foran, 'The Constitutional Foundations of Reasonableness Review: Artificial Reson and Wrongful Discrimination' (2022) 26 *Edinburgh Law Review* 295; AD Boyer, '"Understanding, Authority, and Will": Sir Edward Coke and the Elizabethan Origins of Judicial Review' (1997) 43 *Boston College Law Review* 43.

for the colony under the British Indian Ocean Territories Order 1965, made an Immigration Ordinance in 1971, providing that no one could enter or remain in the territory without a permit, which would not be granted as by this time the British government had already removed the population of the island to make way for the construction of a military base by the United States of America. In 2000, the High Court quashed this provision, holding that this exclusion was not within the Commissioner's power to make law for the 'peace, order and good government' of the territory.[60]

Initially the government accepted the ruling, lifting the restrictions, but subsequently reimposed them by Order in Council. The Court of Appeal upheld the conclusion of the High Court that these restrictions were invalid, but eventually a majority of the House of Lords disagreed. The Court agreed that the legality of the Order in Council was subject to judicial review, rejecting the argument that this exercise of the royal prerogative was immune from judicial oversight: the ordinary principles of legality, reasonableness and natural justice applied.[61] Nevertheless, the majority concluded that the Order was not irrational. The decision of the majority reflected a refusal to accept that the legislative powers of the Crown were limited by the requirement that laws must be ordered towards the 'peace, order and good government' of the territory. Rather than placing restrictions on government power, informed by the rule of law, this clause was construed exclusively as an empowering provision, 'the traditional formula by which legislative powers are conferred upon the legislature of a colony or a former colony upon the attainment of independence'.[62]

Even though it is claimed that a power to make laws for the peace, order, and good government of a territory connotes 'the widest law making power appropriate to a Sovereign',[63] it is nevertheless necessary to ask whether there are inherent limits to 'sovereign' legislative power.[64] As such, Sedley LJ was correct to distinguish in *Bancoult (No 2)*, between what the British government claimed to be in the well-being of the colony and what, as a matter of law, fell within the constitutional limits of a legal order directed towards furthering the interests of its citizens. It is not appropriate for the court 'to substitute their own view of what is best for a colony'. But it is nevertheless 'their constitutional function to decide whether what has been enacted, or what it is proposed to enact, is rationally and legally capable of providing for a colony's well-being'.[65]

It is simply not possible to conceive of this constraint if one remains neutral as to what constitutes the well-being of legal subjects. The protection of fundamental rights is a centrally important aspect of this. But this does not capture

[60] *R (Bancoult) v Secretary of State for Foreign and Commonwealth Affairs* [2001] QB 1067.
[61] ibid [57].
[62] ibid [47].
[63] *Ibralebbe v R* [1964] AC 900, 923.
[64] See Allan, *The Sovereignty of Law* (n 4) 291–92.
[65] *Bancoult (No 2)* [2007] EWCA Civ 498, [51].

those considerations of peace, order and good governance which are not confined to individual rights claims, and which are instead grounded in considerations of the collective well-being and flourishing of the polity. The *Bancoult* cases can be described exclusively by reference to an individual constitutional right of abode, but this would be an impoverished account that would not give due regard to the requirements of peace, order, and good government. It is only when examined by reference to the effect this policy had on the community as a whole that it can be said that the Orders fell foul of standards which, while generally requiring comity, demand that the authority of political bodies rests on their legitimate and reasonable pursuit of the common good.

One cannot make full sense of requirements of good governance if one refuses to think critically about the good. Properly understood, legislative and governmental action cannot be utilitarian or aggregative, sacrificing the minority for the sake of the majority. Instead, legal officials, including courts, must proceed from the presumption that political authority is exercised reasonably as acts of law: not brute will, not unmoored reason, but the careful fusion of each. When viewed in that manner, law *qua* law is properly ordered towards the best interests of the governed, duly respectful of their fundamental rights but not aloof to the quality of their lives. Legality demands that presumptions are made about the reasonableness of public authority, rejecting any attempt to conflate law with the mere will of a sovereign. This cannot be confined to rights analysis on the basis that rights are the product of principled reason and that legislation or executive policy is not.

Once we accept that policy is also the product of reasoned deliberation about how best to achieve peace, order, and good governance, then reason is demanded from judges: presumptions are and have been made on the basis that acts purported to be in the public interest are simply not in any such interest. This is so, not necessarily because they have breached fundamental rights, but because they are not directed towards any plausible vision of the common good. Our legal practice has all of the resources needed to facilitate reasoned interpretation of the requirements of peace, order and good government. Our administrative law principles of legality, reasonableness, and natural justice can just as easily enable the pursuit of the public good as they restrict abuses of power. That is the foundation of our law, grounded in the customs and traditions of the community, founded upon principles of justice and fairness.

At the level of political morality there exist values which must be honoured or respected but also values which must be promoted or advanced.[66] As Simmonds notes, 'some values provide *goals*, while others constitute *constraints* upon the pursuit of goals'.[67] The value of equality can plausibly provide both. Indeed, it

[66] See Simmonds (n 12) 179–80; E Holmes, 'Anti-Discrimination Rights without Equality' (2005) 68 *Modern Law Review* 175, 175–76.

[67] Simmonds (n 12) 180.

must if it is to live up to the aspirational ideals inherent within the rule of law. Law, in its fullest sense, cannot be separated from the ends that to which it is to be put. It is not a mere means to pursue whatever ends a political authority wishes. Rather, to rule through law is to adopt a distinctive attitude towards legal subjects, one which views their collective flourishing as a central feature of the system's success as law. The common good is thus the proper end of any juridical order, manifesting within legal officials a requirement to act as guardians or custodians for the interests of the governed.[68]

A theory of legal equality must account for both the comparative aspects of wrongful discrimination and the comparative aspects of the rule of law. It must be attuned to how the moral equality of persons sets limits on action in the form of anti-discrimination rights. But it must also be attuned to the aspirational aspects of equality which demand that public authority be genuinely public, directed towards advancement of the collective interests of all members of a political community. There is significant room for determination within that sphere and constitutional theory must afford appropriate respect for the role of legitimate political authority in concretising abstract moral principle to meet the context within which it is operative. But it cannot abandon the idea of the common good either. A legitimate constitutional order is one which strives for the flourishing of all legal subjects, respecting their rights but also taking the flourishing of their lives as a constitutive aspect of its own success.

[68] See Raz (n 21).

Bibliography

Albertyn, C, 'Substantive Equality and Transformation in South Africa' (2007) 23 *South African Journal of Human Rights* 253
—— 'Substantive Equality' (2007) 23 *South African Journal on Human Rights* 209
Alexander, L, 'What Makes Wrongful Discrimination Wrong? Biases, Preferences, Stereotypes, and Proxies' (1992) 141 *University of Pennsylvania Law Review* 149
Alexy, R, 'A Defence of Radbruch's Formula' in D Dyzenhaus (ed), *Recrafting the Rule of Law: The Limits of Legal Order* (Hart Publishing, 1999)
Allan, TRS, 'Constitutional Rights and Common Law' (1991) 11 *Oxford Journal of Legal Studies* 453
—— *Law, Liberty, and Justice: The Legal Foundations of British Constitutionalism* (Clarendon Press, 1993)
—— 'Dworkin and Dicey: The Rule of Law as Integrity' (1988) 8 *Oxford Journal of Legal Studies* 266
—— 'Procedural Fairness and the Duty of Respect' (1998) 18 *Oxford Journal of Legal Studies* 497
—— *Constitutional Justice: A Liberal Theory of the Rule of Law* (Oxford University Press, 2001)
—— 'The Constitutional Foundations of Judicial Review: Conceptual Conundrum or Interpretative Inquiry' (2002) 61(1) *Cambridge Law Journal* 87
—— 'Constitutional Dialogue and the Justification of Judicial Review' (2003) 23 *Oxford Journal of Legal Studies* 563
—— 'Questions of Legality and Legitimacy: Form and Substance in British Constitutionalism' (2011) 9 *International Journal of Constitutional Law* 155
—— *The Sovereignty of Law: Freedom, Constitution, and Common Law* (Oxford University Press, 2013)
—— 'The Rule of Law as the Rule of Private Law' in LM Austin and D Klimchuk (eds), *Private Law and the Rule of Law* (Oxford University Press, 2014)
—— 'Law, Democracy, and Constitutionalism: Reflections on Evans v Attorney General' (2016) 75 *Cambridge Law Journal* 38
—— 'In Defence of Radbruch's Formula: Injustice, Interpretation, and Invalidity' in M Borowski, SL Paulson and J-R Sieckmann (eds), *Rechtspjilosophie und Grundrechtstheorie* (Mohr Siebeck, 2017)
—— 'The Moral Unity of Public Law' (2017) 67 *University of Toronto Law Journal* 1
—— 'Principle, Practice, and Precedent: Vindicating Justice, According to Law' (2018) 77 *Cambridge Law Journal* 269
—— 'Political Obligation and Public Law' in L Crawford, P Emerton and D Smith (eds), *Law Under a Democratic Constitution: Essays in Honour of Jeffrey Goldsworthy* (Hart Publishing, 2019)
—— 'Law as a Branch of Morality: The Unity of Practice and Principle' (2020) 65 *American Journal of Jurisprudence* 1
—— 'Why the Law Is What It Ought to Be' (2020) 11 *Jurisprudence* 574
Anderson, E and Pildes, R, 'Expressive Theories of Law: A General Restatement' (2000) 148 *University of Pennsylvania Law Review* 1503
Aristotle, 'Nicomachean Ethics' in J Barnes (ed), *The Complete Works of Aristotle* (Princeton University Press, 1984)
—— 'Politics' in J Barnes (ed), *The Complete Works of Aristotle* (Princeton University Press, 1984)
Arneson, RJ, 'What Is Wrongful Discrimination?' (2006) 43 *San Diego Law Review* 775

—— 'Discrimination, Disparate Impact, and Theories of Justice' in D Hellman and S Moreau (eds), *Philosophical Foundations of Discrimination Law* (Oxford University Press, 2013)
Arrigo, JM, 'A Utilitarian Argument against Torture Interrogation of Terrorists' (2004) 10 *Science and Engineering Ethics* 543
Atrey, S, 'Comparison in Intersectional Discrimination' (2018) 38 *Legal Studies* 379
Austin, JL, *How to Do Things with Words* (Clarendon Press, 1962)
Baber, HE, 'Gender Conscious' (2001) 18 *Journal of Applied Philosophy* 53
Bagaric, M and Allan, J, 'The Vacuous Concept of Dignity' (2006) 5 *Journal of Human Rights* 257
Bagaric, M and Clarke, J, *Torture: When the Unthinkable Is Permissible* (State University of New York Press, 2007)
Balog, K, 'Equal Protection for Homosexuals: Why the Immutability Argument Is Necessary and How It Is Met Note' (2005) 53 *Cleveland State Law Review* 545
Bamforth, N, 'Conceptions of Anti-Discrimination Law' (2004) 24 *Oxford Journal of Legal Studies* 693
Barnard, C and Hepple, B, 'Substantive Equality' (2000) 59 *Cambridge Law Journal* 562
Bedi, S, 'The Scope of Formal Equality of Opportunity' (2014) 42 *Political Theory* 716
Berkowitz, R, 'Dignity Jurisprudence: Building a New Law on Earth' in D Cornell (ed), *The Dignity Jurisprudence of the Constitutional Court of South Africa* (Fordham University Press, 2013)
Bingham, T, *The Rule of Law* (Allen Lane, 2010)
Blum, L, 'Racial and Other Asymmetries: A Problem for the Protected Categories Framework for Anti-Discrimination Thought' in D Hellman and S Moreau (eds), *Philosophical Foundations of Discrimination Law* (Oxford University Press, 2013)
Bourn, C and Whitmore, J, *Anti-Discrimination Law in Britain*, 3rd edn (Sweet & Maxwell, 1996)
Boyer, AD, '"Understanding, Authority, and Will": Sir Edward Coke and the Elizabethan Origins of Judicial Review' (1997) 43 *Boston College Law Review* 43
Brink, D, 'The Separateness of Persons, Distributive Norms, and Moral Theory' in RG Frey and C Morris (eds), *Value, Welfare, and Morality* (Cambridge University Press, 1993)
Burton, SJ, 'Comment on "Empty Ideas"; Logical Positivist Analyses of Equality and Rules' (1982) 91 *Yale Law Journal* 1136
Byk, C, 'Is Human Dignity a Useless Concept? Legal Perspectives' in M Düwell (ed), *The Cambridge Handbook of Human Dignity: Interdisciplinary Perspectives* (Cambridge University Press, 2014)
Cane, P, 'Theory and Values in Public Law' in P Craig and R Rawlings (eds), *Law and Administration in Europe: Essays in Honour of Carol Harlow* (Oxford University Press, 2003)
—— *Administrative Law*, 5th edn (Oxford University Press, 2011)
Casey, C, 'Common-Good Constitutionalism and the New Battle over Constitutional Interpretation in the United States' [2021] *Public Law* 765
—— 'An Administrative State for the Common Good' (*Ius & Iustitium*, 28 July 2022) https://iusetiustitium.com/an-administrative-state-for-the-common-good/ accessed 16 May 2023
Chaskalson, A, 'Human Dignity as a Foundational Value of Our Constitutional Order' (2000) 16 *South African Journal of Human Rights* 193
Chemerinsky, E, 'In Defence of Equality: A Reply to Professor Westen' (1983) 81 *Michigan Law Review* 575
Clarke, JA, 'Against Immutability' (2015) 125 *Yale Law Journal* 2
Cohen, G, *If You're an Egalitarian, How Come You're So Rich* (Harvard University Press, 2000)
Collins, H, 'Discrimination, Equality and Social Inclusion' (2003) 66 *Modern Law Review* 16
Collins, H and Khaitan, T, 'Indirect Discrimination Law: Controversies and Critical Questions' in H Collins and T Khaitan (eds), *Foundations of Indirect Discrimination Law* (Hart Publishing, 2018)
Craig, P, 'Formal and Substantive Conceptions of the Rule of Law' [1997] *Public Law* 467
—— 'Ultra Vires and the Foundations of Judicial Review' (1998) 57 *Cambridge Law Journal* 63
—— 'Theory and Values in Public Law: A Response' in P Craig and R Rawlings (eds), *Law and Administration in Europe: Essays in Honour of Carol Harlow* (Oxford University Press, 2003)

—— 'The Nature of Reasonableness Review' (2013) 66 *Current Legal Problems* 131
—— 'Proportionality and Constitutional Review' (2020) 3 *University of Oxford Human Rights Hub Journal* 87
Crossley, M, 'Reasonably Accommodation as Part and Parcel of the Antidiscrimination Project' (2004) 35 *Ruthers Law Journal* 861
Dahl, R, *On Political Equality* (Yale University Press, 2006)
Daly, P, 'Wednesbury's Reason and Structure' [2011] *Public Law* 237
Dan-Cohen, M, 'Dignity and Its (Dis)Content' in M Dan-Cohen (ed), *Jeremy Waldron, Dignity, Rank, and Rights* (Oxford University Press, 2012)
Darwall, S, *The Second-Person Standpoint* (Harvard University Press, 2006)
Daum, CW and Ishiwata, E, 'From the Myth of Formal Equality to the Politics of Social Justice: Race and the Legal Attack on Native Entitlements' (2010) 44 *Law & Society Review* 843
de Koninck, C, 'The Primacy of the Common Good against the Personalists: The Principle of the New Order' in R McInerny (ed), *The Writings of Charles de Koninck*, vol 2 (Notre Dame Press, 2016)
de Lazari-Radek, K and Singer, P, *Utilitarianism: A Very Short Introduction* (Oxford University Press, 2017)
Dicey, AV, *An Introduction to the Study of the Law of the Constitution* (JWF Allison ed, Oxford University Press, 2013)
Dupré, C, 'Human Dignity in Europe: A Foundational Constitutional Principle' (2013) 19 *European Public Law* 319
Duxbury, N, *The Nature and Authority of Precedent* (Cambridge University Press, 2008)
Dworkin, R, 'Social Sciences and Constitutional Rights – the Consequences of Uncertainty' (1977) 6 *Journal of Law and Education* 1
—— *Taking Rights Seriously* (Harvard University Press, 1977)
—— 'Liberalism' in S Hampshire (ed), *Public and Private Morality* (Cambridge University Press, 1978)
—— *A Matter of Principle* (Clarendon Press, 1986)
—— *Law's Empire* (Harvard University Press, 1986)
—— *Sovereign Virtue: The Theory and Practice of Equality* (Harvard University Press, 2000)
—— *Is Democracy Possible Here?* (Princeton University Press, 2006)
Eidelson, B, 'Treating People as Individuals' in D Hellman and S Moreau (eds), *Philosophical Foundations of Indirect Discrimination* (Oxford University Press, 2013)
—— *Discrimination and Disrespect* (Oxford University Press, 2015)
Elliott, M, 'The Ultra Vires Doctrine in a Constitutional Setting: Still the Central Principle of Administrative Law' (1999) 58 *Cambridge Law Journal* 129
—— *The Constitutional Foundations of Judicial Review* (Hart Publishing, 2001)
—— 'The Human Rights Act 1998 and the Standard of Substantive Review' (2001) 60(2) *Cambridge Law Journal* 301
—— 'Standing, Judicial Review and the Rule of Law: Why We All Have a "Direct Interest" in Government According to Law' (*Public Law for Everyone*, 2013) https://publiclawforeveryone.com/2013/07/29/standing-judicial-review-and-the-rule-of-law-why-we-all-have-a-direct-interest-in-government-according-to-law/ accessed 16 May 2023
—— 'Beyond the European Convention: Human Rights and the Common Law' (2015) 68 *Current Legal Problems* 85
—— 'Consistency as a Free-Standing Principle of Administrative Law?' (*Public Law for Everyone*, June 2018) https://publiclawforeveryone.com/2018/06/15/the-supreme-courts-judgment-in-gallaher-consistency-as-a-free-standing-principle-of-administrative-law/ accessed 16 May 2023
Elliott, M and Thomas, R, *Public Law*, 3rd edn (Oxford University Press, 2017)
Endicott, T, 'Arbitrariness' (2014) 27 *Canadian Journal of Law and Jurisprudence* 49
—— *Administrative Law*, 4th edn (Oxford University Press, 2018)
Etzioni, A, 'The Common Good and Rights: A Neo-Communitarian Approach' (2009) 10 *Georgetown Journal of International Affairs* 113

Fallon, RH and Weiler, PC, 'Firefighters v Scotts: Conflicting Models of Racial Justice' [1984] *The Supreme Court Review* 1
Feinberg, J, 'The Nature and Value of Rights' (1970) 4 *Journal of Value Inquiry* 243
Fiddes, E, 'Lord Mansfield and the Sommersett Case' (1934) 50 *Law Quarterly Review* 499
Finnis, J, *Natural Law and Natural Rights* (Oxford University Press, 1980)
—— 'Equality and Differences' (2012) 2 *Solidarity* 1
Fiss, OM, 'Groups and the Equal Protection Clause' (1976) 5 *Philosophy & Public Affairs* 107
Fleurbaey, M, 'Equality Versus Priority: How Relevant Is the Distinction?' (2015) 31 *Economics and Philosophy* 203
Foran, M, 'The Rule of Good Law: Form, Substance and Fundamental Rights' (2019) 78 *Cambridge Law Journal* 570
—— 'Grounding Unlawful Discrimination' (2022) 28 *Legal Theory* 3
—— 'Rights, Common Good, and The Separation of Powers' (2022) 86 *Modern Law Review* 599
—— 'The Constitutional Foundations of Reasonableness Review: Artificial Reason and Wrongful Discrimination' (2022) 26 *Edinburgh Law Review* 295
—— 'The Cornerstone of Our Law: Equality, Consistency, and Judicial Review' (2022) 81 *Cambridge Law Journal* 249
Fourie, C, Schuppert, F and Wallimann-Helmer, I (eds), *Social Equality: On What It Means to Be Equals* (Oxford University Press, 2015)
Frankfurt, HG, 'Equality and Respect' in *Necessity, Violation and Love* (Cambridge University Press, 1994)
Fredman, S, *Women and Law* (Oxford University Press, 1997)
—— *A Critical Review of the Concept of Equality in UK Anti-Discrimination Law* (Cambridge University Press, 1999)
—— *Discrimination and Human Rights: The Case of Racism* (Oxford University Press, 2001)
—— *Human Rights Transformed: Positive Rights and Positive Duties* (Oxford University Press, 2008)
—— *Discrimination Law*, 2nd edn (Oxford University Press, 2011)
—— 'Breaking the Mold: Equality as a Proactive Duty' (2012) 60 *The American Journal of Comparative Law* 265
—— 'Substantive Equality Revisited' (2016) 14 *International Journal of Constitutional Law* 712
—— 'Direct and Indirect Discrimination: Is There Still a Divide' in H Collins and T Khaitan (eds), *Foundations of Indirect Discrimination Law* (Hart Publishing, 2018)
Fuller, L, 'Reason and Fiat in Case Law' (1946) 59 *Harvard Law Review* 376
—— 'Positivism and Fidelity to Law – A Reply to Professor Hart' (1958) 71 *Harvard Law Review* 630
—— *The Morality of Law*, rvsed edn (Yale University Press, 1969)
—— 'The Forms and Limits of Adjudication' in K Winston (ed), *The Principles of Social Order: Selected Essays of Lon L Fuller*, rvsd edn (Hart Publishing, 2001)
—— *The Principles of Social Order: Selected Essays of Lon L. Fuller*, rvsd edn (K Winston ed, Hart Publishing, 2001)
Galligan, D, *Due Process and Fair Procedures: A Study of Administrative Procedures* (Oxford University Press, 1996)
Gamauf, R, 'Slaves Doing Business: The Role of Roman Law in the Economy of a Roman Household' (2009) 16 *European Review of History* 331
Gardner, J, 'Liberals and Unlawful Discrimination' (1989) 9 *Oxford Journal of Legal Studies* 1
—— 'Discrimination as Injustice' (1996) 16 *Oxford Journal of Legal Studies* 353
—— 'The Supposed Formality of the Rule of Law' in *Law as a Leap of Faith: Essays on Law in General* (Oxford University Press, 2012)
Gerhardt, MJ, *The Power of Precedent* (Oxford University Press, 2008)
Gewirth, A, 'Rights and Virtues' (1985) 38 *Review of Metaphysics* 739
Goldberg, SB, 'Discrimination by Comparison' (2011) 120 *Yale Law Journal* 728

Goldsworthy, J, 'The Myth of the Common Law Constitution', *Parliamentary Sovereignty* (Cambridge University Press, 2010)
Gordon, M, *Parliamentary Sovereignty in the UK Constitution: Process, Politics, and Democracy* (Hart Publishing, 2015)
Green, L, 'Two Worries about Respect for Persons' (2010) 120 *Ethics* 212
Greenawalt, K, 'How Empty Is the Idea of Equality?' (1983) 83 *Columbia Law Review* 1167
—— '"Prescriptive Equality": Two Steps Forward' (1997) 110 *Harvard Law Review* 1265
Griffin, J, *On Human Rights* (Oxford University Press, 2008)
Hale, B, 'The Quest for Equal Treatment' [2005] *Public Law* 571
—— 'Who Guards the Guardians?' (14 October 2013) https://www.supremecourt.uk/docs/speech-131014.pdf accessed 16 May 2023
Hare, R, *Moral Thinking: Its Levels, Method, and Point* (Clarendon Press, 1981)
Harlow, C and Rawlings, R, *Law and Administration*, 4th edn (Cambridge University Press 2022)
Harsanyi, JC, 'Morality and the Theory of Rational Behaviour' in A Sen and B Williams (eds), *Utilitarianism and Beyond* (Cambridge University Press, 1982)
Hart, HLA, 'Positivism and the Separation of Law and Morality' (1958) 71 *Harvard Law Review* 593
—— *The Concept of Law*, 2nd edn (Oxford University Press, 1994)
Havelkova, B, 'Judicial Scepticism of Discrimination at the ECtHR' in H Collins and T Khaitan (eds), *Foundations of Indirect Discrimiantion Law* (Hart Publishing, 2018)
Hayek, FA von, *The Road to Serfdom* (Routledge, 1944)
—— *The Constitution of Liberty* (Routledge & Kegan Paul, 1960)
Heinrich, R, *The Natural Law* (Liberty Fund, 2012)
Hellman, D, 'The Expressive Dimension of Equal Protection' (2000) 85 *Minnesota Law Review* 1
—— *When Is Discrimination Wrong?* (Harvard University Press, 2011)
—— 'Equality and Unconstitutional Discrimination' in D Hellman and S Moreau (eds), *Philosophical Foundations of Discrimination Law* (Oxford University Press, 2013)
—— 'Two Concepts of Discrimination' (2016) 102 *Virginia Law Review* 895
—— 'Indirect Discrimination and the Duty to Avoid Compounding Injustice' in H Collins and T Khaitan (eds), *Foundations of Indirect Discrimiantion Law* (Hart Publishing, 2018)
Hellman, D and Moreau, S (eds), *Philosophical Foundations of Discrimination Law* (Oxford University Press, 2013)
Helmholz, RH, *Natural Law in Court: A History of Legal Theory in Practice* (Harvard University Press, 2015)
Hepple, B, *Race, Jobs and the Law in Britain* (Penguin, 1970)
—— 'The Aims of Equality Law' (2008) 61 *Current Legal Problems* 1
—— *Equality: The Legal Framework*, 2nd edn (Hart Publishing, 2014)
Herzog, D, 'Aristocratic Dignity?' in M Dan-Cohen (ed), *Jeremy Waldron, Dignity, Rank, and Rights* (Oxford University Press, 2012)
Hoffman, S, 'The Importance of Immutability in Employment Discrimination Law' (2011) 52 *William and Mary Law Review* 1483
Hohfeld, W, *Fundamental Legal Conceptions* (W Cook ed, Yale University Press, 1919)
Holmes, E, 'Anti-Discrimination Rights without Equality' (2005) 68 *Modern Law Review* 175
Holtug, N, 'Egalitarianism and the Levelling Down Objection' (1998) 58 *Analysis* 166
—— *Persons, Interests, and Justice* (Oxford University Press, 2010)
—— 'Theories of Value Aggregation: Utilitarianism, Egalitarianism, Prioritarianism' in I Hirose and J Olson (eds), *The Oxford Handbook of Value Theory* (Oxford University Press, 2015)
Ibbetson, DJ, 'Natural Law and Common Law' (2001) 5 *Edinburgh Law Review* 4
Jowell, J, 'Is Equality a Constitutional Principle?' (1994) 7 *Current Legal Problems* 1
Juratowitch, B, 'Torture Is Always Wrong' (2008) 22 *Public Affairs Quarterly* 91
Kant, I, 'Groundwork of the Methaphysics of Morals' in M Gregor (ed), *Immanuel Kant, Practical Philosophy* (Cambridge University Press, 1996)

Karlan, PS and Rutherglen, G, 'Disabilities, Discrimination, and Reasonable Accommodation' (1996) 46 *Duke Law Journal* 1
Karst, KL, 'Why Equality Matters' (1983) 17 *Georgia Law Review* 245
—— *Belonging to America: Equal Citizenship and the Constitution* (Yale University Press, 1989)
Kelman, M, 'Defining the Antidiscrimination Norm to Defend It' (2006) 43 *San Diego Law Review* 735
Kershnar, S, *For Torture: A Rights-Based Defence* (Lexington Books, 2011)
Khaitan, T, 'Dignity as an Expressive Norm: Neither Vacuous Nor a Panacea' (2012) 32 *Oxford Journal of Legal Studies* 1
—— *A Theory of Discrimination Law* (Oxford University Press, 2015)
—— 'Indirect Discrimination' in K Lippert-Rasmussen (ed), *The Routledge Handbook of the Ethics of Discrimination* (Routledge, 2017)
Khaitan, T and Steel, S, 'Wrongs, Group Disadvantage and the Legitimacy of Indirect Discrimination Law' in H Collins and T Khaitan (eds), *Foundations of Indirect Discrimination Law* (Hart Publishing, 2018)
Kolani, A, 'Dignity' (1976) 51 *Philosophy* 251
Kramer, M, *In Defence of Legal Positivism: Law without Trimmings* (Oxford University Press, 1999)
Laws, J, 'Law and Democracy' [1995] *Public Law* 72
—— *The Common Law Constitution* (Cambridge University Press, 2014)
—— *The Constitutional Balance* (Hart Publishing, 2021)
Lee, P and George, RP, 'The Nature and Basis of Human Dignity' (2008) 21 *Ratio Juris* 173
Lester, A and Bindman, G, *Race and Law* (Penguin, 1972)
Lewis, P, 'Pregnant Workers and Sex Discrimination: The Limits of Purposive Non-Comparative Methodology' (2000) *16 International Journal of Comparative Labour Law and Industrial Relations 55*
Lippert-Rasmussen, K, 'The Badness of Discrimination' (2006) 9 *Ethical Theory and Moral Practice* 167
—— *Born Free and Equal: A Philosophical Inquiry into the Nature of Discrimination* (Oxford University Press, 2013)
Lord Carnwath, 'From Judicial Outrage to Sliding Scales – Where next for Wednesbury?' (ALBA Annual Lecture, 12 November 2013) https://www.supremecourt.uk/docs/speech-131112-lord-carnwath.pdf accessed 16 May 2023
MacIntyre, A, *After Virtue* (University of Notre Dame Press, 1981)
Marcosson, S, 'Constructive Immutability' (2001) 3 *University of Pennsylvania Journal of Constitutional Law* 646
Marshall, G, *Constitutional Theory* (Clarendon Press, 1971)
Mayerfield, J, 'In Defence of the Absolute Prohibition on Torture' (2008) 22 *Public Affairs Quarterly* 109
McColgan, A, 'Cracking the Comparator Problem: Discrimination, "Equal Treatment" and the Role of Comparisons' (2006) 6 *European Human Rights Law Review* 650
—— *Discrimination, Equality and the Law* (Hart Publishing, 2014)
McCrea, R, 'Squaring the Circle: Can an Egalitarian and Individualistic Conception of Freedom of Religion or Belief Co-Exist with the Notion of Indirect Discrimination?' in H Collins and T Khaitan (eds), *Foundations of Indirect Discrimination Law* (Hart Publishing, 2018)
McCrudden, C, 'Institutional Discrimination' (1982) 2 *Oxford Journal of Legal Studies* 303
—— 'Changing Notions of Discrimination' in S Guest and A Milne (eds), *Equality and Discrimination: Essays in Freedom and Justice* (ARSP Beiheft 21, 1985)
—— 'Equality Legislation and Reflexive Regulation: A Response to the Discrimination Law Review's Consultative Paper' (2007) 36 *Industrial Law Journal* 255
—— 'Human Dignity and Judicial Interpretation of Human Rights' (2008) 19 *European Journal of International Law* 655
McCrudden, C, Smith, D and Brown, C, *Racial Justice at Work: Enforcement of the Race Relations Act 1976 in Employment* (Policy Studies Institute, 1991)

McMahan, J, 'Torture in Principle and in Practice' (2008) 22 *Public Affairs Quarterly* 111
McSweeney, TJ, *Priests of the Law: Roman Law and the Making of the Common Law's First Professionals* (Oxford University Press, 2019)
Mill, JS, 'Utilitarianism' in JM Robson (ed), *The Collected Works of John Stuart Mill, Vol X, Essays on Ethics, Religion and Society* (University of Toronto Press, 1969)
Moreau, S, 'Discrimination as Negligence' (2010) 40 *Canadian Journal of Philosophy* 123
—— 'What Is Discrimination?' (2010) 38 *Philosophy & Public Affairs* 143
—— 'In Defense of a Liberty-Based Account of Discrimination' in D Hellman and S Moreau (eds), *Philosophical Foundations of Discrimination Law* (Oxford University Press, 2013)
—— *Faces of Inequality: A Theory of Wrongful Discrimination* (Oxford University Press, 2020)
Morris, AJ, 'On the Normative Foundations of Indirect Discrimination Law: Understanding the Competing Models of Discrimination Law as Aristotelian Forms of Justice' (1995) 15 *Oxford Journal of Legal Studies* 199
Nagel, T, *The Possibility of Altruism* (Princeton University Press, 1970)
—— 'Equality' in M Clayton and A Williams (eds), *The Ideal of Equality* (Palgrave Macmillan, 2002)
Nozick, R, *Anarchy, State, and Utopia* (Basic Books, 1974)
O'Cinneide, C, 'Equality: A Constitutional Principle?' (*UKCLA Blog*, 14 September 2011) https://ukconstitutionallaw.org/2011/09/14/colm-ocinneide-equality-a-constitutional-principle/ accessed 16 May 2023
—— 'The Uncertain Foundations of Contemporary Anti-Discrimination Law' (2011) 11 *International Journal of Discrimination and the Law* 7
—— 'Justifying Discrimination Law' (2016) 36 *Oxford Journal of Legal Studies* 909
—— 'Equality: A Core Common Law Principle, or "Mere" Rationality?' in M Elliott and K Hughes (eds), *Common Law Constitutional Rights* (Hart Publishing, 2020)
Oliver, D, *Common Values and the Public-Private Divide* (Butterworths, 1999)
Parfit, D, *Reasons and Persons* (Oxford University Press, 1984)
—— 'Equality and Priority' (1997) 10 *Ratio* 202
—— 'Equality or Priority' in M Clayton and A Williams (eds), *The Ideal of Equality* (Palgrave Macmillan, 2000)
Peters, C, 'Equality Revisited' (1997) 110 *Harvard Law Review* 1210
—— 'Slouching Towards Equality' (1999) 84 *Iowa Law Review* 801
Peters, CJ, 'Foolish Consistency: On Equality, Integrity, and Justice in Stare Decisis' (1996) 105 *Yale Law Journal* 2031
Pettit, P, *Republicanism: A Theory of Freedom and Government* (Clarendon Press, 1997)
Pinker, S, 'The Stupidity of Dignity' (*The New Republic*, 28 May 2008)
Polyviou, PG, *The Equal Protection of the Laws* (Duckworth, 1980)
Poole, T, 'Dogmatic Liberalism? T.R.S. Allan and the Common Law Constitution' (2002) 65 *Modern Law Review* 463
—— 'Back to the Future? Unearthing the Theory of Common Law Constitutionalism' (2003) 23 *Oxford Journal of Legal Studies* 435
Poser, NS, *Lord Mansfield: Justice in the Age of Reason* (McGill-Queen's University Press, 2013)
Postema, G, *Bentham and the Common Law Tradition* (Oxford University Press, 1986)
—— 'Integrity: Justice in Workclothes' (1997) 82 *Iowa Law Review* 821
Radbruch, G, 'Statutory Lawlessness and Supra-Statutory Law' (2006) 26 *Oxford Journal of Legal Studies* 1
Ramelli, ILE, *Social Justice and the Legitimacy of Slavery: The Role of Philosophical Asceticism from Ancient Judaism to Late Antiquity* (Oxford University Press, 2016)
Rashdall, H, *The Theory of Good and Evil: A Treaties on Moral Philosophy*, 2nd edn (Oxford University Press, 1924)
Rawls, J, *A Theory of Justice*, rvsd edn (Harvard University Press, 1971)
Raz, J, *The Morality of Freedom* (Clarendon Press, 1988)

—— *Value, Respect, and Attachment* (Cambridge University Press, 2001)
—— 'The Rule of Law and Its Virtue', *The Authority of Law: Essays on Law and Morality*, 2nd edn (Oxford University Press, 2009)
—— 'On Respect, Authority, and Neutrality: A Response' (2010) 120 *Ethics* 279
—— 'The Law's Own Virtue' (2019) 39 *Oxford Journal of Legal Studies* 1
Réaume, D, 'Dignity, Equality, and Comparison' in D Hellman and S Moreau (eds), *Philosophical Foundations of Discrimination Law* (Oxford University Press, 2013)
Reynolds, W, 'Individualism vs Group Rights: The Legacy of Brown' (1984) 93 *Yale Law Journal* 995
Rommen, H, *The Natural Law: A Study in Legal and Social History and Philosophy* (Thomas Hanley tr, Liberty Fund, 1998)
Rosen, M, *Dignity: Its History and Meaning* (Harvard University Press, 2012)
—— 'Dignity Past and Present' in M Dan-Cohen (ed), *Jeremy Waldron, Dignity, Rank, and Rights* (Oxford University Press, 2012)
Rundle, K, *Forms Liberate: Reclaiming the Jurisprudence of Lon L Fuller* (Hart Publishing, 2012)
Sadurski, W, *Equality and Legitimacy* (Oxford University Press, 2008)
Sangiovanni, A, 'On the Relation between Moral and Distributive Equality' in G Brock (ed), *Cosmopolitanism versus Non-Cosmopolitanism* (Oxford University Press, 2013)
—— *Humanity without Dignity: Moral Equality, Respect, and Human Rights* (Harvard University Pressb 2017)
Sarnoff, J, 'Equality as Uncertainty' (1999) 84 *Iowa Law Review* 377
—— 'I Come to Praise Morality, Not To Bury It' (1999) 84 *Iowa Law Review* 819
Scanlon, T, *What We Owe to Each Other* (Harvard University Press, 1998)
Schymyck, A, 'Vulnerable Detainees in Prison Illustrate the Need for Consistency as a Ground of Review' (*UKCLA Blog*, 24 February 2020) https://ukconstitutionallaw.org/2020/02/24/alex-schymyck-vulnerable-detainees-in-prison-illustrate-the-need-for-consistency-as-a-ground-of-review/ accessed 16 May 2023
Selmi, M, 'Was Disparate Impact Theory a Mistake?' (2001) 53 *UCLA Law Review* 701
Sen, A, 'Rights and Agency' (1982) 11 *Philosophy & Public Affairs* 3
—— *Inequality Re-Examined* (Clarendon Press, 1992)
Shin, P, 'Is There a Unitary Concept of Discrimination?' in D Hellman and S Moreau (eds), *Philosophical Foundations of Discrimination Law* (Oxford University Press, 2013)
Shyllon, F, *Black Slaves in Britain* (Oxford University Press, 1974)
Simmonds, N, *Law as a Moral Idea* (Oxford University Press, 2008)
—— 'Rights at the Cutting Edge' in M Kramer, NE Simmonds and H Steiner, *A Debate Over Rights* (Clarendon Press, 1998)
—— 'Constitutional Rights, Civility and Artifice' (2019) 78 *Cambridge Law Journal* 175
Simons, K, 'The Logic of Egalitarian Norms' (2000) 80 *Boston University Law Review* 693
Singer, P, 'Is Racial Discrimination Arbitrary?' (1978) 8 *Moral Matters* 185
—— *Practical Ethics*, 2nd edn (Cambridge University Press, 1993)
Skinner, Q, *Liberty before Liberalism* (Cambridge University Press, 1998)
Smith, N, *Basic Equality and Discrimination: Reconciling Theory and Law* (Ashgate, 2011)
Stanton-Ife, J, 'Should Equality Be a Constitutional Principle?' (2000) 11 *King's Law Journal* 133
Sunstein, C, 'On the Expressive Function of Law' (1996) 144 *University of Pennsylvania Law Review* 2021
Temkin, L, *Inequality* (Oxford University Press, 1993)
—— *Equality or Priority in Health Care Distribution* (Mimeo, Department of Philosophy, Rutgers University, 2000)
Thomsen, FK, 'Concept, Principle, and Norm – Equality before the Law Reconsidered' [2018] *Legal Theory* 1
Townshend-Smith, R, *Discrimination Law: Texts, Cases and Materials* (Cavendish, 1998)
Vallentyne, P, 'Against Maximizing Act Consequentialism' in J Dreier (ed), *Contemporary Debates in Moral Theory* (Blackwell, 2006)

Vermeule, A, 'Contra Nemo Iudex in Sua Causa: The Limits of Impartiality' (2012) 122 *Yale Law Journal* 384
—— 'Rationally Arbitrary Decisions in Administrative Law' (2015) 44 *The Journal of Legal Studies* S475
—— *Common Good Constitutionalism* (Polity Press, 2022)
Vlastos, G, 'Justice and Equality' in Louis Pojman and Robert Westmoreland (eds), *Equality: Selected Readings* (Oxford University Press, 1984)
Wade, W and Forsyth, C, *Administrative Law* 7th edn (Oxford University Press, 1994)
Waldron, J, 'The Concept and the Rule of Law' (2008) 29 Sibley Lecture Series
—— 'The Rule of Law and the Importance of Procedure' (2011) 50 *Nomos* 3
—— *Dignity, Rank, and Rights* (Oxford University Press, 2012)
—— 'How Law Protects Dignity' (2012) 71 *Cambridge Law Journal* 200
—— 'Stare Decisis and the Rule of Law: A Layered Approach' (2012) 111 *Michigan Law Review* 1
—— *One Another's Equals: The Basis of Human Equality* (The Belknap Press of Harvard University Press, 2017)
Wasserman, D, 'Distributive Justice' in A Silvers, D Wasserman and MB Mahowald (eds), *Disability, Difference, Discrimination: Perspectives on Justice in Bioethics and Public Policy* (Rowman & Littlefield, 1998)
—— 'Is Disability Discrimination Different?' in D Hellman and S Moreau (eds), *Philosophical Foundations of Discrimination Law* (Oxford University Press, 2013)
Webber, GCN and Yowell, P, 'Securing Human Rights through Legislation' in GCN Webber et al (eds), *Legislated Rights: Securing Human Rights through Legislation* (Cambridge University Press, 2018)
Weinrib, J, *Dimensions of Dignity: The Theory and Practice of Modern Constitutional Law* (Cambridge University Press, 2016)
Westen, P, 'The Empty Idea of Equality' (1982) 95 *Harvard Law Review* 537
—— *Speaking of Equality: An Analysis of the Rhetorical Force of 'Equality' in Moral and Legal Discourse* (Princeton University Press, 1990)
Williams, B, 'Persons, Character, and Morality' in *Moral Luck* (Cambridge University Press, 1981)
—— 'The Idea of Equality' in L Pojman and R Westmoreland (eds), *Equality: Selected Readings* (Oxford University Press, 1997)
Wood, AW, *Kant's Ethical Thought* (Cambridge University Press, 1999)
Woodward, J, 'The Non-Identity Problem' (1986) 96 *Ethics* 804
Wright, RG, 'Arbitrariness: Why the Most Important Idea in Administrative Law Can't Be Defined, and What This Means for the Law in General' (2010) 44 *University of Richmond Law Review* 839
Wu, JCH, 'The Natural Law and Our Common Law' (1954) 23 *Fordham Law Review* 13
Wu, T, 'Aquinas on Human Personhood and Dignity' (2021) 85 *The Thomist* 377
Yowell, P, 'A Critical Examination of Dworkin's Theory of Rights' (2007) 52 *American Journal of Jurisprudence* 93

Index

www.ingramcontent.com/pod-product-compliance
Ingram Content Group UK Ltd.
Pitfield, Milton Keynes, MK11 3LW, UK
UKHW020812290926
15470UKWH00003B/1106